Nandita Dogra is a postdoctoral fellow at Goldsmiths, University of London, UK. She holds an MSc. in NGO Management and a PhD in Social Policy from the London School of Economics and has extensive professional experience in development and social policy.

REPRESENTATIONS OF GLOBAL POVERTY

Aid, Development and International NGOs

NANDITA DOGRA

FOREWORD BY STANLEY COHEN

I.B. TAURIS
LONDON · NEW YORK

Paperback edition published in 2014
6 Salem Road, London W2 4BU
175 Fifth Avenue, New York NY 10010
www.ibtauris.com

Distributed in the United States and Canada
Exclusively by Palgrave Macmillan
175 Fifth Avenue, New York NY 10010

First published in hardback in 2012 by I.B.Tauris & Co Ltd

ISBN 978 1 78076 773 4

A full CIP record for this book is available from the British Library
A full CIP record for this book is available from the Library of Congress

Library of Congress catalog card: available

Typeset by Newgen Publishers, Chennai
Printed and bound by CPI Group (UK) Ltd, Croydon, CR0 4YY

Dedicated to my parents Dr Kamal Johri Dogra and Suresh Chander Dogra and to Vijay Koushal

The publishers wish to thank the following organisations for permission to use copyright material:

ActionAid UK, 33-39 Bowling Green Lane, London EC1R 0BJ, UK

Oxfam GB, Oxfam House, John Smith Drive, Cawley, Oxford OX4 2JY, UK
The material on pages 60, 70, 76, 79, 90 and 102 from sources indicated in the list of images is reproduced with the permission of Oxfam GB, Oxfam House, John Smith Drive, Cawley, Oxford OX4 2JY www.oxfam.org.uk. Oxfam GB does not necessarily endorse any text or activities that accompany the materials.

Plan International UK, Finsgate 5-7 Cranwood Street, London EC1V 9LH, UK

War on Want, 44-48 Shepherdess Walk, London N1 7JP, UK

Photo credits are indicated in the list of images. All colour images changed to black and white.

CONTENTS

Part III – Reflexivity

FIGURES

IMAGES

ABBREVIATIONS

Terms and Organisations

AA	ActionAid UK
AAH	Action Against Hunger
BOND	British Overseas NGOs for Development
CA	Christian Aid
CAF	Charities Aid Foundation
CAFOD	Catholic Agency for Overseas Development
CARE	Care International UK
Concern/CW	Concern Worldwide UK
DEC	Disasters Emergency Committee
DFID	Department for International Development, UK
DW	Developed World (also West/ North/ Global North/ First World/ developed countries/ rich countries/ Self/'we'/ 'us' (our)/ 'here')
FA	Farm Africa
G-8	Group of Eight (forum of eight major economies)
INGO	UK-based or British international development non- governmental organisation
MDGs	Millennium Development Goals

MPH	Make Poverty History
MW	Majority World (also South/non-West/the Rest/ underdeveloped/developing/ 'others'/ 'them'/ 'there'/ Third World/ poor countries, world, regions, communities)
NCVO	National Council for Voluntary Organisations
NGO	Non-governmental organisation
Oxfam	Oxfam GB (Great Britain)
Plan	Plan International UK
SCF	Save the Children UK
VSO	Voluntary Services Overseas
WFP	World Food Programme
WOW	War on Want
WV	World Vision

Audience Respondents

ME-1	Male, Elderly Respondent 1
FE-1	Female, Elderly Respondent 1
MM-1	Male, Middle-aged Respondent 1
FM-1	Female, Middle-aged Respondent 1
MY-1	Male, Young Respondent 1
FY-1	Female, Young Respondent 1
ME-2	Male, Elderly Respondent 2
FE-2	Female, Elderly Respondent 2
MM-2	Male, Middle-aged Respondent 2
FM-2	Female, Middle-aged Respondent 2
MY-2	Male, Young Respondent 2
FY-2	Female, Young Respondent 2

ACKNOWLEDGEMENTS

Once upon a time, I was an economist. During this research I missed being one, especially when I had to use many words to describe what could be explained through a simple equation. So I will wear my economist hat and begin the acknowledgements with money matters. The book primarily draws upon my PhD (2004–09) at the London School of Economics (LSE) which was made possible with financial support from LSE – the Dorothy Hodgkin Post Graduate Award (DHPA). I am grateful to the Economic and Social Research Council (ESRC) for the postdoctoral fellowship held at the Centre for Cultural Studies, Goldsmiths, University of London, which allowed me to write this book. These were merely the first order conditions necessary for survival. All those who went on to contribute to the second order condition which enabled me to get through have my deepest appreciation and thanks.

I owe thanks to many over the years at my department of Social Policy at LSE including Professor David Lewis, Dr Hakan Seckinelgin, Professor Julian le Grand, Professor Jude Howell, Professor Alistair McGuire, Professor Anne West, Dr Sarabajaya Kumar, Dr Sunil Kumar, Dr Armine Ishkanian, Dr Nuno Themudo, Jane Schiemann, John Wilkes and Sue Roebuck. And my special thanks to Professor Hartley Dean for his generous support.

I also drew heavily upon other departments and disciplines both within and outside LSE. Dr Derek Hook from the Social Psychology Department and the late Professor Roger Silverstone, Dr Shani Orgad and Dr Raka Shome from the Media and Communications Department at LSE, Dr Bruna Seu at Birkbeck College, London and Dr Lynda Reaich at London Metropolitan University deserve many thanks for their help and guidance. So does Professor Lilie Chouliaraki for her comments and feedback. I have also drawn inspiration and guidance from the works of, and my brief encounters with, Professor Stan Cohen and Professor Stuart Hall.

Photographers Susi Arnot and Crispin Hughes for some early breaks and ideas deserve many thanks. My PhD lists the many library staff members of Barnet Council who helped me with the extensive newspaper searches. I repeat my thanks to all of them and single out Ian Cutts at the Chipping Barnet Library for his exceptional support.

I am sincerely grateful to all the audience respondents, strangers who agreed to talk to me *gratis* and the photographers and NGO staff members for their valuable time and interest in the project and the kind permissions to reproduce their messages. As a practitioner and policymaker, I am well aware of the demands upon them and the constraints they face. The critical attitude that I personally witnessed amongst many NGO staff makes me optimistic about change.

Goldsmiths has provided a supportive, stimulating and radical home for writing this book as well as deepening my connections with immigration and education, issues that I have become increasingly involved in. All academics and staff members who have helped me have my gratitude and thanks. These include Dr Bhaskar Mukhopadhyay, Dr Matthew Fuller, Professor Les Back and Lisa Rabanal. My wonderful mentor Professor John Hutnyk has my heartfelt thanks not just for his invaluable academic support but also for his personal warmth, innate informality and inclusivity. I owe thanks to my prompt and helpful editor at I.B.Tauris, Tomasz Hoskins, picture editor Martin Shoesmith and copyeditor Allison McKechnie.

I thank all my family members and close friends for their unflinching faith and support. My father for his customary acceptance of my decisions (this time to study yet again) and for keeping the soul-inspiring discussions on music running, my mother for all the questions and comparisons with her own PhD, my brother Dr Ajay Dogra for showing the humour and irony in our different circumstances, my sister-in-law Anamika for worrying about the state of our health and nutrition, my niece Aastha for her bafflement at her aunt's continuation in university education ('do you study or teach in the college?'), my in-laws Vijayalakshmi and Shri Nath Tiwari for giving us the space to follow our ever-changing paths, Shashi *masi* and Tinku for always being there for me and the late Veeri *bhaiya*, whom I miss so much, and Rajni *bhabhi* for their help and encouragement.

My friends Yesim Akici, Shamsul Alam and Abdul Momen in London and Shikha and Dora Mukherjee in India cannot be thanked enough. London would not have been the same without the picnics with Shamsu, Georgie, Ishan and Akashi and the visits to art exhibitions and movies with Momen *bhai* and Yesim. The warm friendship, moral and intellectual support of Dr Georgie Wemyss has been invaluable. My 'twin' Shikha and Dora, of course, have remained true friends throughout. Other friends who have always been there to listen include Sawako, Anil, Anjan, Uday, Kacker uncle and auntie, Abhinav, Mudit, Bhuvana, Norma, Roshni, Prakash, Carlos, Eri, Du Jie, Nahid, Nisrine and Nidhi.

The research and relocation have extracted a high personal price: the sacrifice of two excellent careers and a hugely comfortable, and affordable, upper middle-class life with a large sea-facing apartment in south Mumbai, proximity to family and the sheer modernity, warmth and openness of India for a life of struggle in expensive London, staying in a distant suburb in a cramped room surrounded by mounds of old, dusty newspapers (my data) and mouldy walls, and, constantly being at the mercy of the UK's race and immigration politics. It is not possible to echo the usual stuff about 'self' that one comes across in so many research projects where a 'Western', usually 'white', researcher expresses the privileges (and discomfort) that stem from her identity. The research has meant giving up so many privileges that I often took for granted earlier. On the other hand, the travails happened in London, a city that I have lived in for the longest period of my peripatetic life, a city whose diversity lessened our homesickness and a city that I have come to love almost as much as I love Mumbai.

Above all, I owe everything, especially 'all that is good in me', to my country India; the poet Kashmiri Lal Zakir eloquently expresses my sentiments – *mujh mein jo kuch accha hai sab uska hai, mera jitna charcha hai sab uska hai.* And to my husband Arun Tiwari. If there is one person who made the research and writing possible, it is Arun. I need not add anything and embarrass him further, he *knows.*

Parts of this book have been presented or published elsewhere and are reproduced here with the permission of the original publishers, whom I thank. Substantial parts of chapter 2 were published in the *Third World Quarterly,* 32(2), 2011: 333–348. Parts of chapters 2 and 5 were incorporated in a paper presented at a conference on 'Cultural Difference and Social Solidarity' in the Middle East Technical University, Northern Cyprus Campus in July 2011 and subsequently published by the conference organisers.

The book was written during a Postdoctoral Fellowship granted by the Economic and Social Research Council (PTA-026-27-2546) at the Centre for Cultural Studies, Goldsmiths, University of London.

FOREWORD

In the conventional narrative of the discourse on global poverty, the Ethiopian famine crisis of 1984 heralded a 'crisis in imagery' or a 'crisis in representation'. The term 'crisis' was (as usual) over-used and imprecise. But clearly some radical differences were appearing, some of them – like the celebrity rock star appearance – instantly contested and divisive (and astonishingly long lasting). One of the changes most disturbing to the older generation was the ready acceptance of the power assigned to representation in its populist sense. A campaign against injustice and inequality becomes part of the spectacle. The collage of Bob Geldof, the Band Aid and Live Aid events and the iconic tableau of the dying African child saved by a Madonna, far from being marginal, constituted the problem itself.

International NGOs (INGOs) like Oxfam became generators and carriers of material and cultural knowledge about global poverty. They now became exposed to all sorts of demanding questions: how close was their imagery to the truth? Or are there only multiple regimes of truth? Is it true that the INGO world view was constituted primarily by 'negative images' – a 'pornography of suffering' assembled by 'merchants of misery' ? And how far was it driven by guilt about the legacy of colonialism?

Nandita Dogra's scrupulous and penetrating study of recent British INGOs avoids both journalistic hype and political denunciation. The descriptive detail is always theorised; the micro-world of the humanitarian organisation given its historical context; the slogans taken seriously, yet ruthlessly deconstructed: MAKE POVERTY HISTORY; SPONSORSHIP GIVES HER A HELPING HAND, NOT A HANDOUT; YOU DON'T HAVE TO BE A SAINT TO MAKE A DIFFERENCE; THERE'S NOTHING FREE ABOUT FREE TRADE; DON'T LOOK, DON'T READ, WALK AWAY; SKIP A LUNCH, SAVE A CHILD. The agencies' strategy – even marketing and PR discussions about video-technology, branding and sponsorship – is located in the 'outside' political history.

Alongside causal questions (not, for some, 'why does massive global poverty exist?' but 'why does it *still* exist?') there are the relentless policy questions about 'what works?' or what strategies work better than others. Terms like 'alongside' give the game away: the construction of categories of knowledge does not innocently run 'alongside' the exercise of political power. The most anti-theoretical activist at a demonstration will appreciate Foucault's conceptual explanation – bowdlerised as it may be – about the link between knowledge and power.

In one sense this link is abstract and universal. In the commonsense sense, however, a campaign, say, about children starving to death within miles of a tourist resort needs an utterly 'local' narrative, located in the history of this particular instance of the remains of colonialism. In the representation of social problems like global poverty – whether in organised campaigns, media coverage, UN-type reports or academic studies – the same tension between the universal and specific appear and even dominate the discourse.

The book is built around a related but more complex tension. Dogra argues that a dual logic of *difference* and *oneness* is the master code to understand INGO messages and also the ways we all deny the obvious and utterly unbearable statistics of global poverty. This message enables most of its audience 'to show the global poor as different and distant from the developed world and yet like us by virtue of their humanity'. The INGOs' condemnation of social injustice rests on the assumption of oneness. But histories of the world are dominantly histories of difference, notably the difference that results from and then perpetuates social inequality and global poverty – a conclusion all the more remarkable when it wholly understates the over-arching significance of colonialism, imperialism and slavery.

But another book is needed to unravel this thesis. What concerns Dogra here are the discursive strategies used to 'contain' the paradoxical links between difference, distance and othering 'versus' oneness and universality. Although I have stressed these theoretical and rhetorical concerns, the book is resolutely empirical; the findings lie in the angle of the child's head in a photo and its caption.

Although Dogra is consistently balanced and undogmatic, she has less sympathy for the 'oneness' language of universal humanism. The message (sometimes kitsch) from 'the family of mankind' asks the audience to look beyond their immediate surroundings of family, tribe, region or nation. The globe is one home. Dogra sees this as complacency: a home without a history of the differences in power that made the modern world. Poverty is not under the skin, the same everywhere. She is particularly scathing about what is now called the 'new liberal cosmopolitanism' (with its new liberal military interventionism?).

There is no foreseeable future when the tensions between oneness and difference will somehow fade away. Meantime there will indeed be crises of representation, gaps that become unsustainable: first, the gap between the thing itself – such as global poverty – and its representation and second, the gap between people's knowledge of distant suffering and what they do with this knowledge.

Stanley Cohen
London School of Economics
June 2011

CHAPTER 1

INTRODUCTION

Food Crisis across Africa ...
Make Poverty History ...
Sponsorship gives her a helping hand, not a handout ...
You don't have to be a saint to make a difference ...
There's nothing free about free trade ...

In our deeply connected but unequal world, what do these messages tell us about global poverty? International charities or non-governmental organisations (NGOs) bombard us with many such messages through our letter boxes, newspapers and television screens. How do they help us visualise and understand global poverty? How do we connect them with our own lives? This book addresses these questions through a study of recent representations by international NGOs (INGOs).

The book is about representations, global poverty and INGOs. We come to know the world through its representations. Representations do not simply re-present facts but also constitute them. It is imperative that we engage with world poverty and inequalities that affect, and often implicate, us all. We derive our understandings of global poverty from our 'stock of knowledge' which includes what we see, hear, know, believe and feel about it. Representations, which include what aid agencies and NGOs tell us, are key ingredients of this knowledge, our awareness of global inequalities and our very conscience.

INGOs form an important segment of institutions engaged in poverty reduction and development globally. They are not just important global development actors but also carriers of material and cultural knowledge about poverty across the globe. While they are based in the 'developed world' (DW) where they raise most of their funds, they work in and for the 'majority world' (MW) or 'Third World' or 'developing countries' mainly of Asia, Africa and South America. They also represent the MW to audiences in DW nations where they are seen as legitimate and proxy voices of the MW. This distinctive feature of international NGOs lends immense importance to their representations. The book conceptualises this set of development actors as 'media institutions' or 'institutions of representation'.

INGOs' representations not only influence our understandings of the world, but they also have significant implications for the management of NGOs. There are three main areas of NGO management – internal structures and processes, activities or roles of NGOs, and relationships of NGOs with other actors and communities (Lewis, 2007: 15), and NGOs' public messages have implications for all these aspects. Representations have a special significance for INGOs due to competing concerns of fundraising and advocacy linked to internal coherence within these organisations and their role, as institutions of representation, in feeding into wider discourses about poverty, development, inequalities and the MW in general, as well as engaging DW publics and governments to inform broader relationships between DW and MW. Representations are also important to INGOs in the light of concerns about their present and future, encompassing multiple accountabilities towards 'stakeholders' in both donor and receiving countries and legitimacy questions about their rights as the representative or authentic voice of MW countries – issues I engage with in greater depth in the book.

To unpack the opportunities, challenges and consequences of INGOs' representations in the global context, the book examines three interlinked levels of messages of UK-based international development NGOs – representation, production and reception. It first reviews the annual cycle of INGOs' public fundraising and advocacy messages for the year 2005/6 to understand the connections and relationships they mediate between DW and MW. Drawing on interviews with INGO staff and British audiences, it further probes the broader environment to understand why the messages take the form that they do.

The book focuses on 2005/6, which was a big year for INGOs. It was a year of summits and disasters leading to a flood of public messages by INGOs with visual imagery at its heart. The Asian Tsunami had occurred on Boxing Day in 2004 and its tremors still lingered in the new year.[1] The unprecedented public response to the appeals of the Asian Tsunami boosted the coffers and profile of INGOs in a similar way to the Ethiopian crisis of 1984–85. 2005 was also the year of 'Make Poverty History', a high-profile joint campaign by INGOs under the aegis of an independent coalition.

The central argument of the book is that a dual logic of 'difference' and 'oneness' characterises INGOs' messages. The analysis of a full annual cycle of INGOs' recent public messages finds that they construct, and connect, DW and MW through a double logic of 'difference' and 'oneness' which enables them to show the global poor as different and distant from the DW and yet like us by virtue of their humanity. INGOs' messages project many colonial discourses even as they ironically erase this period of our connected history and its legacies which continue to shape existing global economic structures, power relations and the current state of poverty and prosperity across various regions. Shared world history is the central plot in the story of global inequalities. *History makes poverty*. Any reflexivity about 'charity' and 'justice', hence, requires engagement with both the material and cultural legacies of global history. The book also highlights the sparse but crucial exceptions to INGOs' dominant messages which provide novel ways to foster reflexive understandings of global poverty and development amongst DW publics.

International NGOs and representations

It is estimated that that there are currently over 600 INGOs, more than half of which were established between 1991 and 2000; making the 1990s the boom period for INGOs (CAF and BOND, 2004).[2] Some INGOs have existed since the end of the First World War. The oldest INGO is Save the Children Fund (now Save the Children), which was founded in 1919. Another INGO, Plan, was established in 1937. Some INGOs were formed during the Second World War, including Oxfam (1942) and Christian Aid (1945). Many INGOs such as the Catholic Agency for Overseas Development (CAFOD) and War on Want came into being during the decolonisation period of 1950s and early 1960s, and numerous new agencies have been formed since then. A 25-year comparison between 1977–78 and 2002–3 also shows a remarkable jump both in the number and total income of INGOs, from less than £100 million to around £625 million (CAF, 2004).[3]

While the early remit of many of these organisations was respond-ing to disasters in the MW, from the mid-1960s on they began to support 'development'. There is now a wide variety of organisations involved in a range of activities from disaster relief, development projects, development education and advocacy to policy research, with a shared aim of poverty alleviation and human rights. Many INGOs simultaneously contain within them what David Korten calls 'gen-erations' of relief, community-level development, policy changes and advocacy, and wider alliances with social movements and are, hence, 'multi-generational' (Korten, 1990; Senillosa, 1998).

There are considerable variations among INGOs in their size and funds. In the financial year 2002/3, 36% of INGOs had an income of less than £100,000, 26% between £100,000 and £499,999, 20% between £500,000 and £1.9 million, and 13% between £2 and £19.9 million. Only 4% of INGOs had an annual income above £20 mil-lion (CAF and BOND, 2004). This shows a very high concentration of income in the hands of the larger INGOs. Nevertheless, the con-centration of income has not hindered the growth in the number of smaller INGOs, making the subsector increasingly diverse, although the hegemony of larger INGOs remains. In terms of public messages, this implies that the reach of smaller INGOs is rather limited and it is the messages of large INGOs such as Oxfam that reach wider audiences.

While INGOs' activities are diverse, their income and profile have invariably risen most dramatically during disasters, which makes their fundraising especially reliant on disaster imagery. For example, the Ethiopia crisis of 1984–85 raised between £110 and £140 million

(Smith cited in Robinson, 1994). More recently, the Asian Tsunami crisis of 2004–5 resulted in phenomenal donations worth around £500 million (CAF and NCVO, 2005). The Haiti earthquake appeal by the Disasters Emergency Committee (DEC), the UK umbrella organisation that coordinates disaster appeals, raised a total of £103 million (CAF and NCVO, 2010).

The profile of many INGOs is so high that they have transformed into valuable 'brands' across the NGO sector and the public at large, with significant political influence and responsibility (Anheier, 2005: 329). 'Brand', a marketing term, suggests a set of ideas associated with an organisation encompassing the organisation's name, logo, symbols, reputation, product, qualities and marketing (Jones, 2007). The public messages, including visual images, of INGOs play a significant part in these brand activities.[4]

The academic literature on INGOs' imagery is fairly small and peaks just after the Ethiopian crisis of 1984, which marked a watershed in the study and practices of INGOs' representations of MW countries in general, and Africa in particular. It led to what can be termed the 'imagery debate' during the late 1980s and early 1990s and several consequent policy changes within INGOs. Drawing largely upon Jørgen Lissner's earlier criticisms of images of starving children during the 1970s, academics and development practitioners argued that negative images of Africa had reproduced colonial stereotypes of a 'dark continent' of misery and hunger (Benthall, 1993; Lidchi, 1999).[5] Lissner famously called such images 'pornographic' (1981: 23). The story of the Ethiopian famine in 1984–85, with its powerful emotional imagery, led to unprecedented donations followed by efforts to raise funds through a 'Cultural Revolution' led by singer Bob Geldof, who co-wrote and organised the recording of *Do they know it's Christmas?* under Band Aid and then followed it by organising the Live Aid concert.

The 1980s were also characterised by a parallel phenomenon of the rise of 'development education' within INGOs. The broad framework of development education includes a three-pronged process of information, promotion of humanitarian values and spurring of community action. The informational aspect involves dissemination of information not only about poverty in the MW and its root causes, but also its link with affluence in the DW. This implies that acknowledging global interdependence is an integral part of the dimension of value promotion. The third dimension of action aims to motivate citizens to address both short- and long-term development issues and also influence public policy (Minear, 1987).

The focus on development education from the 1980s onwards led the INGOs to produce a wide variety of publications and materials on development issues and global problems which were, and still are, used especially in schools in the UK. In addition, there was resistance within INGOs to the use of starving child images in view of 'the new emphasis on solidarity with the Third World' (Black, 1992: 164).[6]

While INGOs have taken up distinct and varied advocacy roles, which are considered more 'political' in nature, no strict distinction has been made between education and advocacy. Advocacy is quite often used as an umbrella term for a range of activities like lobbying, development and public education, campaigning and mass communications (Minear, 1987; Eade and Williams, 1995). Many INGOs now accord high value to their education and advocacy roles. For instance, Oxfam claims that 'all of (its) work has an advocacy dimension' (Eade and Williams, 1995: 817). INGOs now also consider advocacy as an essential indicator of their non-conservatism (Hudson, 2002).

The considerable interest in imagery during the 1980s along with concerns of development education and advocacy, post Band Aid fundraising and the tensions of fundraising versus operations and awareness-generation, led to considerable introspection and action on the part of INGOs. Oxfam and War on Want set up working groups to develop guidelines on visual communications. A workshop on 'Visual images of colonised people' was held in Oxford in 1984 (Benthall, 1993).

The interest in imagery, development education and advocacy in the 1980s also had many management and policy consequences for INGOs. Apart from direct advocacy and education efforts, many INGOs developed guidelines on visual communications, published focus papers on imagery and adopted codes of practice on representation. Christian Aid outlined its views on images in its educational leaflet titled 'Images of Development, Links between Racism, Poverty and Injustice' in 1988 (Lidchi, 1999). Save the Children Fund published 'Focus on Images' in 1991 and Oxfam released 'Oxfam 50: Our World in Photographs' in 1992. In 1989 the General Assembly of European NGOs adopted its Code of Conduct on images and messages related to the MW. In Australia the NGO coordinating agency, ACOFA, adopted a Code of Ethics in 1989 that incorporated respecting the dignity of recipient communities in advertising, audiovisuals and other communications. In the United States, too, similar codes were laid down for member agencies by InterAction in 1993 (Smillie, 1995). Greater use of logos for TV coverage and of in-house photographers also became more common among INGOs.

Structural reorganisation such as the merger of fundraising and campaigning divisions under the marketing arm within many INGOs was another response to address the longstanding debate over clashing priorities (Fenton et al., 1993). INGOs also began to discard 'negative' visual images in favour of what was considered to be more 'positive' imagery and a policy of 'deliberate positivism'. This aimed to show self-reliant and active people of the MW, to attain greater coherence between the objectives of fundraising and development education and practice.[7]

Inherent in the criticisms of representations and consequent policy changes were the discourses of 'charity' versus 'development' and the privileging of education over fundraising. Fundraising, with its target of giving to the poor, promoted the idea of 'charity' while education and advocacy, by emphasising DW appropriation of MW wealth, advanced the idea of 'social justice' (Lidchi, 1999: 90). Fundraising is also often associated with short-term gains as against the long-term aims of education and advocacy, such as generating awareness (VSO, 2002: 2). This perceived antagonism between fundraising and education and advocacy continues to be seen as an important source of internal tension within NGOs.

The widespread interest in INGOs' imagery and concerns of advocacy both among the NGO community and researchers during the 1990s gradually petered out due to budget constraints on education and advocacy within INGOs, the political nature of advocacy and the growing complexities of developmental issues (Edwards et al., 2000). The last two major studies were undertaken in the early 1990s (Benthall, 1993; Lidchi, 1994). Recently there has been a renewal of interest in this area with a few new studies, but these remain small-scale and scattered. There has also been no attempt to consolidate previous studies (Smith and Yanacopulos, 2004). Studies have also tended to focus more on disaster-related messages even though INGOs' communications encompass a much wider range across both fundraising and advocacy messages (Dogra, 2007a).

A review of the more recent studies indicates a fairly limited and unclear status of INGOs' current imagery. Some of these studies suggest that INGOs' messages are becoming increasingly mixed and ambivalent. Matt Smith argues that traditional 'negative' views of need are increasingly being combined with a contradictory, 'positive' agenda; such as the theme of empowerment as seen in recent child sponsorship messages of the INGOs Plan and ActionAid (2004). A survey on how INGOs use and source photography indicates that many INGOs nowadays have picture policies (Clark, 1993 and 2003). Based on responses to questionnaires from 63 INGOs, the survey also finds that INGOs believe their visual imagery has improved over time. Their comments indicate that they avoid 'negative' and 'helpless' imagery and use 'positive' and active images. However, another set of critical scholars, working broadly within postcolonial theories (Shaw, 1996; Shohat and Stam, 1998; Hutnyk, 2004) argue that INGOs' messages remain simplistic and occasionally 'negative', which contradicts the studies of the early 1990s claiming that 'positive' images were, by and large, replacing 'negative' imagery. On the 'negative' side, the issues of spectacle, simplification and decontextualisation have been raised by Stanley Cohen (2001). He is critical of disaster images of helplessness and dependence that lead to the 'view of the developing world as a spectacle of tragedy, disaster, disease and cruelty' (Cohen, 2001: 178). This is also reflected in Lilie Chouliaraki's analysis of specific disaster news on television: what she refers to as 'adventure news: suffering without pity', which dehumanises sufferers through the absence of their agency (2006: 97).

Although some of these recent illustrations can cautiously be seen as examples of continuing arguments of 'negative' representations, they do not permit generalisations across a broader set of INGO messages. In empirical terms, the focus of most studies has been on disaster images or images of children, and other types of INGO representations have been neglected. The strong reactions to disaster imagery, stemming from the Ethiopian crisis, and the neglect of other forms of NGO messages, have restricted the scope of discussions. This has also resulted in a polarised, narrow, simplified and generalised conceptualisation of imagery across a 'negative'/'positive' divide that lumps complex images into one category or the other instead of viewing them in detail and considering a deeper investigation of the practices and potential of INGOs' public messages.

This book pays attention to both the empirical and conceptual aspects. To provide empirical rigour INGOs' public messages were studied for a full year to cover a large, representative and diverse range of both fundraising and advocacy representations. Conceptually, the discussion on INGOs' messages is broadly organised around 'positive' and 'negative' elements which, in turn, are rooted in certain world views and 'ways of seeing' such as humanism, humanitarianism and human rights on the 'positive' side and colonial discourses on the 'negative', with different scholars focusing on specific aspects. John Berger's phrase 'ways of seeing' addresses the connection between the image and the viewer (1972). A complex term, it includes not just what is shown and how it is constructed but its relation to other things and the positioning of the viewer that it invites, signifying deeper links between thought and action.

Global poverty, world history and representations of 'Others': Colonialism, Orientalism and Development

World history is deeply connected and shapes the current global order of MW poverty and DW prosperity. This is true both of the material links, located in the *realpolitik* of slavery, colonialism and imperialism, and the production of knowledge through representations, namely the cultural effects of colonial history which invented various constructs such as 'race',[8] 'Africa', 'Orient' and later 'development'.

History is a continuous chain and though the world was linked long before the colonial era, the nature of connections altered fundamentally to become greatly skewed and exploitative during colonialism. The literature on slavery, colonialism and imperialism is vast and diverse, and a detailed review is beyond the scope of this book. A host of historians have documented that the colonial period greatly harmed the colonies and benefited the colonising nations, and the current state of poverty, and affluence, in different parts of the globe is a legacy of this period (Chandra, 1992; Davis, 2001; Pogge, 2002; Hobson, 2004; Luxemburg, 2004; Easterly, 2006). The European slave trade, for instance, 'haemorrhaged' and depopulated Africa over four centuries (Inikori and Engerman, 1992; Heuman and Walvin, 2003: 4). Although figures vary, it is estimated that around 12 million Africans were forced into Atlantic slave ships to America and countless died during the slavery period. William Easterly provides a comprehensive account of the historical role of 'the West' in the creation of current global poverty through what he calls 'the mess left behind by the old White Man's Burden' of 'five centuries of European violence, slavery, paternalism, colonialism, exploitation' (Easterly, 2006: 239, 255). Calling it the 'Secret History of the Nineteenth Century', Mike Davis draws attention to the history of droughts, famines and diseases during colonialism in the nineteenth century and shows that the total human death toll could have been anywhere between 30 and 50 million across Asia and Africa (2001: 6). He contrasts this with the earlier accounts of many travellers across East and Central Africa, and Asia, who describe the variety of crops and evident prosperity of these regions and their gradual transformation into dependent colonies tied to the world markets they had no control over.

More than three-fourths of the world's population today is shaped by its experience of European colonialism and imperialism in economic, political, social and cultural spheres, which makes it imperative to engage with it to understand the modern world (Ashcroft et al., 1989; Lloyd, 2001). The historical processes are not simple or linear but complex and widespread and affect all aspects of our lives today – institutions, structures, national boundaries, citizenship, production and consumption patterns and our very understandings about ourselves. The spread and legacies of colonialism clearly suggest the need to treat the globe as one interconnected analytic category.

It is easy to slip into generalised statements about 'good East' and 'bad West', which Easterly rightly cautions against, and imply, for example, that 'the West' was the only contributory factor to bad governments in other parts of the world (2006). Hence, at this stage it is vital to state that my emphasis on the historical role of DW in the current situation in MW is not aimed at suggesting that the colonial experiences of all regions were homogeneous, or denying the responsibility or culpability of these regions, particularly their elites. Instead it aims to unveil the gauze of 'collective amnesia' about history and to emphasise how closely DW and MW are linked so that any portrayal of their separation into discrete zones is a flawed one.[9] Such portrayals are not uncommon for there is no dearth of 'Eurocentric historians', as revealed by James Blaut in his fine analysis of eight influential historians, who have constructed a vast complex of beliefs and theories all suggesting 'European superiority or priority in everything from climate and topography to demography, technology, state, family, and mentality' to explain Europe's present prosperity (2000: 3).[10] These accounts not only exclude the central role of the non-European world during the colonial period but also the historical connectivity predating this period that lies across other areas, notably science and technology, as reflected in the significant role many scientific inventions and discoveries made in Asia played in Europe's technological and industrial advancements (Frank, 1998).[11] There is also the 'revisionist' school that argues that colonialism was, in fact, a 'Good Thing' for the 'empire[s] enhanced global welfare' (Ferguson, 2004: xxi).[12]

Eurocentric historical accounts are particularly significant in the context of what Catherine Hall terms 'the amnesia of empire' that prevails in Britain (2002: 5) and arguably across most nations of DW. To be sure, there were some Europeans, such as journalist William Digby and naturalist Alfred Russel Wallace, who recorded and vehemently criticised the famines, along with slum poverty in cities during the nineteenth century. However, while the latter 'Dickensian slums' remain in the world history curriculum, the former have disappeared. These missing pages from Western textbooks that show the links and continuities among different parts of the world (Davis, 2001; Shohat and Stam, 1994) enable specific readings and understandings of current situations and their narratives, including those of INGOs. These absences work in varying ways as the 'invisible empire' (Wemyss, 2008: 23), selective history, ambivalences and 'postimperial melancholia' (Gilroy, 2004: 98) about Britain's imperial past.

Valentin Yves Mudimbe eloquently describes history as 'a legend, an invention of the present' (1988: 194). Whether considered 'true' or 'mythical', history undoubtedly has immense significance in shaping our consciousness and understandings of the past, present and even the future. Historical knowledge and praxis are related because history does not merely enumerate facts but explains why and how things happened (Preiswerk and Perrot, 1978). The dominant version of history taught, and known, in Britain is either selective or revisionist and, thus, 'mythical', which tends to exclude or gloss over the accounts of what Young calls the 'long, violent history of colonialism' (Young, 2001: 4; Newsinger, 2006).[13]

The division of the world into DW and MW has its roots in historical processes, especially of colonialism. Simultaneously, 'othering' – namely the construction and maintenance of 'difference' between categories such as 'us' and 'them' or 'the West' and 'non-West'/ 'East'/ 'Orient' – is a central tenet of colonial discourses. These categories and the differences assigned to them are not geographical but historical constructs, represent immensely complex ideas and have no simple or single meaning (Hall, 1992a: 276–277). These discourses still linger and inform the ways of seeing and representing 'Other' cultures (Mudimbe, 1988 and 1994; Said, 1994 and 1995). The substreams of colonial discourses are distinct, yet closely interlinked, and I have organised them under the headings of colonialism, Orientalism, Africanism and 'development', for the sake of analytical clarity and to build up a framework to analyse the public messages of INGOs. As none of these discourses of colonialism or 'development' is monolithic, the lens does not aim to generalise but to cull out dominant themes and narratives, including essentialisations if any, within INGOs' messages.

The colonial discourse of 'difference', reflected particularly in the textual and visual representations of Europe's 'Others', became quite widespread and institutionalised from the eighteenth century onwards.

This has been argued by Edward Said in his highly influential idea of 'Orientalism', and its counterpart, often called 'Africanism', which is the focus of scholars such as Mudimbe.[14] While both highlight various modalities of colonial discourses applicable to 'the Orient' or 'East' and 'Africa' respectively, the concept of Orientalism serves to bring to the surface *more* difference or 'distance'; that is, an exaggerated sense of difference between 'the West' and 'non-West'. These colonial discourses in turn influenced later discourses, particularly that of 'development', with the predominance of modernisation theories in the post Second World War era and an overall 'top-down' approach, as argued by the 'post development' school led by Arturo Escobar (1995).[15]

Colonialism deployed many modalities such as classifications and stereotypes[16] to explain, produce and project knowledge about colonies in specific ways in order to show difference between 'us', i.e. European colonisers, and 'them' or 'Others', i.e. the colonised regions, and to justify the colonial project (Hall, 1992a; Breckenridge and Van der Veer, 1993; Cohn, 1996; Dirks, 1996). Historically continuous, this process of 'knowing' and projecting 'Others' as 'different' began earlier during the slave trade. European commercial slave trade from the sixteenth century onwards not only supplied a cheap labour force for plantation economies but also constructed Europeans as 'civilised' *vis-à-vis* the 'native savage' as an inherent part of the ideology of racism (Ashcroft et al., 1998). The 'science of race' was invented gradually to attribute values and characteristics to people based on their biological traits. The one thing Africa was said to have is nature, shown as wild landscape particularly in the explorers' imagery and as *terra nullius* in the form of uninhabited land that could be colonised. This was in marked contrast to previous accounts of Africa's courts and cities, all signs of which disappeared from the narratives during colonialism and continue to remain absent from mainstream Western imagery of Africa (Nederveen Pieterse, 1992).

Bernard Cohn's analysis of representations of India during British colonialism also provides useful illustrations of the ways of seeing inherent in colonialism (1996).[17] Cohn indicates that many 'investigative modalities' of gathering, ordering, classifying and using knowledge about India were adopted by the British during their colonial project from the eighteenth century onwards. These included the survey modality of mapping, inspection and exploration; the museological modality, India being a vast museum filled with ruins, antiquities and people representing [European] past eras such as the classical, biblical or feudal era; the surveillance modality, surveying India from a distance or height such as atop a horse, train or elephant, and the observational and travel modalities of following predetermined routes and seeing in predictable ways to make it all seem familiar (Cohn, 1996: 6–8). These modalities adopted by a range of British institutions and scholarship resulted in the projection of India as 'different' in certain definitive ways.

In order to understand India, the British 'reduced vastly complex codes and their associated meanings to a few metonyms' (Cohn, 1996: 162). Instead of engaging with the complex societies they came into contact with on their own terms, colonisers, in general, attributed characteristics to them (Hall, 1992a). Such interpretative strategies included comparative methods of history which implied linearity and showed 'regression, decay and decadence' in the colonies (Cohn, 1996: 55). Progressive refinements to the comparative model could project India within historical developmental stages based on 'markers of progress' (Cohn, 1996: 79) such as the presence or absence of communal or private property, pastoralism or settled agriculture, centralised state or kingship and, thus, static as against a progressive Europe (Hall, 1992a). In other words, the idea combined the notion of 'Others' who were not just 'different' but at a stage already crossed by the 'developed' Europeans. These notions also inherently assumed that the colonies were capable of being changed by the imperial powers, thereby justifying the colonial project.[18] They resonate later in the 'development' discourse through Mark Hobart's idea of 'agentiveness', which suggests a static MW that can be developed with outside (DW) intervention.

Drawing upon the work of Michel Foucault, especially his notion of discourse as 'power/knowledge', Said showed the link between knowledge and power through 'Orientalism', the process of which constructed and dominated Europe's 'Others' (Ashcroft and Ahluwalia, 2001: 49). Said describes Orientalism as a 'discourse which both assumes and promotes a sense of fundamental difference between a Western or Occidental "us" and an Oriental "them"' (Schech and Haggis, 2000: 71).

Orientalism works through a widespread network of institutions and disciplines including anthropology, linguistics, history and physical sciences (Said, 1995).[19] The varied and complex ways or modalities of Orientalism project a heightened sense of 'difference' that can also be called 'distance'. These differences are usually seen, and shown, through binary oppositions and polarisations of distinctions so that 'the Oriental becomes more Oriental, the Westerner more Western' to 'limit human encounters between different cultures, traditions, and societies' (Said, 1995: 46). So by enhancing difference, such representations also create and stretch the distance between 'us' and 'them'.

Other ways to show difference and distance include the reproduction of stereotypes which allow the production and maintenance of myths about 'the West' as superior – rational, progressive and civilised in contrast with the inferior 'disorder', 'irrationality' and 'primitivism' of non-Europe (Fanon, 1990; Ashcroft and Ahluwalia, 2001; Eriksen, 2001).[20] This is akin to the objectification of the Orient which can be 'known' and seen based on the assumption that it is monolithic, static and passive in comparison with the 'active' and 'dynamic' Europe (Ashcroft and Ahluwalia, 2001: 64). These representations not only distort through caricature but also generalise across a group (Preiswerk and Perrot, 1978: 174). Besides, the ideological nature of representation lets 'powerful representations become the "true" and accepted ones, despite their stereotypical and even caricatured nature' (Ashcroft and Ahluwalia, 2001: 56).

Mudimbe's work adds to this discussion by illuminating both the similarities and differences in the ways in which 'Africa' was 'invented' through the 'ethnocentrism' of 'colonial discourse' (1988: 19). Locating representations of 'Africa' in the institutional context that includes 'the colonial state, science and Christianity', he shows their links to power through various ideological strategies and 'methodological rules' (Mudimbe, 1988: 76 and 1994: 4–5). For instance, colonial rule's 'ideological model' is based on the assumption of 'primitiveness' symbolised by 'pagan (evil)' or 'naked (child)' who can be converted or transformed into 'Christian (good)' and 'civilised (adults)' through 'Christianity' and 'Education' (Mudimbe, 1988: 50). Similarly, a study on the representations of plantation workers in Jamaica illustrates that African men and women were shown as 'fundamentally different from, and inferior to, their white superiors' — they were 'evasive, lazy, childlike and lacking judgement ... and in that sense linked to established colonial discourse' (Hall, 2002: 108).[21] The 'discourse on idleness' of 'the natives' was common in colonialism (McClintock, 1995: 252). In the same way, 'missionary theology of salvation' works to establish 'order' out of 'disorder (... corruption)'; thereby converting 'primitiveness' into 'Western Civilisation and Christianity' (Mudimbe, 1988: 53).[22]

'Development' is more than a technical term. It is also a 'cast of mind' and a 'perception which models reality' (Sachs, 1997: 1). The enormous attention paid to representations of development by the anti- or post-development school of thought, which argues that the language and imagery of development is informed by and reflects the long history of colonialism, makes this school of ideas a key focus of my analysis of INGOs' messages. According to Escobar, the DW has constructed a hegemonic form of representation through a 'discursive homogenisation' which erases the diversity, complexity and historicity of the MW, thereby allowing DW to exercise its power over MW (1995).[23] In addition, the subtlety of the ideology is able to project this discourse as rational and detached. Escobar deconstructs the discourse of 'development' through the analyses of key words such as market, environment, participations, needs and poverty to argue that images and themes of famine, poverty and illiteracy in the 'Third World' have crystallised as signifiers for development.

The 'post-development' critique of development does bring to the surface many, hitherto mostly neglected and unspoken, discourses related to power relations which have special significance for representations and their interplay with theory and practice. However, it is a limited approach in many ways and has been widely criticised. Critics argue that it takes an anti-modern stance and is based on a narrow view of Foucault's concepts of power and discourse; a criticism similar to that levelled against Orientalism (Brigg, 2002; Ziai, 2004). Ralph Grillo is particularly critical of Escobar for being too political and ethnocentric (1997). The main critique of 'post-development' is its essentialisation and oversimplification of 'development' as a single, monolithic 'Western' discourse (Corbridge, 1998).

A major reason for the strong criticisms of 'post-development', in my view, is its implicit conspiratorial tone which suggests that the sins of development are deliberate, i.e. of commission, not of omission. This is obviously problematic and hard to support. Nevertheless, the dominant strategies in development such as labelling and tropes that post-developmentalists argue against provide many useful insights to study representations. These must, of course, be used along with other alternative discourses of development which highlight the role of grassroots movements, indigenous knowledge, participation and community, and a more people-centred and bottom-up approach to emphasise the agency of people (Nederveen Pieterse, 1998). These discourses have also been promoted and adopted by many INGOs, which makes it important to explore whether, and how, they inform INGOs' messages and imagery.

Given the range of complex modalities employed in colonial discourses and later in development, I have summarised these in a 'postcolonial lens' (see Figure 1.1). It is a conceptual framework of the ways in which DW/'Self' and MW/'Others' were seen and projected in these discourses. The development of this lens was an iterant and evolving process that took place along with the data analyses.

This lens is primarily a heuristic tool and its application to the visual analyses later in this book shows both its usefulness and limitations. It is not a mechanical checklist but an evolving framework. Further, 'othering' includes portrayals of cultural 'Others' – which is the focus of postcolonial literature – and all 'others' such as women and those who are poor, gay or have disabilities, as discussed in sociology and social policy literatures. I use both sets of strategies of 'othering' in my analyses.

Methods and terminologies

This study takes a constructivist approach emphasising the constructed and pluralistic nature of reality, which assumes that 'self-evident' truths 'are actually the product of complicated discursive practices'

Discourse	Modalities and mechanisms	Illustrations and themes
Colonialism *Modalities projecting the non-West as static, regressive and 'different' in specific and simplistic ways*	Simplifications	
	Classifications and Stereotypes	People as primitive, lazy, irrational
	Infantilisation	Metaphor of children
	Spatial metaphors	Wild, empty land/*terra nullius*
	Surveillance	Seeing from a superior position, e.g. camera angle
	Museological	Exhibit, spectacle
	Linear representations	
Orientalism and Africanism *Assuming and promoting 'difference' between 'us'/West and 'them'/non-West usually with subtle exaggeration to enhance 'distance'*	Binary oppositions of 'Self'/'us'/'the West'/ 'Occident' and 'Others'/ 'them'/'the East'/ 'Orient'/ 'non-West'/ 'Africa'	Superior–Inferior Rational–Irrational Order–Disorder Safe–Dangerous Civilised/Christian–Naked/ child/pagan
	Idealisation	Child-like 'Africa'
	Romanticisation (feminisation)	Exotic 'Orient'
Development *Erasing the diversity, complexity and historicity of the 'Third World' through monochromatic and ahistorical depictions*	Homogenisation	
	Classification and Labelling	'Third World Woman'
	Spatial metaphors and imagery	Barren land, overcrowding, ruins
	Tropes	Famine, war
	Binary (and Linear)	Developed/Underdeveloped Modern/Traditional Setting – rural/urban
	Commodification/ Fetishism	Predominant display of decontextualised body parts such as eyes
	Decontextualisation and Discontinuity	(Lack of) Local–Global links: historical and current

Figure 1.1   The postcolonial lens

(Schwandt, 1994: 125). It also goes beyond a discursive approach to incorporate political economy and the material context of global poverty through the historical background of colonialism and imperialism and its continuities with current MW poverty, thereby mingling 'discursive history with textual analysis' (Shohat and Stam, 1994: 7).

Any text (including images) simultaneously represents as well as sets up identities and relations (Fairclough, 1995). Hence any comprehensive and dynamic study of public messages needs to explore the entire 'representational field', which encompasses the message, its origins, its reception and the inter-relations among these elements. I explore the representational field of INGOs' public messages covering three levels or stages and their inter-linkages: 1) representation – texts and images in the public messages; 2) production – views of relevant INGO staff or source of origin of the messages; and 3) reception – how audiences receive these messages.

The dearth of recent empirical research on INGOs' communications led me to collect a large and wide-ranging corpus of primary data from national newspapers in the UK for a period of one year instead of restricting the data to a single case study. Providing rigorous empirical evidence, I believed, was critical for both practitioners and academics as it would allow evidence-based assessment of the output of INGOs' messages shown in the public domain over an annual period. Looking at messages over such a long period would also add to knowledge in substantial ways by mapping the entire range of public messages of INGOs over a year to reveal the *collective* representations from this subsector. Constructing an annual corpus of messages was important not only for its empirical 'representativeness' but also for the purpose of analysing messages intertextually; that is, seeing a message alongside other similar messages.

The INGOs under study have these characteristics in common: they are based in the UK, operate overseas in more than two countries, and share a common aim of poverty reduction – poverty being a complex phenomenon that incorporates factors such as physical weakness, vulnerability, isolation, powerlessness and poverty itself (Chambers, 1983). The INGOs also combine elements of short-term and long-term work such as relief aid and development[24] and have an advocacy/

education element in addition to their operational element (namely the provision of grants and services). Finally, they have a presence in the printed press through direct advertising and/or inserts in newspapers which gives them a wide reach across audiences.

The book focuses specifically on public messages used for fundraising and advocacy by INGOs in still or printed format. It excludes moving images such as television appeals and video ads and includes only still images. The exclusion of audio-visual messages may be considered a shortcoming of the study but INGOs often use the same image and theme for a given campaign across print and multi-media and, thus, the print data are fairly representative and the *range* of INGO imagery is adequately covered. I also selected one year (12 months) as the period because a year covers all the regular seasons of fundraising and publicity of NGOs such as Easter and Christmas. The main sources of data were INGOs and newspapers.[25] In addition, inserts, direct mail and leaflets were collected through the year and web images were also searched. The overall visual analysis consists of a total of 88 messages of twelve INGOs in the newspapers containing 276 images/texts and approximately 7,000–8,000 still images in other formats.

Of the three interlinked levels of the representational field, the 'production' and 'reception' components are based on in-depth qualitative interviews while 'representation' uses mixed methods of content analysis, discourse analysis, compositional visual analysis and semiotics (study of signs) for the visual and textual analyses of INGOs' messages. This is aimed to optimise the relative advantages of each method and counteract their disadvantages (see Annex I). The quantitative content analysis complemented the detailed qualitative visual analyses as the richness of a message could be captured while simultaneously locating it intertextually in relation to the overall INGO messages. The study is guided theoretically by the conceptual framework of 'postcolonial lens' that I developed iteratively as I undertook the visual analyses.

Many terms in this study have been used interchangeably by various academics and practitioners at different points in time to broadly mean 'majority world' and 'developed world'; my current preferred terms. These terms have been varyingly used as shorthand constructs for geographical locations, labelling, dividing and uniting and to convey complex, and shifting, ideas. While being aware of the problematic nature of these terms and their varying shades of meanings, it was not possible to replace them with other words retrospectively in the original quotations and citations. This means that it is an unavoidable challenge for the readers to keep in mind the many terms that have the same or similar meaning, as illustrated below:

Developed world (DW): West/ North/ Global North/ First World/ developed countries/ rich countries/ Self/we/ us (our)/here

Majority world (MW): South/Global South/ non-West/the Rest/underdeveloped/developing/less-developed/ Others/ them/ there/Third World/ global poor/poor (countries, world, regions, communities)

I use the expressions 'developed world' and 'majority world' in the study to the extent possible to avoid the problematic nature of other terms. The former is in common use and not devoid of its share of problems, particularly with its connotation of being 'developed' as in 'advanced' compared to other implicitly 'non-developed' countries/ world. I chose not to use the term 'minority world' to avoid the binary opposition it evokes in relation to 'majority world'. The term 'majority world' is aimed to avoid the negative connotations of 'Third World' as well as to highlight that it is a factually correct term given that the majority of the world's population does indeed live outside the 'developed world'. However, 'majority worlds' also exist in 'developed worlds' and vice versa in view of the fluidity and closeness of global connections. These terms are, hence, not capable of conveying global realities to the fullest extent and should be viewed as porous categories that are perhaps simply less problematic today than others.

Lastly, the terms 'discourse' and 'ideology' are used interchangeably. Louis Althusser defines Marx's notion of ideology as 'the system of ideas and representations which dominate the mind of a man or a social group' (1984: 32). It is 'the system of ideas that explains, or makes sense of a society' (Ashcroft et al., 1998: 221). Discourse, in Foucault's theorisation, 'is a system of statements within which the world can be known' (Ashcroft et al., 1998: 42). The definitions of both are similar and mean way(s) of knowing and talking about something. However, the word 'ideology', particularly in view of its Marxist association, can suggest a lack of agency while 'discourse' seems more fluid. Keeping in mind these subtle but important distinctions I use the two terms interchangeably as fluid, not fixed: ideology as crystallised or crystallising discourse and discourse as ideology in motion.

Chapter outlines

This book contains eight chapters and is divided into three thematic parts that follow this introductory chapter. The empirical material is organised, chapter-wise, across the three aspects of the representational field as follows: representation in chapters 2, 3, 4 and 5, production in chapter 6 and reception in chapter 7.

This chapter has highlighted the importance of connected histories in shaping current global inequalities. It has also discussed the cultural legacies of colonialism which are the focus of various postcolonial and development schools of thought and important to the ways in which 'Others' have been represented and perceived. Drawing on these studies I have developed a conceptual framework, termed a 'postcolonial lens', in order to locate specific ways of seeing by INGOs. This lens guides the visual and textual analyses presented in chapters 2 to 5.

This book shows that a dual logic of 'difference' and 'oneness' characterises INGOs' messages. The first part of this dualism – 'difference' and 'distance' – is the focus of Part I. The Introduction to Part I presents the concepts of 'intertextuality' and 'palimpsest', which are integral to the study. It also reviews INGOs' messages of 2005/6 by summarising the main findings of the content analysis. Each chapter in Part I reveals how difference is projected through the representations of characters and people (chapter 2), spaces (chapter 3) and the causes of, and solutions to, the problems of global poverty (chapter 4). These chapters show that global poverty is imagined as 'out there', without any real connections with 'us'.

The second part of the dualism – 'oneness' – is explored in Part II of this book. Chapter 5 concludes the visual analysis by demonstrating the ways in which INGOs' messages connect 'us' and 'them' through specific notions of humanism, cosmopolitanism and human rights. There are, however, some messages which break out of these dualistic representations to highlight connected histories and structures, and these too are explored. Chapter 5 also summarises the main findings of the visual analyses and discusses further implications of dualism and the consequent fetishism. Chapter 6 begins to examine the setting of INGOs to understand why the images are the way they are. It looks 'inside' the INGOs (production in the representational field) and discerns distinctive forms of 'oneness' that permeate INGOs. Based on interviews with key INGO staff, it demonstrates that oversimplification and decontextualisation in INGOs' messages stem from both institutional factors of isomorphism and societal factors that include definite assumptions by INGOs about Western, particularly British, audiences as a homogenised mass.

The focus of Part III is on 'reflexivity'. Chapter 7 moves 'outside' the INGOs to explore audience perspectives (reception in the representational field) through interviews conducted with members of the British public or audience. Based on their responses to specific INGO messages, it finds clear links between knowledge and emotions, and the personal and collective. The simultaneously divergent and shared audience responses both question the generalised form of Eurocentric 'Britishness', the public's inability to engage with historical connections, and reveal its deep structures and durability. Chapter 8 draws together the threads of 'difference', 'oneness' and 'reflexivity'. It underlines the key implications for the management of NGOs. It argues that INGOs, as highly trusted institutions, must go beyond 'the human', engage more with the consequences of their representations and inculcate a more reflexive understanding of global poverty and development amongst Western publics.

A diagrammatic summary of the multi-directional links that emerge from the research around the public messages of INGOs is mapped out in Figure 1.2. The schema provides a useful map to guide the readers through the wide and intricate web of diverse actors and connectivities that impact upon, and are reflected through, INGOs' public messages in complex and fluid ways.[26]

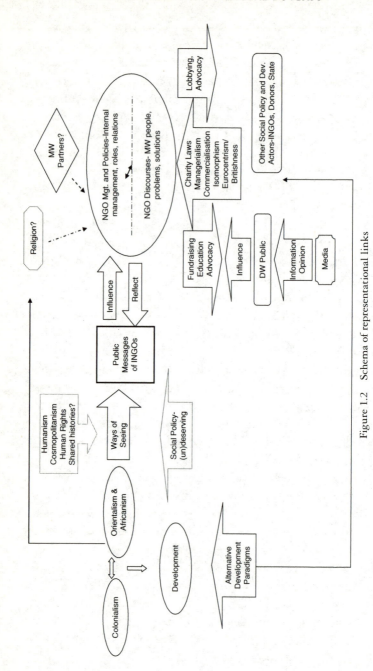

Figure 1.2   Schema of representational links

PART I

DIFFERENCE AND DISTANCE

What is 'out there' is, in part, constituted by how it is represented.

(Stuart Hall, 1992b: 14)

Introduction

The book shows that INGOs' public messages construct and connect the developed and developing worlds through a dualism of 'difference' and 'oneness'. This projects the global poor as separate from the West while still being like us through our shared humanity. This part focuses on the first theme of 'difference'. It demonstrates that difference, as seen in INGOs' predominantly oversimplified, decontextualised and ahistorical narratives, is projected through specific characters, space, causes of global poverty and its solutions in the shape of easy, do-able development.

Part I demonstrates that INGOs' public messages construct ideas of 'difference' and 'distance' (more difference) through the presence/inclusion and absence/exclusion of different characters, spaces and issues, and the discursive positioning of the developed and majority worlds as oppositional especially through the use of binaries and distinctive framings of global poverty and development. The categories of 'difference' and 'distance' overlap and have been divided only for the purpose of analytical clarity.[1] The overlaps also support the argument that INGOs' messages (just like *any* message) are polysemous, which implies that they have multiple meanings, but the polysemy is circumscribed in two ways – across space and time. The concepts of 'intertextuality' and 'palimpsest' are useful here. First, messages are *intertextual*; that is, they are produced and read within the context of other messages including INGOs' other messages and wider messages available in a given society at a given time. Second, messages are also linked to time as they are in relation to messages prevalent in a society *across* time. This means that just like a palimpsest, a parchment that has been written over but still reflects previous writings, messages contain traces of the 'past'. The messages may also be understood by the audiences within the context of historical ways of seeing that they are accustomed to.

Difference and distance, shown through binary positioning, takes many forms in INGOs' messages. But why are binaries so problematic? The concept of 'liminality' illustrates this well. Deriving from the word 'limen', which means threshold, it is an 'interstitial or in-between space' (Ashcroft et al., 1998: 130). Binary systems of representation 'suppress ambiguous or interstitial spaces between the opposed categories' (Ashcroft et al., 1998: 23). And such liminal spaces are where understanding and change can take place. Widespread use of binaries in INGOs' messages suppresses liminality or in-between spaces, thereby constructing more difference or 'distance'.

Part I of this book shows that INGOs' messages work within dominant themes of difference and distance albeit in manifold, intricate, overlapping and paradoxical ways. Chapter 2 shows how this is achieved by way of discursive strategies of infantilisation and feminisation through portrayals of children and women; and through binary depictions of the DW and MW as 'active givers' and 'passive receivers' respectively.

In addition to people or characters, space features in INGOs' messages to enhance the difference and lengthen the distance between the DW and the MW where the latter are shown as lands of famines and disasters, and as an infinite, unchanging village. Distance, thus, becomes exaggerated across both time and space through 'biblical' depictions of starvation and rurality that project a timeless and ahistoric 'Third World' as against a modern, urban 'First world'. Chapter 3 maps how the discursive strategies of geographical symbolism, cartography, different settings, homogenisation and the absence of urban life, modern symbols, historical context and linkages are used to achieve this.

Finally chapter 4 explores representations of the core issues of global poverty – the causes of the problems and their solutions in the form of development. It shows that INGOs' messages circumvent the historical context of global poverty and construct it in two ways – global poverty as a consequence either of 'internal' factors such as corruption, overpopulation and violence in MW or a result of God-given 'natural' factors. Further, in contrast to the massive scale of global problems, these messages suggest that solving global poverty through development is actually simple, easy and technical, not systemic or political.

Overview of INGOs' annual messages: 2005/6

A summary of the content analysis of INGOs' public messages in UK's national press, and the dominant features of themes and characters, is given here.

During the year (February 2005 to January 2006) there were a total of 88 INGO fundraising and advocacy items in UK's national newspapers, of which 5%, i.e. 13 messages, were purely textual and did not carry an image.[2] Many messages contained more than one image and the total number of images was 263, which clearly shows the predominance of image-based messages and the overall importance of images *vis-à-vis* text in INGOs' messages.

There were twelve INGOs with press presence in terms of adverts and/or inserts in the national newspapers. The largest NGO, Oxfam, had the highest number with 29 messages followed by Christian Aid (CA) with 17 messages. Of the other INGOs, Plan International UK (Plan) showed ten messages, Concern Worldwide UK (Concern/CW) carried nine messages while ActionAid (AA), Save the Children (SCF), World Vision (WV), Care International UK (CARE), Catholic Agency for Overseas Development (CAFOD), Farm Africa (FA) and Action Against Hunger (AAH) showed two to six messages each. War on Want (WOW) did not have any press advertisements, but it had a single insert.[3] The high press presence of larger INGOs such as Oxfam and CA highlights an in-built selectivity of messages as a result of the dominance of large INGOs over smaller ones.[4] While the small size of an NGO is not an indicator of its radicalism, the relatively low power of smaller organisations to reach mass audiences compared to the giant INGOs does have implications for the overall plurality of messages. The high concentration of income in the hands of the larger NGOs has also been a growing trend since the 1990s (Smillie, 1995). This trend of oligopoly and concentration of resources is also reflected in their public messages, suggesting a clear link between income and publicity and the consequent crowding out of minor INGO voices. When seen in terms of 'brands', a larger INGO has more users than a smaller INGO, which gives it an added advantage. As consumers are inclined to use large brands more often than small brands, the advertising of large brands becomes relatively more productive and less expensive as a proportion of their income (Jones, 2007: 105, 109–110).

With regard to the intended purpose of the messages or the 'type' of messages, fundraising messages clearly dominate. Although 50% of total messages were hybrid as they gave information and raised funds, in all 80% to 85% of messages were aimed at fundraising. Only 15% of the total messages could be categorised as advocacy/campaign and awareness-generation messages. The hybridity of messages might suggest that INGOs have responded positively to the criticisms that they separated fundraising from awareness-generation and advocacy, as was suggested in the 'imagery debate' literature. Closer analysis, however, reveals that usually only limited information, most commonly about the INGOs' own work and projects, is added to the fundraising message, which means that their response is in fact somewhat limited. Only seven out of a total of 139 hybrid messages were about awareness-generation of deeper contextual issues; the remaining 132 merely gave information about the INGO's activities and simply publicised the INGO's own achievements. This specific form of combined messaging seems to echo a similar trend in the United States where 'self publicity comes to masquerade as "raising awareness"' (Sogge, 1996: 12).

A mere 12% of overall messages were related to advocacy, which includes political mobilisation and awareness-generation about a specific issue. These included the issues of Make Poverty History (MPH)

– debt, trade and aid – and showed individuals, mostly from the DW, campaigning over MPH issues. There were also specific issues such as universal registration for children and some messages that attempted to bust 'myths' and stereotypes of MW. Three percent of messages were information-giving and contained information about or updates on work carried out by the INGO without directly asking for any funds. Many advocacy appeals contained fundraising elements, thereby making the actual purpose of these messages ambivalent.

The blurring of lines exists not just between fundraising and advocacy but also between the themes of disasters and development, with many images falling within more than one category. A broad theme-based analysis indicates that 'development' is the most common theme of INGO messages, followed by disasters. Nearly half of INGO messages can be categorised under 'long-term developmental' messages. These include developmental activities such as education, health, water and livelihood as shown directly in the form of INGO projects or Christmas gifts and in child sponsorship appeals. This is a loose categorisation because the focus varies in each message. For instance, while many child sponsorship messages show developmental activities, the spotlight is generally on a child, which makes such messages people-oriented or character-based rather than activity-based.

While most messages can be said to show an issue or activity, around 7% of messages are more people-oriented in that they do not show an issue directly but focus on MW people, mainly women and children, to project a sense of childhood, motherhood or womanhood which, in turn, characterises the MW in specific ways. Similarly, disasters including food crises, natural disasters and political conflict, form the second most prominent theme at 27% of the total messages. However, while many of the emergency messages do not show any image, there are many developmental items such as supplements in newspapers which include images of, say, HIV/AIDS that would fall under the category of disaster images.

The high incidence of hybrid messages in terms of intention and content, with unclear lines between disaster/emergency/crisis imagery and developmental imagery, has important implications for both the debate and practices of INGOs' communications. Hybridity dissolves any clear-cut distinction between fundraising and advocacy. The mixed, and occasionally inconsistent, nature of messages also makes it hard to categorise advocacy and fundraising under the respective labels of 'positive'/'good' and 'negative'/'bad', as was argued in the imagery debate of the late 1980s and early 1990s.

CHAPTER 2

CAST OF CHARACTERS

The spectacle is not a collection of images, but a social relation among people, mediated by images.

(Guy Debord, 1994: 12)

A review of INGOs' public messages in the UK national press during 2005/6 shows that people are the main subject of these messages. I argue in this chapter that INGOs' messages work within dominant themes of 'difference' and 'distance' (more difference) through the representations of characters. This is implemented by way of discursive strategies of infantilisation and feminisation through portrayals of children and women respectively, as well as depictions of DW as active and giving and MW as passive and receiving. The first and second sections respectively analyse portrayals of the most popular characters in INGOs' messages – children and women. The third section illustrates forms of binary positioning of DW and MW through the representations of people.

INGOs' messages are people-centred with nearly four-fifths of the messages showing characters. Ordinary MW people are the most commonly used characters, in tune with the most common themes of development and disaster in the messages showing the involvement of MW people in 'passive' or 'active' modes. Ordinary MW inhabitants formed the subject of 71% of messages while 14% of messages showed MW landscape, animals, maps or 'developmental' products. Ordinary DW individuals and famous persons (DW leaders and celebrities) were shown in 7% and 3% of the messages respectively and 5% of messages did not contain any images but were text-based.

The proportions of different types of characters within the total people shown in INGOs' messages are given in Figure 2.1.

Figure 2.1 shows that 42% of all characters are MW children, making them the most popular character in INGOs' messages. These are followed by MW women at 30%: a category that includes images of mother and children at 17% of all characters. The dominance of children and women in INGOs' messages also lends strong support to the arguments of 'infantilisation' and 'feminisation' of MW. In terms of characters, these also set up MW as 'different' – inhabited mainly by children and women and usually without men, who form only 9% of total characters.

MW characters also appear mostly in fundraising and information-giving messages. Further, when they appear within advocacy messages, they are used for awareness-generation, not political mobilisation. For example, CAFOD's 'Ethiopia Lives' photographic project aims to bust

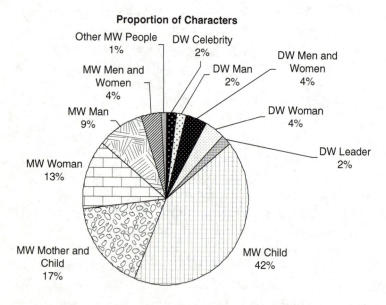

Figure 2.1   Breakdown of characters in INGOs' messages
NB: Other MW People: mixed groups of people, children with adults, and crowds that cannot be seen clearly.

stereotypes of Ethiopia by showing Ethiopians engaged in 'normal' activities such as going to school and sipping tea. 'Normality' here becomes defined as ordinary day-to-day or non-disaster life. DW people, on the other hand, mostly appear in advocacy images. The use of MW and DW people for different purposes also partially explains their active–passive characterisation because advocacy messages, in general, show more active images compared to fundraising and other messages.[1]

Several important findings emerge from the content analysis. The messages are dominated by MW characters, particularly children and women, who also tend to appear more in fundraising and information-giving messages when compared to their DW counterparts. Furthermore, developmental activities and disasters form a large percentage of INGOs' overall messages. This analysis is useful to gain an overview of INGOs' messages that also aids the following qualitative analysis.

Innocent children

MW children's images form an overwhelming proportion of INGOs' messages at 42% of the total messages showing characters. Seen in terms of their popularity, children truly are the 'development candy' of INGOs' messages. The 'universal' appeal of children to evoke visceral emotions, irrespective of their ethnicity, as in the slogan 'A Hungry Child Has No Politics' (Cohen, 2001: 178), is a part of their apparent attractiveness. Children's images, however, work in complex and divergent ways as metaphors to symbolise childhood and MW across axes of 'need', vulnerability, universal appeal, 'hope' and, above all, infantilisation.

A single child's face, seemingly caught unawares, staring passively, and without any clear expression, at the camera is the quintessence of many sponsorship appeals. The issue of eye-contact with the camera (and thus the viewers) is a blurry area. On the one hand, it can convey 'need' via an appeal through the eyes, which places the person photographed in a 'low' position compared to the viewer, connoting the subject's availability and servitude (Nederveen Pieterse, 1992: 131). On the other hand, it can suggest the faith the photographed subjects show in their photographer, as argued by Comaroff and Comaroff in the case of anthropologist Isaac Schapera's photographs of children in

Image 2.1   ActionAid, AA-6 'Sponsorship will give her the time of her life.
Childhood' (Saima)

Botswana taken during his fieldwork between 1929 and 1934 – '*Bana*:
Children at Play and Work' (2007).

Given the close-up of the face, such expressions may be read by various viewers as sad, hurt, appealing or complaining (as if saying 'why
don't you help me?'), thus making the children look needy. The need
quotient of these images is enhanced by two factors – the removal or
blurring of the background including any other person in it, and the
relatively large space occupied by the image in the total space of the
advert. The image, cropped to hide the background, lends a quality of
isolation to the child and decontextualises her, thus adding to the overall sense of need and urgency. A child sponsorship brochure (AA, 2005)
illustrates how 'cropping' is used as a strategy to enhance vulnerability.
The cover, with the title 'You have the chance to change this child's
life forever', and some colourful patterns, has a window through which
one can see the next page where a girl from 'Africa' wearing a frock
stands alone on a mud surface looking slightly downcast. Interestingly,

when one turns the page to see the whole picture, one can see shadows of three people on the muddy ground, implying that the girl was not alone but standing in a group or with her family. So the cover photo, which usually works as a 'hook' to attract readers, cleverly heightens the vulnerability and isolation of the child by hiding parts of the image and achieving a cropped effect on the cover.

When repeated on different dates, some of the messages in newspapers reduce the space used by the image in comparison with that occupied by the written text. Comparing these sets of adverts illustrates the effect of the varying percentage of space occupied by the images in the total advert. The 'up close' and big images lend a magnified effect, thereby objectifying the subjects. On the other hand, an attempt is made to individualise or personalise them by 'naming' them so that they do not seem to be the unnamed and undifferentiated faces of 'the "teeming masses" of Third World' (Escobar, 1995: 70).

Another contradiction is linked to the single child versus community debate. Child sponsorship schemes favouring a single child instead of the overall benefits to a greater number of people have been criticised for being 'possessive and patronising'. This has led many INGOs to move towards a more 'community-oriented approach' (Smith, 2004: 743) which is attempted by emphasising the benefits of sponsorship to communities as in the following message:

> Sponsorship will give Saima and her community access to safe, clean water, healthcare and education. These basics which we take for granted, are so vital in making sure they have a chance of making their dreams of becoming self sufficient come true.
>
> You'll soon notice the difference that you'll make to a community like Saima's, with regular updates from local fieldworkers and messages from the child you sponsor.
>
> (ActionAid, AA-6 showing 'Saima')

This message is laden with contradictions. The 'needy' look of Saima, in the picture, is symbolically linked to her unnamed community that would gain basic services through the sponsor's help which, in turn, will make it 'self sufficient'.[2] Here, community, empowerment and autonomy are emphasised but a quick and easy solution to poverty is also offered. The 'gain' to sponsors through regular updates accentuates its 'win-win' suggestion. Such messages suggest that the lack of self-sufficiency of this community is because of a lack of basic services and not linked to any wider structures and global relations which make this community economically poor in the first place.

Another set of contradictions is revealed in the appeal titled 'Sponsorship gives her a helping hand, not a handout' (AA-1, 'Amita') which reflects 'competing ideas of assistance' through 'a critique of both welfare dependency and the demeaning character of handouts' (Smith, 2004: 744).[3]

Images of children are also used to project childhood as a state of 'need,' i.e. lacking something, as in the case of Saima's image, and in an idealised form, as it ought to be. The smile is an important way to achieve 'idealisation of the other, permitting the projection of the ideal of the happy life' (Lutz and Collins, 1993). Children such as 'Manu' by AA and a girl child in many press ads and direct mailings of Plan (P-2 and P-3) are shown smiling broadly.

'Photogenic poverty' is projected through the healthy looks and happy and naughty expressions of these children (Hutnyk, 2004: 87). Apart from the feel-good and 'post NGO intervention' scenario such images evoke, they also, perhaps, make the viewers identify with them as the children shown look as if they could come from anywhere in the world including the DW. However, all images ensure that this identification, if any, remains partial. This is achieved through projections of some obvious, visible differences between 'our' children and 'theirs' that take the form of the facial features of the children, darker colour of hair and eyes, unkempt state of hair, 'ethnic' jewellery such as earrings and safety pins typically worn in the Indian subcontinent as in the image of 'Saima'. These features not only show 'them' as distinct but also prove their authenticity and the INGO's presence and intervention by combining docu-realism with a happy, idealised childhood. So on the one hand, there is emphasis on the children *looking* 'different' or 'ethnic' to show that they are 'Other' children, while on the other hand they are also supposed to *be* like children anywhere and doing things children must do, connoting a universal sense of *childhood*. In other words,

Image 2.2   Plan 'Sponsor a child with Plan'

images of children are used to show childhood in two main ways – as a state of lacking or needing something or, in a normative sense, how it should be – idealised, happy, engaged in play and study.

Children are also equated with emotions. This is not just in terms of adults' 'natural' emotional reactions to children but children *themselves* being emotional, natural and playful and thereby symbolising these qualities. The overall depictions of children are as needy (as they should *not* be) or as idealised and happy (as they *should* be). With the sole exception of a SCF photograph in an insert that shows a group of MW children campaigning, they rarely speak for themselves to demand their rights.

On the other hand, apart from being seen as embodiments of childhood that evoke universally 'natural' and 'human' emotions of nurturing in the audiences, irrespective of their 'race' or cultural background, children also symbolise MW, as contended by both colonial and development discourses (Nandy 1983; Mudimbe, 1988; Escobar, 1995). There is also a whole history of colonial imagery that *did* infantilise the non-West (Mudimbe, 1988; Shohat and Stam 1994; McClintock, 1995). When seen purely in this light, the use of children as symbols of MW arguably infantilises the developing world and attributes to it several contradictory ideas associated with children such as 'positive' notions of innocence and a child-like state and 'negative' connotations of paternalism, ignorance and under-development. These will be explored further below.

The 'infantilisation' argument is supported by Ashis Nandy through the metaphor of childhood in colonial discourse as 'a blank slate on which adults must write their moral codes'. This then links it with ideas of growth and development to draw parallels between primitivism and childhood (Nandy, 1983: 15). This suggests, and justifies, that MW symbolised by a child can, and must, be intervened upon, as indeed the NGO is already doing. Such portrayals also fit into Rostow's model of economic growth that puts MW at the first stage of 'under-development'/infancy that should evolve into a 'developed', adult-like stage just like 'the West'. Nandy (1987) highlights this development discourse that draws on colonial metaphors as 'the representation of the Third World as a child in need of adult guidance ... The infantilisation of the Third World' (cited in Escobar, 1995: 30).

Following Nandy, Escobar argues that the portrayal of a hungry MW child to be adopted for a donation of some small change every month signifies a whole discourse of inequality between, and the power of, the 'First World' over 'the Third' (1995). Another study, discussing the ads of private corporations that use smiling children from Asia and Africa, echoes this to show their symbolic helplessness and dependence – while children are 'enchanting, they present those children as helpless creatures dependent on the bounty provided by corporate conglomerates' (Ramamurthy, 2003: 186). Children symbolically project MW as 'toddlers' still needing the help of the 'adult'/developed nations (Shohat and Stam, 1998). John Hutnyk adds that such 'charitable' images, in fact, work as 'trinketisation' of poverty and conceal power and inequality behind 'morsels of aid' (2004: 87).

Deserving 'Third World women'

The infantilisation of MW is linked, and runs parallel, to the 'feminisation of MW' which is realised in four main ways in INGOs' messages: 1) the numerical dominance of MW women; 2) specific ways in which they are portrayed; 3) an exclusion of men that is a simultaneous de-masculinisation of MW; and 4) binary opposition of DW and MW women.

MW women form the second most popular group represented in INGOs' messages (30%) with images of mother and children forming 17% of all characters, supporting the argument of the 'feminisation' of MW in INGOs' messages. But surely more stories about women also makes for a good change? From the perspectives of the feminist schools which have criticised the invisibility of women in development, this could *prima facie* be considered a positive trend. Early gender and development critiques argued for making women, until then missing, visible as authentic socio-economic actors and this gradually resulted in the 'mainstreaming of gender'. Recognising the centrality of gender to socio-economic change, almost all development agencies and international organisations now incorporate gender analyses and programmes. Women are present everywhere in INGOs' messages – not just MW women but also DW women. Is there a sisterhood at play here or the old colonial hierarchies and differences? And what about men? As all identities are gendered, multiple and interconnected

(Plantenga, 2004), examining the representations of men is equally important.

A common characterisation of MW women is as mothers. Most mothers appear in disaster appeals where they are shown with an infant or child in a feeding station or in a health centre. Margaret Kelleher calls the representation of famine and its effects through the images of women as the 'feminization of famine' (1997: 2). It leads to the naturalisation of problems in two main ways. First, the graphic and shocking nature of many images of women works as a spectacle which places their plight 'within the realm of "nature"', with occasional sub-human or superhuman features, safely removed from the "human" and political spheres'. This has important implications because the form of the female figure, akin to that of a child, can project ideas of 'nature' while hiding other ideas such as the historical background and politics of famines. Such images in essence project the women (and children) as a homogeneously powerless group of innocent victims of problems that just 'happen to be'. Portraying 'manmade' food crises through the apolitical victim-like figure of MW women, thus, tends to depoliticise and de-historicise extreme poverty.

Second, the crises are naturalised through raw portrayals of physical and emotional bonds between mothers and children. For example, Concern's many images of 'Food Crisis in Sub-Saharan Africa' show infants clinging to their mothers. Similarly, a WV pamphlet shows a mother in a loose pink gown that has slipped off a shoulder as she feeds her child a glass of water. These are reminiscent of the many iconic Madonna and child images images where a shoulder or another body part of the mother is revealed to signify a physicality and bond between mother and child (Fowle, 2002).

Motherhood is depicted through such messages as a common and universal 'condition'. While on the one hand mother and children project MW as 'different' in terms of its extreme vulnerability shown through its most vulnerable characters, on the other hand such images also show the 'timeless and sacred' relationship between mother and child to evoke universal, positive feelings (Lutz and Collins, 1993). Iconic images of motherhood have connotations of soft, 'touchy-feely' emotions that encompass a 'universal' and 'natural' order. These also signify 'nature' and 'private'. Melhuus and Stolen (1996) argue that images of young mothers can be read as literal representations of a female-in-nature and epitomise the private sphere as against the male public and social sphere. Further, MW women are also shown doing domestic chores, which again arguably raises sensitive issues about bringing the private/domestic sphere into the public domain for the consumption of Western audiences as well as feeding into a patriarchal culture by showing the women in 'their place'.

At the same time, these images also reflect the colonial discourses of the 'fecundity' of 'Other' women which were transformed within the development discourse into the over-crowded MW with its over-reproductive women who have a 'tendency to breed like rabbits' (Parmar, 2003: 289). Sander Gilman highlights its racial aspect by linking this to 'the association of blacks with concupiscence' (1985: 79). The coalescence of primitivism and sexuality was seen during the nineteenth century in the humiliating display across Europe of people from Southern Africa as fetishised body parts, in particular those of Saartjie Baartman as the 'Hottentot Venus'. Gayatri Chakravorty Spivak has recently highlighted this discourse by arguing that blaming poor MW women for 'all the world's problems' disguises that 'one Euro-American child consumes 183 times what one Third World child consumes', a fact that is never thought of, let alone articulated (2007: 194). Treating every new born as an equivalent addition to the world population, irrespective of the location, is misleading because it hides this extreme disparity in consumption that makes one child in DW equivalent of nearly 200 additions to the world population. Such a logic of MW overpopulation implicitly constructs the knowledge of MW problems as 'internal' to MW and 'out there'. By reproducing such myths, such portrayals not only limit any 'outside the box' thinking about MW problems and solutions, but also contradict INGOs' own messages, especially their portrayals of MW women as 'good' and 'deserving'. This leads to inconsistencies and incoherence in their messages.

Apart from their role as mothers, which simultaneously and contradictorily projects the 'goodness' of 'universal' motherhood with problems of over-reproduction, the 'womanhood' of MW women is depicted in complex ways to highlight not just their 'difference' but also their 'deservedness'. Richard Dyer's term 'typifaction' for stereotypes of gay portrayals is useful here (1993). Typifications are 'visually recognisable images and self-presentations' that have a clear advantage of being 'immediate and economical' and establishing the character 'literally at first glance' (Dyer, 1993: 21–22). The following analysis locates some ways in which MW women are often typified as 'good' and occasionally as 'religious', which resonate with the development discourse of MW women as 'traditional'.

Chandra Mohanty's observation that a homogeneous and universal notion of woman as a group has been constructed under the social category of an 'average third world woman' who has 'needs' and 'problems' is invaluable here:

> This average third world woman leads an essentially truncated life based on her feminine gender (read: sexually constrained) and her being 'third world' (read: ignorant, poor, uneducated, tradition-bound, domestic, family-oriented, victimised etc.) ... in contrast to the (implicit) self-representation of Western women as educated, as modern, as having control over their own bodies and sexualities, and the freedom to make their own decisions (Mohanty, 1995: 56).

Oxfam's 'Call for Change' advert titled 'After the earthquake – a struggle to survive winter' (O-22, *Metro*, 14 December 2005, page 33) showed two images – 'Rubina Abbasi' with her children outside a camp, and boys in an outdoor class, in addition to a regional map. The main image is a posed photograph showing a woman wearing a bright red and golden *salwar-kameez*, a dress of the Indian subcontinent. Her head is covered by a red *dupatta* (long scarf) or a shawl and she holds a notebook and pen in her hand. She is surrounded by another lady, similarly dressed, who holds a well dressed boy, a young girl and two boys in the background. Rocky hills with loose stones can be seen in the background.

Rubina's character is established at first glance as 'different' by virtue of being dressed in a 'traditional' (non-Western and colourful) dress. In Orientalism, clothes, or their absence, were frequently used to project 'difference' and 'distance' (Lewis, 1996: 146). The narrative and form of portrayal then go on to reaffirm Rubina's 'goodness' within a broad frame of the 'development' discourse that draws heavily on one of the stereotypes of the 'Oriental' woman as 'sweet' (Trinh, 2003: 153). The accompanying story tells us that 'Rubina Abbasi has five children and no husband', signifying her 'need' due to many children and lack of any male support in her life. The message then mentions that she has set up a makeshift school to teach the children in camps, where she also educates them about hygiene and praying to God. The other photograph in the message supports this by showing a few children staring with a boy in the front holding a pencil in his hand. It is captioned 'Children study outdoors at Thuri Park camp's school'.

While the 'different' femininity of Rubina's character is established at first glance by virtue of her being an MW woman dressed in a 'traditional' dress located in an exclusive gendered setting *sans* men, the narrative and form of portrayal go on to reaffirm her 'goodness'. This is achieved through the description of her activity of teaching children about hygiene and prayers. It is also reported that she has five children and no husband; as such she is 'typical' of poor MW women who have too many children and no support from their own men. There is no explanation of where her husband is. All these details are invoked through the outwardly simple face of an MW woman. As Dyer eloquently states, typification 'condenses a wealth of social knowledge into a few striking and vivid signs' (1993: 50). The story is also sentimentalised with elements such as the soft expressions of those photographed and depictions of their 'goodness' through their deeds and prayers. The image also differs remarkably from other media and INGO website images of this South Asia earthquake which usually showed ordinary men and male officials from the region carrying out the rescue and rehabilitation work.

Another Oxfam 'Call for Change' (O-19, *Metro*, 7 December 2005, page 37) appeal titled 'Trade talks are key to tackling poverty' contained images and story of 'Agnes Maseko' with her family on her cane sugar plot in Zambia and inside her living room. Her story commendably mentions the 'EU threat to sugar farmers' through dumping and unfair prices that adversely impacts small farmers like Agnes. The message, however, focuses more on 'positive' aspects of her life such as the benefits of electricity to her family and the electrical goods they purchased, narrated in her own 'voice'. We get to know that her 'day begins by praying to the Lord'. On the whole, the story establishes her as a nice, god-fearing (Christian in this case) 'good' MW woman.

These depictions are also based on the Western assumption of the MW as 'traditional' and 'religious'. Amartya Sen, for example, demonstrates that the Western imagination focuses on India's exoticism, mysticism and religion (but not atheism, which is also a part of its 'religious' traditions) to imply that it lacks 'Western' values of secularism and scientific, rational and materialist traditions (2006: 159–160, 285). Similarly Mohanty explains that the 'Third World woman' as a homogenised social category is defined as religious to imply that she is 'not progressive'. INGOs' messages contradictorily valorise individual MW women as 'heroines' while keeping their portrayals strictly within what is expected of MW women as a group.

The feminisation of MW, which is achieved through the sheer dominance of MW women in INGOs' messages (30% of messages) as well as the ways in which they are portrayed as 'traditional', 'needy' and 'deserving', is also heightened by a simultaneous de-masculinisation through the 'missing' MW men. The quantitative review shows the extremely low presence of MW men (only 9%) in INGO messages. A remarkable example of this is Concern's supplement on the Millennium Development Goals (MDGs) in the *Guardian*. In the entire supplement containing 39 images there was only one MW man shown on the pages on Education. These pages showed classroom scenes and students from Bangladesh, Uganda and Sierra Leone, and a male teacher was shown in the feature on Uganda. Showing families without a father or male provider figure was done earlier by documentary photographer Lewis Hine to signal the family's 'lack or neediness' and invoke a 'paternalistic impulse' (Clark, 1997: 23).[4] This is a common feature of INGOs' messages as well.

It is also relevant that many MW men appear elsewhere as 'bad' men, such as corrupt leaders and local rebel fighters. Reverting to Mohanty's scathing criticism of depictions of MW women with 'needs' and 'problems', in INGOs' messages MW men themselves become an added 'problem' for MW women by way of abandoning their women or being 'bad' towards them.

MW men usually appear in developmental activities and rarely with MW women. Similarly, it is rare to find the image of an adult MW male helping a fellow citizen in a crisis. One of the rare exceptions in this regard was Oxfam's 'Call for Change' update on Haiti (O-11/16, *Metro,* 2 November 2005, page 54), which contained an image of a flooded street with a couple helping a woman, although the image was dwarfed by the caption eulogising Oxfam: 'Oxfam's help has changed my life'. The man was also shown looking sideways instead of at the woman in the water who he was trying to help, as if he himself was waiting for help (from Oxfam), which conveyed that he was not doing a very effective rescue job.

The bulk of images, thus, clearly project MW as 'different' through gender segregation as the norm in the MW, a likely hangover of the Orientalist discourse where the 'harem' or women's living arrangements in Islamic households came to signify, among other things, separation of men's and women's spaces (Lewis, 1996), applied here across the entire MW in INGOs' messages.

It should not be simplistically concluded that showing MW women in the ways described above is entirely negative, for it does take care of the gender dimension by showing their contribution to eco-social lives. In fact, 'feminisation of poverty' is a common term, used varyingly to capture patterns of women's poverty in terms of both incidence and experiences (Lister, 2004: 56). However, the fact that they make up a disproportionately high number of the people shown in the images, are typified as 'Third World women' and are usually shown without any men around paints a distorted picture. Paul Gilroy demonstrates a racist discourse in the lack of family or inter-generational group representations of British blacks in the media, which presents the black family as 'incomplete, deviant and ruptured' (1995: 59). In INGOs' messages the connotations are contradictory – women without men signify both their 'traditional' nature (as in perceived gender-segregated cultures) and nurturing role as mothers which, in turn, connotes their family values and again makes them 'traditional', not deviant. However, the deviance of MW men is signified through both their absence and violence, shown elsewhere as 'war lords' and 'rebels' (Cohen, 2001: 176). Similarly, MW families are shown as 'incomplete' in contrast to a 'normal' DW family which contains both male and female members.

Such images have a long history in the DW. Development has borrowed these images from colonial repertoires. An Oxfam appeal from the 1970s containing two images illustrates this well.[5] The first is a sketch of a white man sitting on a sofa with his wife in a t-shirt and shorts sitting on the arm of the sofa with her arm around him. Both look smilingly at the camera and at their two children, a boy and a girl, who sit on the floor playing. Erving Goffman argues that '[t]he nuclear family as a basic unit of social organisation is well adapted to the requirements of pictorial representation' (1979: 37). This image of an ideal, happy, nuclear, small family is contrasted with another image, a photograph of an MW family. It shows a woman, presumably the mother, sitting on a chair with a child in her lap and five other children of varying ages sitting or standing around her. The woman wears a *sari* and has her head covered, connoting her origins in the Indian subcontinent. The father is missing. The text mentions Oxfam's concern about population explosion and the family planning projects it supports in MW. The use of the sketch for the first family also suggests that it could be any (or every) Euro-American family while the photograph suggests a 'real' MW family (Dogra, 2007b).

The vulnerability of MW women is enhanced by either de-linking them from MW men (and the familial support they provide, like men across the world), who are not shown at all, or by attributing their vulnerability to MW men who, in such cases, are demonised as 'bad' and/or 'irresponsible'. The division essentialises and naturalises notions about MW men and women. The men are shown to lack the good male values but have all the bad values and dangers associated with the male in general, and the African male in particular. Meanwhile, MW women become more virtuous and are valorised for imbibing all good feminine values and some masculine ones through the non-traditional roles they take up mainly because their men abandon these tasks.

The rare appearance of MW women in non-traditional roles is usually found in their attempts to earn a livelihood through activities such as farming or small-scale trading. It takes the form of success stories of women who become self-sufficient through these activities, proving that such help is a good 'investment'. Such messages project a neo-liberal logic of good economic sense where the woman is shown as an instrument of development. Many scholars and practitioners have criticised such functionalist approaches to women's issues, saying that they do not serve women's long-term wellbeing and often even contradict them, for example providing short-term employment programmes for women to mitigate the effects of male unemployment or considering women's education as a means to increase household and market productivity (Beneria, 2003: 11). Mary John (2004) astutely observes how the initial feminist agenda of giving voice and visibility to poor women for their empowerment has been converted by neo-liberals for instrumental purposes to use them as easy, efficient, less risky constituencies of developmental interventions and to increase women's overall work burdens primarily in the unprotected self-employed and informal sector. Such instrumental use of these, largely true, characteristics of women turns the argument of these women's struggles for survival into a question of *efficiency* rather than of *exploitation* for specific political and economic ends. Further, these 'myth[s] of women as the most effective anti-poverty agents', and the consequent instrumentalisation of women, lead to specific developmental interventions such as self-help micro-credit groups, and both individual- and group-level investments in women by INGOs. These interventions, as shown in the representations of INGOs, nurture 'a depoliticised collective action that is completely non-threatening to the power structure and political action' (Batliwala and Dhanraj, 2007: 32).

A brief discussion on gender frameworks provides a useful background here. Three distinct paths in the field of gender shape the works of various scholars and practitioners – Women in Development [WID], Women and Development [WAD] and Gender and Development [GAD] (Rathgeber, 1990). WID makes assumptions of modernisation theories to stress Western values and targets individuals as catalysts of social change (Visvanathan, 1997). This approach has been heavily criticised by scholars such as Chandra Mohanty and Catherine Scott (1995) for being implicitly gendered and portraying MW detrimentally as 'traditional' and male-dominated as against a democratic, egalitarian and 'modern' West. WID also wrongly assumes that MW women must be integrated into economic systems but, as shown by WAD, which draws on Marxist and dependency theories, women have always *been* a part of development and its international structures. While WAD makes a valuable contribution by highlighting the embedding of gender within structural socio-economic factors, its overemphasis on structures and neglect of household-level relations has, in turn, faced criticism.[6] Incorporating these reflections GAD emerged in the 1980s with a more radical and holistic approach that considers gender relations both in workplace and other contexts instead of focusing narrowly on 'women' as a category. It acknowledges both economic and political concerns of women and advocates strategies for activism and transformation (Young, 1992). It therefore looks at varied factors such as capitalism, patriarchy and racism.

INGOs' messages are still largely projecting WID, as seen in their choice of individual stories of women who are either seen solely as mothers and nurturers or as means to achieve developmental goals by taking up 'women's jobs' and supplementing their household incomes. Such approaches were criticised decades ago, as seen in the following comment by McCarthy et al.:

> Agencies conceive of helping women by shunting them into handicrafts or programs for cookery, nutrition, child care and a model of housewifery that is basically Western in design ... The foreign agency idea of a good program for rural women is some specialized project like charka spinning, sericulture or bee-keeping. These are done in the home, and may bring some income into the family, but only small amounts and only at the costs of extending the actual labor of women. These programs do not encourage rural women into new ventures, to develop new social roles and skills, or to increase their independence.

Rather most programs implicitly assume that the best place for a woman is in the home and hence indirectly support the present status quo in the villages (McCarthy et al., 1979: 368–369).

The lack of portrayals of men in general, their implicit depiction as bad or irresponsible and the rarity of women and men shown together are other throwbacks to the WID perspective that was dominant in the 1970s, unlike the more current GAD which considers social relations within their contexts and acknowledges men as potential supporters of women.

Maxine Molyneux's (1985) conceptualisation of 'interests', which often become conflated both in theoretical works and policymaking, is also useful here. She distinguishes between women's interests, strategic gender interests, and practical gender interests. The first term assumes a commonality of interests based simply on biological homogeneity. It is a false and contentious concept because the interests of women are shaped, in complex and even contradictory ways, by their particularities such as social positioning (class, ethnicity), age, chosen identities and so on. So Molyneux considers the concept of gender interests to be more helpful, wherein she distinguishes between strategic and practical gender interests. The former aim to overcome women's subordination while the latter seek concrete interests within the existing gendered systems such as division of labour. Caroline Moser has applied these concepts into gender planning through the distinction between strategic and practical gender *needs*. She defines strategic needs as 'the needs women identify because of their subordinate position to men in their society', and practical needs as 'the needs women identify in their socially accepted roles in society' (Moser, 1993: 39–40).

While at the broad level, INGOs' conceptualisation of the needs of MW women is in terms of strategic needs as indicated in their aims and missions and the rhetoric of the rights-based approach now taken by many of these organisations (Cornwall and Molyneux, 2006), the solutions shown fall into the practical category such as small projects, healthcare, training and so on, which were also a major focus of WID.

There are, however, some rare representations of strategic interests, as found in a few Christmas Gifts catalogues by Oxfam and WV. These include 'gifts' such as the cost of running a training kit for women to combat domestic violence. However, the assumption conveyed is that if only the MW women get to know that domestic abuse is wrong they will protest against it, as if a timeless, fixed notion of female inferiority exists in the MW (and MW alone). The second implicit assumption stems from the Western decontextualised approach which considers rights as individual and hence in conflict with MW cultures usually seen as repressive. It makes this rights discourse 'victim-centred and retrospective' but 'removed from broader frames of analysis, engagement, and action' (Lyon, 2005: 174). In real life all women, including poor MW women, constantly negotiate their practical interests *vis-à-vis* their strategic interests and attempt to meet the needs which they consider most important at a particular point in time, even if it involves sacrificing other priorities. This negotiation is not a result of a lack of awareness, as reflected in these representations. Colonial cultural assumptions of ignorance may partly account for muddling up the strategic and practical needs. There is no denying that the two interests are intertwined. However, a training project to sensitise MW women about domestic abuse merely lists a problem supposedly endemic only to the MW to which a Western solution in the form of a technical outside intervention is offered. At its best this is another success for the NGO and at its worst an erasure of the complex ways in which MW women negotiate their interests *by themselves*, as well as the long history of feminism, awareness and conscientisation *within* MW nations. Instead of interventions aimed at sensitisation, the portrayal of MW women as protestors, for example, could show both agency and knowledge on their part, but such a portrayal is rare. The existing representations merely become yet more examples of MW women as 'the passive dupes of patriarchal culture' (Kabeer, 2000: 40) and 'inherently incapable of solving their own problems' (Alam and Matin, 1984: 8).

There are also other deeper assumptions about survival and what it entails. It is assumed that MW women are too busy trying to survive to have time for anything else. At the same time, the act of survival is shown as heroic to make them worthy of help. In other words, the overall messages assume that MW women are concerned only with survival and not political activism, a myth that has been refuted by many such as Saskia Wieringa (1995).

Thus, we see that in INGOs' messages global poverty itself is used to reinforce patriarchal norms. The vulnerability of women, which is a product of multiple factors including their specific circumstances and age, is used to show MW women, in general, as vulnerable and hence worthy of help. The agency of women and how they negotiate their interests on their own becomes invisible in these representations. When shown in the non-traditional roles of traders, they are not shown in their own right or because they want to work in these areas but out of necessity; for instance because their men have abandoned them. The multiple burdens of women, then, merely add to their feminine values of long-suffering nature and sacrifices. Additionally, the fact that these non-traditional roles remain small-scale, confined to survival issues and within the 'good' female discourse, ensures that the future possibilities remain limited and thus non-threatening to the DW.

The vulnerability and incapability of MW, shown through children and women, and its consequent 'distance' from 'us' is further heightened in subtle and complex ways through the binary opposition of DW and MW women. The illustrations of DW women shown as 'surrogate' mothers to MW children demonstrate a remarkable selectivity and exclusion in INGOs' messages to achieve this. When compared to overall fundraising ads, the child sponsorship brochures contain an interesting difference: the near erasure of images of mothers. As most children shown are not infants, this could be considered as a plausible reason but it is still perplexing given the plethora of mother and child images elsewhere, especially in disaster appeals and developmental appeals. Images are often cropped from a group or family photograph to show a single child or children on their own. For instance, in two images in an AA brochure the hands of a woman, possibly the mother, can be seen in the background holding the child and washing clothes respectively, but the mothers are not shown.

In the same detailed brochure of AA, only one photograph from Bangladesh is of a mother and child smiling at the camera. She is the only MW woman shown in the brochure as against four DW women sponsors. So while the MW women are erased from the brochure, DW women who are helping the MW are brought in simultaneously.

When read inter-textually in relation to INGOs' messages taken as a whole, the overall chain of signification is as follows:

- Missing MW Men: MW men, in general, are not shown except in a few developmental appeals
- MW women, mother and child are dominant characters, often shown in fundraising appeals
- MW women vanish from the child sponsorship appeals
- DW sponsors, mostly women, make their appearance

The European paradigm of sexual difference constructs women as the 'other-within'; 'the symbolic inferior' as against an inherently superior masculinity (Lewis, 1996: 17). Furthermore, through their symbolism, women are often constructed to signify nations, national cultures and their difference from other nations (Anthias and Yuval-Davis, 1989) though they are 'denied any direct relation to national agency' (McClintock, 1995: 354). Seen accordingly, the given chain of signification stretches across socio-gender hierarchies to locate the Western 'other'/inferior, namely DW women, in a strong position *vis-à-vis* all the cultural 'others'. It transforms the DW women into the helpful *de facto* 'parent' to MW children and enhances their agency, which specifically positions DW women as superior to MW women – capable of not just looking after themselves and their own children but others' children as well. This classificatory gaze, rooted in Orientalism, gives DW women access to 'the enunciative position of a white superiority that is implicitly male' (Lewis, 1996: 18).

The 'softest' representation of DW women is in the form of child sponsors where their 'feminine' qualities of doing something in a more personal manner and the emotional gratification of such acts are emphasised. However, even this soft and feminine portrayal works to show them as capable parent figures, able to take care of their own as well as other women's children. Their capability is enhanced by removing or reducing the real mothers from the representations. If agency is usually considered a male attribute which is denied to women even when they symbolise nations, then the overall effect of these representations is that of transforming these nice, 'feminine' DW donors into 'masculine' patriarchs of MW.

Simultaneously, through their symbolic value as 'Western' women signifying 'Western' nations and their difference from other nations, the chain connotes the binary of a superior DW in relation to an inferior and incapable MW, suddenly mother-less here, that is unable to look after its children. The *gendering* of MW poverty through the above forms of representations, where images of MW women are used to show vulnerability, feminine qualities and 'otherness' *per se*, does not make any radical or feminist statement. Instead, it is used to reinforce the subordinate status of women and reflect patriarchal values. This is the case even though the specific actors change, with DW women taking on 'masculine' roles and thereby increasing the 'distance' between DW and MW. Rather than emphasising the diversity of women, this representation serves to categorise them in a hierarchical manner.

There are many examples of juxtaposed representations of DW and MW women. For example, Concern's supplement on the MDGs contrasts photographs of white women protestors with a woman in a *sari* squatting in her kitchen and another breaking stones with a child standing next to her. The difference between an 'average' DW woman and an MW woman is universalised, essentialised and carefully constructed – the symbolism of pots and pans, the bare essentials and squatting position of women cooking, the private sphere for MW women against the image of a young white woman raised high above other protestors with a 'Make Poverty History' banner in her hands. She and other DW women are literally clashing with police authority and also symbolically with the two most powerful male 'world' leaders, George W. Bush and Tony Blair, who are shown on the adjoining page. The MW women seem to take their lot as they should, like poor powerless people in the narrow confines of kitchen, survival and child bearing.

DW women are represented in many other forms as ordinary citizens and professionals. DW women are invariably shown doing something, and more importantly doing many things. When they are not busy sponsoring MW children, DW women campaign as seen in many messages such as of CAFOD, CA and Concern. Even the Oxfam Director is seen participating on the forefront, connoting an 'egalitarian' society that does not sit on formal hierarchies. DW women hike with DW men and run marathons to raise funds for the global poor. With the same ease they don suits to become corporate donors.[7] They are journalists such as the white female reporter 'Ros' in Rwanda where she smilingly lays down a foundation stone while being watched by a crowd of Rwandan men and children.[8] They are NGO officials, for example the Oxfam Director.[9] DW female celebrities are not far behind. They too sponsor children; for instance, television actress Shobna Gulati for Plan UK, or are sponsored by NGOs to take up causes. Examples include actress Helen Mirren for Oxfam in

Photo: Jenny Matthews/ActionAid

Image 2.3   ActionAid, Emma Thompson visiting Ethiopia, 2005 an anti-arms campaign where she is shown listening to an arms victim child, or actress Emma Thompson visiting Ethiopia for AA. There is no instance of a female MW celebrity or leader, although 'safe' and 'apolitical' MW personalities such as Nelson Mandela and Archbishop Desmond Tutu do appear occasionally.

While MW women are shown as a similar group by virtue of the commonality of their problems of poverty and vulnerability, DW women are represented as powerful in diverse ways, thereby increasing the distance between the two sets of women in INGOs' messages. These taken-for-granted portrayals of DW women erase the distinction between their traditional and non-traditional roles, making such a distinction a thing of the past 'here' while it still continues in the non-Western world. This argument is bolstered by observing the clothes worn by women. DW women, irrespective of their ethnicity, are shown in 'Western' dresses such as t-shirts, shirts, trousers and skirts. MW women are generally shown in their traditional garments. On the occasions when they are in Western attire, the t-shirts, for instance, show the NGO logo and are generally worn by the NGO's partner staff member, namely a female worker in a non-traditional role, for instance Oxfam worker 'Noni' in Aceh (O-24/2, *Metro*, 22 December 2005, page 39). A female local staff member wearing a Western dress stamped by the NGO's logo quite obviously advertises the NGO. However, it also connotes development and modernity brought by the NGO to the MW through the vehicle of the NGO local staff member, whose dress symbolises her status as being closer to Western women and thus her *legitimacy* to bring development and 'our' non-traditional values to the recipients.

The point here is not that one is less truthful than the other but that both sets of women are constructions. The notions of the 'liberated' DW woman and the 'oppressed' MW woman are equally contentious. What is desired is a greater range of representations of women's subjectivities but INGOs' messages are clearly lopsided. While DW women are portrayed in an array of complexities, both in public and private spheres as individuals and political beings, the same regard is not given to MW women who are shown in limited, largely instrumental, roles. To be sure, they perform these roles across all the settings found in INGOs' messages – disaster, development and campaigning – but as victims, instrumental agents and silent observers being advocated for by others.

To conclude, INGOs' dominant representations of MW women continue to be those of mothers and nurturers. In addition, all qualities and virtues such as hard work and caring which make the recipients worthy of help are shown through them. They are often typified as 'good' through their traditional lives and religiosity. Morality indeed speaks through them. They are seen both as 'backward and the potential sites of radical change' (Melhuus and Stolen, 1996: 26) and hence made to participate in developmental activities and sensitised against male violence. Their participation in developmental activities, however, does not clearly ascribe to them 'modern' values but is represented in terms of survival and compulsion. The diversity and multiple identities of women are made visible to some extent but their portrayals are contained within what is expected of 'third world women' as a category. The contradictions seen in their representations suggest little change, for they leave the status quo clearly intact. Occasional positioning of women from the 'first' and 'third' worlds in binary opposition to each other also enhances the 'difference' between them.

The dominant characters in INGOs' messages and their typifactions evoke implicit binaries of 'good' MW women versus 'bad' MW men. The collective representations also feminise the MW itself and thus implicitly set out a masculine/feminine polarity between the DW and the MW.

This section demonstrates the many ways in which INGOs remain complicit with colonial ways of seeing in their messages. Portraying non-Western women as victims, whether in themselves or in contrast to Western women, reproduces the colonial perception of the backwardness of MW and the advancement of DW while sidestepping the deep connected histories that shape current global inequalities. Such representations 'freeze third world women in time, space, and history' (Mohanty, 1991: 6) and naturalise, depoliticise and dehistoricise their lives and struggles.

'Givers' and 'takers'

The 'difference' between DW and MW is also portrayed through binary oppositions across varied axes that amplify the 'distance' between them. Two prime characterisations are DW as 'active' and 'giver' and MW as 'passive' and 'taker'.

Active–Passive

Figure 2.2 shows how the characters appear in INGOs' messages based on their activity, i.e. whether they are shown as 'passive' or 'active'.[10] It shows that significant fractions of MW characters are shown as 'active'

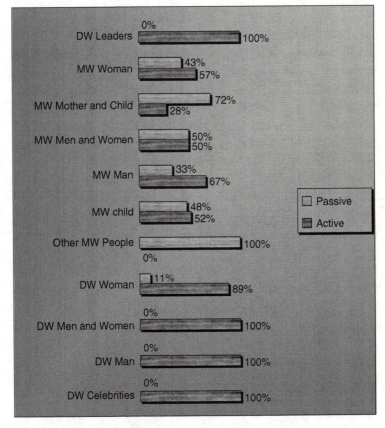

Figure 2.2   Characterisation of ordinary people

in INGOs' messages in tune with the policy of 'deliberate positivism' (Lidchi, 1999). However, there are two main differences between people from DW and MW – the proportion of active people and the type of activity.

Nearly half of MW children, who are the most popular figures in INGOs' messages, fall under the 'active' category as they are frequently shown to be engaged in activities such as play or study. The second most popular figures are those of MW mothers with children, who are generally shown in a passive mode, sitting around waiting for help in a clinic or camp. MW women, when presented alone, are often shown to be engaged in an activity such as agriculture, craft or trade.

MW men, when shown, are also usually portrayed as active in a developmental purpose such as agriculture, water project or shed construction but, while there was no instance of an ordinary DW man shown in a passive mode, ordinary MW men were shown in passive mode in around a third of images. Most DW people were shown as active, which was not the case with MW people. Given that MW characters dominate INGOs' messages with a sizeable proportion shown as passive, a dominant 'difference' of the active DW and passive MW is still invoked by these representations.

Furthermore, the above categories of 'active' and 'passive' do not show the complete picture because their *levels* vary across characters. If seen as a continuum that goes from active to passive and from micro to macro level, it can be mapped as shown in Figure 2.3.

The matrix in Figure 2.3 illustrates that ordinary MW characters are shown to be active at micro level, doing developmental work, but they are rarely seen as political activists which might, *inter alia*, risk suggesting to DW audiences the presence of 'normal' democratic systems or the existence of MW governments and leaders – elements that INGOs tend to avoid. Ordinary people in the DW demand macro-level changes in advocacy messages. In contrast to many MW inhabitants, ordinary DW men and women are shown in active modes – as protestors fighting for MW, raising funds through runs and marathons or as benevolent visitors and sponsors, which connotes their goodness and heroism. Photographs of DW campaigners were found, for example, in

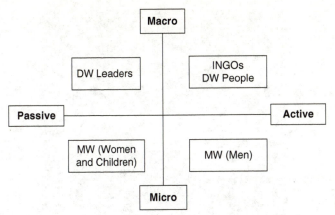

Figure 2.3   Continuum of action from micro to macro levels
NB: The images of DW Leaders are shown to be 'active' but they are often described as not doing enough and hence shown here as 'passive'.

a news item about 'Christian Aid Week' and Concern's supplement on the MDGs in the *Guardian*.

The messages related to events in support of INGOs also show ordinary British individuals taking part in, for example, marathons and countryside walks to raise funds for INGOs. They are invariably depicted as fairly young, healthy and middle-class people who actively support the INGO. DW celebrities are also shown as 'good' celebrities talking about MW problems. So, on the whole, these messages construct a binary opposition of dynamism and action of the DW and the acceptance and passivity of the MW.

MW individuals work hard for their livelihood while DW inhabitants project their goodness through their donations and their dynamism and a higher level of awareness through campaigning. Their difference is thus maintained, and amplified, through the level of activities they undertake and the labels they are assigned – 'farmer'/ 'peasant' for DW and 'campaigner' for MW, the former being a common category in development discourse (Ferguson, 1990; Escobar, 1995). The portrayal of active MW people challenges one colonial discourse, that of 'lazy natives', but reaffirms another which projects a simple, 'low level' MW as against a dynamic, 'high level' DW.[11]

Image 2.4   Oxfam, O-20 'Take a hike!'

Giver–Receiver

A related and common projection is that of DW individuals as concerned givers to MW receivers, who are shown as 'grateful takers'. This is shown through the language of gratitude and thanks and the 'success' of giving through strategies of 'linearity' where 'then'/'before' is contrasted with 'now'/'after', similar to the development discourse where 'underdeveloped' becomes 'developed' after the developmental intervention. The exclusion of historical and current structural context ensures that this relation is always shown as one-way – from DW to MW, but never the other way around.

Oxfam's 'Village of Hope' features in the *Daily Mirror*, for instance, contained many images of gratitude. The first appeal, carried over two full pages on 25 June 2005, had a title in big, bold letters – 'School that Hope Built'. The feature carried a news story from Rwanda by a credited reporter about a school built in Nyamikamba village after the genocide.[12] The message contained a photograph of 'Odette', a 'grateful' student and her letter of thanks.

The second heading of the Oxfam feature promised to reveal 'How your cash has helped bring a village back to life'. While this was a clear written statement that told the readers the effect their donation had had, there were several *visual* depictions of 'before' and 'after' that contrasted the pre- and post-NGO intervention stages. For example, a feature titled 'Village of Hope – Daily Mirror Oxfam appeal' (O-18) was a part of the series of updates by Oxfam detailing how the *Daily Mirror* readers' donations had been used. Spread across two pages, it showed five images and a map. One photograph showed children studying outdoors with a male teacher in December 2004 ('Then'). It was contrasted with an image taken in December 2005 ('Now'), which showed a new classroom with shiny desks and children in uniform with the same smiling teacher. The images showed how the initiative had transformed many lives in MW. The text in the story also emphasised how grateful and happy the villagers were for the help they had received.

A variation of such visual depictions is the use of linearity to show a chain of interventions. One of Plan's inserts in 2005, for instance, contained a series of images on three folds that showed a visual depiction

Image 2.5   Plan 'Learning from the past ...'

of Plan's intervention 'justifying' the use of sadness and happiness in this way – 'Learning from the past ...' (shows a sad black baby with runny nose and dirty frock), 'to solve the problems of the present ...' (an image of a smiling brown child drinking running tap water), 'and build a sustainable future' (this fold shows a laughing brown child holding a notebook, who will be named as 'Trung' in another Plan insert).

One of the interesting things about messages such as those shown in Image 2.5, which are becoming rarer and/or less obvious, is that given their long and extensive use, *all* the stages need no longer be shown in every case. The familiarity with linear narratives means that even seeing one stage can lead to a chain of semiosis and understanding of the whole narrative. The narrative is simple and like a fairy tale, with a situation and protagonists that transform and are transformed by the end of the fable. It also establishes a certain positioning of the DW as saviour by projecting a problem *before* DW intervention that is solved *after* the intervention, leading to a happy ending.

Conclusion

This chapter has critically analysed the key representations of people in INGOs' messages. It showed that the dominance of MW children and women suggests, in divergent ways, the 'infantilisation' and 'feminisation' of MW. This feminisation is intensified by typifying MW women as 'good', 'religious' and 'traditional', i.e. as 'average Third World women' and by a simultaneous 'de-masculinisation' of MW through missing men or 'bad' men – corrupt leaders or violent guerrilla fighters. The dominant characters in INGOs' messages and their typifactions infantilise and feminise the MW as a place inhabited by mostly vulnerable women and children towards whom the male/adult/doer DW can be paternalistic and helpful, thereby setting the scene for what Hobart (1993) calls 'agentiveness' or outside intervention.

This chapter has also shown that a parent/child status is evoked through an infantilised MW represented through its children, who are the most favoured of characters in INGOs' messages. Similarly, feminisation and de-masculinisation of MW sets out a masculine/feminine distinction between the DW and MW. INGOs' messages also heighten difference and distance between DW and MW through binary oppositions of an active, dynamic, concerned and giving DW as against a vulnerable, incapable, low-skilled, gratefully receiving MW. This projection of a one-way relationship reduces liminal or in-between spaces of understanding between DW and MW and also locates them on a superior/inferior axis.

CHAPTER 3

DISTANT SPACES

Space features in INGOs' messages to enhance the distance between DW and MW countries, where the latter are shown as lands of famine and disaster and as an infinite, unchanging village. Distance, thus, becomes exaggerated across both time and space through depictions of extreme hunger and rurality that project a timeless and ahistoric Third World as against a modern, urban First World. This is done through various mechanisms including differentiated settings, geographical symbolism, cartography, homogenisation and the absence of urban life, modern symbols and historical context and linkages.

Lands of famine and disaster

Disaster-related messages, which have faced the most criticism in the 'imagery debate' for being 'negative', continue to form a substantial proportion of INGOs' messages. 27% of themes relate to crises with a high proportion of total images being 'disaster-type' images, given the blurring of boundaries between developmental and disaster images. The iconic images of starving children and mother and child, in particular, seem to have survived in INGOs' messages although many INGOs prefer not to show any image in their emergency appeals. Such images have been criticised for being 'pornographic' (Lissner, 1977 and 1981), 'a spectacle of tragedy, disaster, disease and cruelty' (Cohen, 2001: 178), 'de-humanising' through the absence of the agency of sufferers (Chouliaraki, 2006: 97) and showing famine as a 'blanket phenomenon' without any local initiatives and its 'victims' as needy and dependent on DW (Arnold, 1988).[1] They have widely come to represent Africa in particular and MW in general, and contributed to an enhanced sense of the vulnerability of MW.

Further, in the current disaster images there is no direct depiction of a DW 'saviour' as was shown in INGOs' messages till the late 1980s (Benthall, 1993). The DW saviours have been replaced by local staff, when shown at all. However, these changes in disaster imagery reflected, for instance, by imagery of a skeletal child being cared for by an MW (and not a DW or 'white') health worker, still project merely the end result, namely starvation, without any context or valid explanation of why it has reached this stage. The broader context – historical, social, political and economic – which explains (and often implicates) why such extreme poverty exists around the world and how it is connected to 'us' remains unspoken.

The emergency appeals are the most obvious examples of the large scale and urgency of problems highlighting the vulnerability of MW. This is often shown through the massive scale of problems in terms of statistics and weak and vulnerable characters such as starving children. A series of Emergency Appeals, including many full page adverts, on the 'Food Crisis in Sub-Saharan Africa' by Concern demonstrate this well. One of these (Concern, CW-1) has a quote from the Niger Country Director of the World Food Programme (WFP) as the sub-heading:

Children are dying. We have said this before and we are saying it again – Niger needs help today, not tomorrow.

There are four black and white images in the appeal including two maps, one of Africa with Niger marked on it and another of Niger and two images of infants (*The Times*, 26 July 2005, page 14). The main image is a photograph of a small, almost naked girl ('Halima') lying on a sheet with two pairs of hands holding her head and hips. Her skeletal frame, large head, stretched hands and needy expression projects severe malnourishment and desperation. A fine, barely readable, print contains the caption for the image – 'Halima is a 2 year old girl but is small for her age because of malnutrition. She is in Niamey Hospital, Niamey, Niger.' The text names, and thus specifies, the location of crisis (and help) but Halima's self-evident description is a truism which, when read with her image, shows her and her vulnerability as an object on display supporting nearly all the arguments mentioned earlier of pornography, spectacle, lack of agency and de-humanisation. To these arguments can be added that of 'atmosphere', as made by Colin Barnes in the case of images of disabled people in films and television dramas that are used to 'enhance a certain atmosphere, usually of menace, mystery or deprivation' (1992: 12). Similar 'pathetic and pitiable' (Barnes, 1992: 7) depictions in INGOs' messages also create an ambience of tragedy and suffering in MW that amplifies its distance from DW.

Because disaster messages show extreme examples of poverty that evoke the urgency required to save a life on the threshold of death, the potential and justification for action and 'agentive-ness' is greatest in such messages. There is a straightforward visual symbol ... a clear and direct action is required – simplicity at its best and cruellest. As Terje Tvedt argues, the 'modern version of humanitarianism rests on the image of permanent emergencies and people's inability to help themselves' (1998: 226).

Extreme images of disaster, signifying a vulnerable and incapable MW, often also contain images of celebrities and views of 'experts' that also work as direct binary oppositions to the disaster images – the very worst of MW juxtaposed against the very best of DW. Similarly, binary oppositions are also set up through the medicalisation of famines, which allows INGOs to show themselves, and DW in general, as 'experts'. Quotes from DW 'experts'; for example, senior officials and heads of international bodies such as the UN as well as celebrities like Bono, are used to add weight to the argument and appeal especially in the case of emergencies.[2] For instance, a Concern appeal (CW-6, *Guardian*, 5 September 2005, page 9) with the heading 'Food Crisis in Sub-Saharan Africa – Appeal to help buy Emergency Medical Supplies', focused on medical supplies and Concern's 'years of expertise', which has allowed it to 'develop a specialised Emergency Medical Kit' enabling its 'experienced staff to save lives'.

While there is a general consensus among scholars and practitioners over the 'negativity' of disaster images, Cohen raises an important
question when he asks, 'Surely being dependent on the help of others
is not a shameful state. And if people are portrayed as not asking for
your help, why then should you offer this help? (2001: 180). This question was also discussed in the imagery debate of the late 1980s and
early 1990s where an implicit argument pertained to the 'rightness'
or 'wrongness' of showing distress or 'negative' imagery. The changes
in INGOs' policies and practices are also based on parallel debates
which swing from 'it is wrong to show such (negative) images' to 'it is
important to show reality and starvation *is* real'. In other words, the
central debate lies across an axis of political correctness versus realism
and evidence. In the process, the entire question of 'context' remains
neglected and the core debate remains stuck on 'negative' versus 'positive' with the latter, containing idealised and happy images, becoming a preferred option. There is little investigation of what 'positive'
images say – if they represent a post-NGO intervention scenario or
are merely a safe way out of the criticism of negative imagery (Dogra,
2007a). If INGOs, which unquestionably serve as important 'anti-
denial' organisations by informing DW audiences about suffering in
MW (Boltanski, 1999; Cohen, 2001), do not show 'negative' images,
then who will? Instead of an open rejection of 'negative' images, what
is required is to question why they work as de-humanising spectacles.
The answer, I contend, lies in the 'context' or causes of MW poverty
and its link to DW, a context that is both historical and current, and
is largely missing from INGOs' messages. It is the decontextualisation
of poverty, through dehistoricisation, oversimplification and other discursive strategies in INGOs' messages, that shows the problems and
people as spectacles 'out there', distant from and unconnected to 'us'.

The rural–urban divide

An overlooked form of representation in Orientalism which provides
a valuable perspective is the polarity of city and village that was used
to view, and project, 'the modern, historic West set against the ancient,
timeless East' where 'Western cities displayed the features of the modern

Occident against the stagnant Orient' (McIntyre, 2002: 218). At the same time, the city was shown as 'an archetype by which village-based colonies could be remade to join the modern world' (McIntyre, 2002: 219).

Distance between DW and MW is enhanced through depictions of rurality to project a timeless and ahistoric MW. Anne McClintock locates it as a core element of colonial discourse that projects, and judges, 'Enlightenment in the European metropolis' as the ultimate stage in the 'evolutionary logic of historical progress' and where 'geographical difference across *space* is figured as a historical difference across *time*' (1995: 40). Juxtaposing rural and urban can, thus, project distance across both time and space. This is done through showing different settings for DW and MW, geographical symbolism, maps, the lack of urban life, modern symbols and homogenisation of MW and the exclusion of historical context and global linkages.

The content analysis indicates that most MW characters are shown in a rural setting. This is significant because it supports difference shown through a general rurality of MW, as found in colonial discourses, and also because it sets up a contrast between the rural MW and the urban

Image 3.1   Plan, P-6/7 'Two methods of farming in
Lalibela', Ethiopia

DW, akin to the binaries in Orientalism (Nederveen Pieterse, 1992). In terms of setting, INGOs' messages overwhelmingly depict MW as rural (un-modern) with connotations of timelessness and ahistoricity.

The rurality of MW is also shown through depictions of livestock, as in the Christmas Gifts catalogue. By showing rural development activities that fall into the realm of nature and earth such messages also tend to *naturalise* development. 'Christian Aid Week' messages illustrate this well. These used a 'chain of rural investments' under the theme of 'you add we multiply'.[3] The first in the series is an ad with a pink background that was titled 'A chicken lasts longer than an omelette'. The image shows a sketched chain of development with arrows connecting each stage of the chain. A currency note of the denomination Five goes into the envelope 'Christian Aid Week 15–21 May' which buys two chickens, which in turn produce some eggs which hatch into more chickens. Other messages show a similar chain in the form of donation to CA week being used for a coconut plant which becomes a coconut tree and bears coconuts, or one cow that goes on to produce three which go on to produce six cows.

The CA Week ads are humorous and imaginative with a 'feel-good' element due to the use of light colours in the background and simple sketches as are commonly used in children's books. However, the examples of chickens, cows and coconut are all rural and fall into the realm of an MW of 'timeless villagers', who are close to nature and hard-working tillers of the soil, which sets up implicit binaries with the 'modern' and 'urban' DW (Dogra, 2007a: 169).

There are also instances of clear-cut and explicit binaries, a notable illustration of which is 'Corporate gifts' from Oxfam, where the images include a goat symbolising the MW placed on a shiny office desk while three individuals (both men and women), stand behind in formal 'Western' suits clearly projecting a gulf of difference or 'distance' between the DW and MW. While closeness to nature can also be viewed romantically, these depictions predominantly establish a generalised rurality and lack of or low level of skills.

Further, nature itself is used to show a variety of 'natural-ness'; for example, as barren and hostile or lush green and abundant. So nature here is used as 'an ideological category' to project a 'natural', 'rural',

Image 3.2   Oxfam, 'Corporate gifts: NEW service for companies'

low-skilled, 'other-worldly' sphere (Mitchell, 1989: 2). The overall effect is that of a 'naturally' rural MW with no urban or 'modern' elements, which puts it either in an earlier time period of an 'under-developed' stage, common in development discourse, or in a 'time-less' and 'archaic' state as in Orientalism (Lewis, 1996: 135). Further, this state of 'contemporary international division of labour [that] is a displacement of the divided field of nineteenth century territorial imperialism' (Spivak, 1988: 289), more specifically, the centuries-old colonial connections that brought a significant proportion of MW agriculture into the world economy, are completely erased from these depictions.

The rurality of MW is also commonly displayed through geographical symbolism to show 'Africa' as a vast and endless village, particularly through use of cartographic tools such as maps. Maps work in many ways. They can name a place but also inscribe an ideology. Cartography was a crucial practice of colonialism that was used to classify, organise knowledge and justify various imperial actions (Ashcroft et al., 1998: 30–31). For instance, the blank spaces of early maps signified a *terra nullius* that European explorers could penetrate. Similarly, the Enlightenment conceptualised Europe as Eastern and Western through cartography, among other things, where Eastern Europe was placed in a space between barbarism and civilisation during the eighteenth century (Wolff, 1994).[4] The maps worked as an invitation to conquest as well as proofs of triumph on medallions. They highlighted the distinction between 'well known' and 'less known' lands to fit the cultural differentiation between different parts of Europe.

A prime illustration of cartography in INGOs' messages is a series by Oxfam in the form of joint appeals with the *Daily Mirror* entitled 'Village of Hope'.[5]All these messages use geographical symbolism to connote a homogeneously rural and inexplicably timeless Africa. The context of the colonial-era conversion of these regions into mono-cropping producers to provide for consumption in the colonising nations, their consequent dependence on international markets and poor bargaining position are not made clear. So it remains mysterious why they have not been able to industrialise.

In these appeals, the outline map of Africa was shown in green with the title 'VILLAGE OF HOPE' across it and a donation form. The colour green was also Oxfam's brand colour. This map can be read as Africa = Village (albeit of hope) and/or Oxfam's reach across the entire continent and by association the MW. So the map through its symbolic nature is used to map, label, address and people an entire continent as a homogeneously rural entity. This justifies Oxfam's specific policies and interventions and places 'Africa' *vis-à-vis* DW in a clear relation of difference and distance across time and place.

The timeless ahistoricity of MW is usually accompanied and exaggerated by showing it as spatially homogeneous – 'one' MW World. One feature titled 'How Oxfam is helping around the World' (O-11, *Metro*, 2 November 2005, pages 52–53) contained many images, mostly of disasters, from ten countries, with the accompanying text stating what the situation is, what needs to be done and what Oxfam is doing. The first image shows a near-naked starving, bald child with visible ribs crying in the arms of a woman whose eyes are downcast. It is superimposed on the background image of a world map, showing Africa and parts of other continents, as if it is a free-floating image emerging from the background. The continents, shown in black, are set against the oceans, which are shown not in blue, but in brown 'earth colours', making the overall background of the message appear as barren and parched. Several trouble spots, all in the MW, are shown in red across the landmass of continents seen in the image. Using a mix of popular tropes, the map and the image together signify (and discursively homogenise) a uniformly arid and disaster-laden MW with starving children and women. As in the eighteenth century when maps were used to distinguish and order relations between 'Europe [and] other lands of the world' (Wolff, 1994: 145), the lack of trouble spots in DW makes another visible distinction between DW and MW.

Depictions of rurality, on the whole, signify body, emotions and nature in contrast to connotations of mind, intellect and rationality associated with urban symbols (McIntyre, 2002). When seen alongside the absence of any linkage to macro-level history, such depictions project MW as ahistorical and timeless. Urban life, modern symbols and historical linkages are largely absent from INGOs' messages. The overall representations, thus, continue to validate criticisms of the persistent modern and post-modern depictions of MW societies as 'underdeveloped' and stuck in a past era, even in this global world (Nederveen Pieterse, 1992; Shohat and Stam, 1998). The messages fail to indicate how the situations depicted came about, and how the historical global inter-connections, including the ex-colonies'/MW's integration with, and dependence upon, world markets as producers mostly of farm produce, play a major role in the current situation of global poverty. Excluding historical and structural connections leads to people being depicted 'out there' without any connection to 'us'. In the absence of the historical context, it also freezes MW in an unexplained time warp and situates it within a historical stage already passed by DW.

Conclusion

This chapter has shown that the broad theme of difference continues in INGOs' messages through the use of space which heightens the distance between MW and DW through oppositional representations that project a largely rural MW containing extreme poverty and vulnerability and an urban, modern and prosperous DW. The deep historical connections that created and maintain this visible split among regions across the globe are completely ignored, and this, in turn, pathologises the MW. These portrayals also view societies as homogeneous, self-contained and discrete entities when, in this globalised world, there are no islands left. In the past imperialism and colonialism played a pivotal role in connecting the world, and the structures created at that time continue to enhance this process through various institutions and mechanisms. The tendency to see MW as discrete with its problems caused by 'internal' rationales takes no account of the interconnectedness of issues and people.

Chapters 2 and 3 underlined how characters and space feature in INGOs' messages to project an MW very different from the DW. In varying, and sometimes contradictory, ways the representations depict the contemporary world through colonial themes and project MW as infantilised, feminised, naturalised and dehistoricised, separate and unconnected to the DW. While these representations reflect many ways of seeing, rooted in discourses of colonialism, Orientalism, Africanism and development, they simultaneously, and ironically, erase the historical materiality of the same colonial period that impacts current global poverty. The next chapter focuses on INGOs' specific representations of global poverty – its causes and solutions.

CHAPTER 4

GLOBAL POVERTY – CAUSES AND SOLUTIONS

'Poor rainfall and a locust infestation have destroyed family crops';
'Violence continues to haunt Darfur victims'; 'How on earth do you
wrap a donkey?'

This chapter focuses on such seemingly disparate messages to examine
how INGOs represent the causes and solutions of global poverty in
their messages. Building on the analyses in chapters 2 and 3, which
showed how characters and space are represented, it takes forward the
theme of 'difference' by exploring key issues relating to poverty and
development. It shows that INGOs' public messages construct ideas of
difference and distance through dehistoricised and depoliticised framings of the causes of global poverty. This is achieved through the use
of 'internal' rationales and 'naturalisation', combined with the simplification of development itself, all of which serve to deny continuities of
global inequalities with their historical, geopolitical context.

INGOs' messages tend to construct discourses of global poverty
in two ways. First, the messages suggest that global poverty is a consequence of 'internal' factors such as corruption, overpopulation and
violence in the MW. Second, INGOs are inclined to construct global poverty as a consequence of 'natural' causes. Put together, these
respectively imply that global poverty can be explained pathologically
as either the fault of the MW itself or the problem and responsibility

of no one but Mother Nature. Finally, the messages also suggest that, despite the massive scale of global problems, particularly exemplified in disaster messages, their solutions are relatively easy and simple.

Myths of 'internal' causes

The logic of 'difference' is supported by various myths which deploy depictions of specific features of the MW that are shown to be 'internal' or distinctive to it and cause its problems without any connections to the richer countries. These include corruption, overpopulation and violence. I employ the term 'myth' here in two ways – first, simply as mythical or not true and secondly, in terms of semiotics, as an approximation for ideology; namely ideas that come to mean truth.

Corruption

During July 2005 Oxfam carried a series of appeals on 'African Myths'. The appeals were aimed at busting prevalent myths about Africa in particular, and the MW in general. In a staff booklet titled 'The art of self defence for Oxfam supporters: How to rid the world of those annoying myths about Oxfam', Oxfam lists ten myths that should be countered (Oxfam, 2006a). Most of these myths are about Oxfam and charities in general: it 'spends most of its money on admin', 'not all the money gets there' and 'Oxfam shop staff take all the best stuff for themselves'. There are two myths about the MW: 'Africa's just a basket case – nothing can change that' and 'All African leaders are corrupt'. The 'African myths' series of public messages during 2005 were also a part of Oxfam's attempts to counter such myths. In all these ads, the space was divided vertically into two halves with a myth on the left side and its counter-argument on the right.

'African Myth # 1' states the myth as 'I'M NOT GIVING MONEY TO A CORRUPT LEADER IN AFRICA' (*Telegraph*, 7 July 2005). Oxfam's response on the right side is – 'Neither are we'. The subsequent text clarifies that Oxfam does not give money to governments and challenges corruption. Though the ad aims to bust the myth, it ends up validating it. The message does not refute the existence

AFRICAN MYTH # 1

"I'M NOT
GIVING MY
MONEY TO
A CORRUPT
LEADER IN
AFRICA."

Neither are we.

We never give money to governments. And if
we come across corruption, we challenge hard.

If you have ever meant to do something to
help end poverty, please join Oxfam today.

There's never been a better time to stand
up and be counted.

So make your regular gift now.

Call **0800 312456**

or go to **www.oxfam.org.uk/poverty**

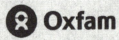

Oxfam GB is a member of Oxfam International. Registered charity no. 202918.

Image 4.1   Oxfam, O-7 African Myth ≠ 1

of corruption in Africa; nor does it mention that corruption is not endemic to Africa alone but is encountered across the globe in varying forms, or that the DW plays a role in engendering corruption in the MW through the arms trade, support of dictators, unequal terms of trade, exploitation of natural resources, tax evasion and havens and conditional aid, to name just a few. All Oxfam states is that it does not give money to corrupt leaders in Africa and is, hence, worthy of support. In addition, Oxfam assures the readers that it will ensure the money goes only to those who are deserving as judged by Oxfam.

The theme of corruption in MW was also used by Plan. Plan's supplement titled 'Futures Valued: What chance for poor children?' contained country-based details along with many images related to disasters, child sponsorship and development (*Guardian*, 19 November 2005). In a section on the advantages of microfinance, Plan mentions that it avoids the 'pitfalls of aid in developing world' where 'large donations can be embezzled'.[1] This feeds into the myth of corruption in the MW, specifically reflecting the 'civilising mission' within the colonial Africanism discourse. As Mudimbe (1988: 53) has shown, the 'missionary theology of salvation' projects 'disorder (... corruption)' to be converted into 'Western Civilisation and Christianity'. The corruption of governments and leaders in MW is also used to justify small interventions as *the* solution. Development is, thus, projected in terms of micro-level initiatives disconnected from, and bypassing, macro-level politics.

The form of representation of corruption is also noteworthy. MW leaders are not given a face or name, which suggests corruption as generic and endemic, prevalent among *all* MW leaders. On the other hand, DW leaders, when shown in advocacy messages as 'bad' leaders, are named and identified which makes it seem that the 'bad' values are applicable only to them and not to all DW leaders. This may well be due to the 'fame' of these leaders in the DW. However, not giving a face to MW leaders unless they are 'dictators' leads to the overall connotation of a generalised state of badly governed MW inhabited by corrupt leaders, without exception. Apart from justifying small-scale solutions, the representations also employ a neo-liberal logic by attributing corruption purely to state actors, particularly MW leaders and governments. This implicitly justifies the need for and importance of non-state actors, such as NGOs, which are also presumed to be non-corrupt and above corruption.

Overpopulation

One of the most widely held beliefs about the causes of global poverty is the Malthusian notion of population explosion. Oxfam's Myth #2 relates to the AIDS epidemic (O-8, *Guardian*, 7 July 2005, page 21). The left side states: 'THERE'S NO POINT IN GIVING TO AFRICA – EVERYONE'S DYING OF AIDS' and the right side counters this with the statement: 'Tell that to the 43 million orphans in sub-Saharan Africa'. It seeks to contradict the view that it is pointless to give as everyone is dying of AIDS and talks of the millions of orphans in sub-Saharan Africa – 'These children are alive. With your support, many can stay alive – and build Africa's future.' The message primarily appeals for funds, with the text urging the readers to give regular gifts and keep the 'orphans' alive. It tries to bust the myth about the whole of Africa being a dying continent by stating that millions of orphans in Africa are alive and they can build Africa's future. While future, potential and hope are connoted here through the children, it also reinforces another myth of the overpopulated MW where millions of orphans await help.

The third myth states that 'AFRICAN FAMILIES HAVE TOO MANY CHILDREN' (O-6, *Guardian*, 4 July 2005). Oxfam's response to that is 'African families have to <u>bury</u> too many children'. It goes on to mention the rate of infant mortality: 'With your support, we can improve their chances of survival. And give them hope for the future.' Raising the issue of infant mortality is highly commendable. However, the message does not mention the relation between high death rates and family size, and thereby falls short of clearly connecting the two issues. So instead of contradicting the myth of too many African children, it ends up agreeing with it when it states that they bury too many children (who were born in the first place). Furthermore, this simplistic overpopulation argument does not reflect the extreme disparity in the per capita consumption by one child in the DW, which

AFRICAN MYTH # 3

"AFRICAN FAMILIES HAVE TOO MANY CHILDREN."

African families have to bury too many children.

One-in-six African children won't reach
their fifth birthday. With your support,
we can improve their chances of survival.
And give them hope for the future.

If you have ever meant to do something
to help end poverty, please join Oxfam today.

There's never been a better time to stand
up and be counted.

So make your regular gift now.

Call **0800 312456**

or go to **www.oxfam.org.uk/poverty**

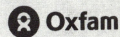

Image 4.2   Oxfam, O-6 African Myth ≠ 3

is equivalent to the consumption by 183 children in the MW, as evidenced by Spivak (2007).

Another illustration is Oxfam's 'Call for Change' (O-19, Metro,[2] 7 December 2005) feature, titled 'Trade talks are key to tackling poverty', which contains two images of a Zambian woman named 'Agnes Maseko'. The first image shows a group of six people standing outdoors in a muddy field. A posed photograph, it shows two women, a young man and three children. A thin manmade water stream can be seen along with some green fields in the far background. It is captioned 'Under Siege: Agnes Maseko, top right, surveys her cane sugar plot with some of her children'. As there are five other individuals in the photograph apart from Agnes and we are told they are only 'some' of her children, the caption at once suggests a very large family and feeds into the myth of too many Africans. Only on reading her detailed story does one find out that she has, in fact, adopted ten AIDS orphans, which explains her exceptionally large family but this is not indicated in the caption. The real-life reading experience of audiences is such that they tend to skim through newspapers, usually noticing only the image and the caption and opting to read the details only if their imagination is captured. As a reader can find out only from the fine print that Agnes has adopted many children, the dominant reading of the message would suggest an overpopulated 'Africa'.

The theme of overpopulation is spread across INGOs' messages. For instance, a message on the South Asia earthquake of October 2005 (O-22, Metro, 14 December 2005) captioned 'Lucky Ones: Rubina Abbasi and her five children are living in Thuri Park camp after their home was destroyed' yet again illustrates a large MW family. Another Oxfam message titled 'Crisis worsens in Darfur – but is the world listening?' (O-14, Metro, 23 November 2005) features the story of Elham Ali Musa's family of fourteen living in a single shelter in an aid camp. The story has a double effect of conveying the difficulties of camps but reiterating the myth of an uncomprehendingly overpopulated MW.

These messages are also linked to, and work within, the recurrent discourse about poor people being 'deserving' or 'undeserving'. A widespread perception is that poverty is caused by the behaviour, including irresponsible reproduction and large families, of many poor people themselves (Golding and Middleton, 1982). The messages signifying large MW families and overpopulation implicitly assign the blame to the global poor, categorising them under 'undeserving' poor. This, ironically, contradicts INGOs' other messages which showcase the innocence, blamelessness and deservingness of the global poor.

Violence

Depictions of the MW as violent and dangerous emerge intermittently. Ordinary MW men make their rare appearance as violent guerrilla fighters, particularly on a few webpages and inserts, supporting Cohen's assertion that 'men are associated with violent "factions" or "war-lords"' (2001: 176). Violent situations and civil wars are staple themes in many messages. For example, a message titled 'Violence continues to haunt Darfur victims' shows a close-up of a mother with her child (O-12, *Metro*, 10 November 2005). In addition to an iconic Madonna and child image, use of the passive tense is a rhetorical device here which conveys the text's meaning as neutral without implicating anyone – a state of being, as it *is*.

Violence and 'distance', shown through selective projection of history, is found in another 'Call for Change' ad (O-14, *Metro*, 23 November 2005), 'Crisis worsens in Darfur – but is the world listening?', which carried a news account of the conflict situation in the Darfur region of Sudan. Apart from the militia details, it also has bullet points on information about Darfur such as ethnicities and history, including slave trade by a particular kingdom to the Arab world. It is noteworthy that such background is rarely, if ever, mentioned in the case of countries/ regions with long Western colonial and imperial histories. The text here too fails to even mention the more recent British colonial rule and significant British involvement in Sudanese history.[3] The conflict is framed purely in terms of 'Africans' (or 'non-Arabs' as labelled in this message) versus 'Arabs' –

- Relations between Arab and non-Arab inhabitants have been tense throughout Darfur's past
- It was the centre of slave trade when the Fur kingdom exported Africans from other parts of Sudan as slaves to the Arab world ...

Erasing the complexity and historicity, the discursive framing as Arabs versus Africans above casts it 'as a tribal war in which the victims appear to the outside world as another set of decontextualised casualties in the long history of African conflict' (Campbell, 2007: 377).

When read, intertextually, with the overall dominance of children in INGOs' messages which infantilise the MW, the generalised 'child-like' and 'primitive' stage of Africa signifies lack of leadership through portrayals of disorder, violence and corruption, and irrationality through representations of overpopulation which, in turn, justifies paternalism and outside leadership. Oxfam's African Myths #2 and #3, in particular, paint a rather desperate picture of the situation in Africa, with emphasis mainly on how much the continent needs Oxfam.

These messages also construct binary oppositions between the developed and majority worlds informed by discourses of Orientalism and Africanism. Portrayals of the MW as distinctively corrupt and violent set up generalised safety/danger and order/disorder polarities while overpopulation signifies the rational/irrational schism between the DW and the MW. In addition, raising the issues of corruption and overpopulation supposedly existing in the minds of the public without really breaking these myths merely reinforces them and gives yet another reminder of these 'internal' problems of the MW. The other appeals connote the myth of an inexplicably overpopulated and corrupt MW. Instead of clearly stating the role of numerous contingent factors, both historical and current, such as international politics, trade regimes, exchange rate, and government and donor policies in issues of poverty and development, the messages rely on 'safe' contingencies 'internal' to the MW such as corruption and overpopulation. In all, the myth-busting ads end up validating myths instead of busting them.

'External' causes – Mother Nature and medicalisation

In addition to 'internal' causes of problems, several discursive strategies are used in INGOs' messages to project poverty as a neutral, apolitical and technical issue and circumvent discussions of its complexities and historical context to take away from its 'manmade' causes. These strategies include naturalisation and technicalisation through medi-calisation and disaggregation. The complexity of poverty is shown by INGOs in their messages in specific, usually oversimplified, ways. I focus on two main issues of poverty – the concept and continuities – using illustrations of extreme poverty, namely disaster messages which still make up a substantial share of INGOs' messages.[4] The high inci-dence of disaster messages also conceptualises poverty or 'underdevel-opment' in a narrow sense of extreme or absolute poverty.

Poverty is a complex and problematic concept that raises diffi-cult questions about aggregation and causation (Sen, 1981: vii). In his various writings, Amartya Sen describes deprivation in terms of capabilities, of which material limitations are only a part, to show that economics cannot be separated from the political sphere, which includes gender equities, form of government and international rela-tions (1995, 1999 and 2001). In order to take into account its complexi-ties, many other scholars, such as Alexander de Waal, also argue for a wider understanding of poverty. Discussing famine, de Waal (1989) rejects the Malthusian idea of famine as mass starvation unto death in favour of the broader spectrum of meanings including hunger, desti-tution and social breakdown, as also encompassed within traditional African understandings of famine. He states that the local people, like his Darfurian friends in western Sudan, do not build definitional boundaries between malnutrition and famine or poverty and starva-tion. Famine, thus, forms a part of a continuum of poverty, an argu-ment that can be stretched to show the continuum of, and continuities between, historical processes of colonialism and current global pov-erty. David Arnold explains the relevance of the 'past', which 'tell[s] us about the causes of today's mass hunger and the historical antecedents of the current division of the world between the starving poor and the stinking rich' (1988: 2).

The well documented impact of colonial rule and imperial policies encompassed all aspects including trade, agriculture, infrastructure and labour (see Chandra, 1992; Davis, 2001; Bagchi, 2002; Kothari, 2002; Pogge, 2002; Hobson, 2004; Luxemburg, 2004; Easterly, 2006 and Newsinger, 2006 – briefly reviewed in chapter 1). The current glo-bal system of production of cash crops by many developing countries for the use of Western nations is a legacy of these rules. More recent works such as that by Stephen Devereux (2007) also focus on politics as causation of current famines and failures to prevent famine. These historical and current contexts of extreme food crises are largely missing from INGOs' messages.

A common way of projecting poverty in INGOs' messages is through 'naturalisation', which shows nature as its cause. This is aided and abetted by the heavy use of children and women, who have 'no politics' and are 'closer to nature'. Naturalisation of problems is most evident in emergency appeals. The two main types of disasters shown are long-term disasters such as famine, and sudden natural disasters. While the latter *are* caused suddenly by natural or environmental factors, they are shown as such.[5] The focus in these cases is on the scale and urgency of the emergency. However, the most extreme form of long-term poverty, namely large-scale food crisis or famine, is also shown as 'natural'.

One of the advantages of naturalising crises is that it saves the trouble of taking sides. In other words, 'natural' can easily stand for 'neutral'. Timothy Mitchell (1991) has shown the developmental portrayal of Egypt through the trope of 'the overcrowded Nile River Valley' wherein problems are understood in terms of topography, natural space and social reproduction. Mitchell (1991: 19) states that

> the more natural the object appears, the less obvious the discursive construction is ... The naturalness of the topographic image sets up the object of development as just that – an object, out there, not a part of the study but external to it.

Oxfam's West Africa Food crisis appeal (O-9, *Independent*, 27 July 2005) exemplifies the naturalisation of famine. The message states that severe drought and locusts have led to the devastation of crops in various West African countries, with millions facing starvation.[6] Similarly, Concern's emergency appeal titled 'Emergency in Niger' (CW-3) states that

> Poor rainfall and a locust infestation have destroyed family crops. As a result people have no food and are in need of our support.

Please help Concern provide food, medicine and healthcare to families struggling to survive in Niger.

The overall text emphasises the massive scale of the problem and Mother Nature as its cause. The naturalisation of disasters in INGOs' messages detracts from their manmade causes. Thus, naturalisation aids an apolitical and ahistorical construction by avoiding the issue of any role of 'Self' and reinventing it as a 'new' problem of 'Others' without any continuity with the past. Roland Barthes would call this myth a 'conjuring trick' that 'has turned reality inside out, it has emptied it of history and has filled it with nature' (1993: 142).

Extreme poverty is also projected as a technical issue. This is done through medicalisation and disaggregation; processes that are often interlinked. Peter Conrad's definition of medicalisation, which 'consists of defining a problem in medical terms, using medical language to describe a problem, adopting a medical framework to understand a problem, or using a medical intervention to "treat" it' (1992: 211), is useful here. There are also numerous instances where elaboration of poverty through details of its components or related dimensions is shown to be its cause, separate from it. This gives the impression that substantial information is being provided but obscures the fact that the 'information' is tautological and circulatory. The information, at best, merely splits up the manifest symptoms of a complex issue to show them as various 'causes'.

Technicalisation through a combination of medical framing and disaggregation is illustrated by this message from Concern (CW-6, *Guardian*, 5 September 2005). Titled 'Food Crisis in Sub-Saharan Africa – Appeal to help buy Emergency Medical Supplies', one of its two images shows a malnourished child with big needy eyes in a woman's arms with a caption in fine print under the photograph that states 'Weakened malnourished children are at great risk of infection and disease'. The fact that an extreme form of poverty, namely famine, is being shown where people are already ill justifies the medicalisation at one level. On the other hand, the entire background of how such a severe stage has been reached and its embeddedness in the region's history is sidelined. This is one of several examples of the disaggregation of a compound concept to show elements of the same problem as having a cause–effect relationship. What appear to be details are self-evident parts of the same complex fact of food crisis split up to show that one leads to another when the reverse is also true: that is, disease can, and does, lead to malnutrition. The complex elements of poverty here are shown as separate causes, *outside of* poverty. Such 'details' also technicalise the issue and divert attention from macro-level politics. This is not to say that wider causes are never mentioned, but they are rare and usually in small, fine print that can easily be missed. For instance, the Concern appeal does point out, in passing and in simple technical terms, that 'Drought, crippling debt and rising food prices have left 30 million facing major food shortages'. In a later text the G-8's decision to cancel debt is mentioned, with the note that it will come too late for people currently at risk – 'and the sad truth is that western governments tend not to give sufficient aid until emergencies hit the headlines'. Thus, some of the contextual and related issues are indicated but these are framed to justify Concern's urgent need for funds.

While a common argument for not showing details might be the lack of room to do so, given the limited space in most appeals, even in newspaper supplements where a significant amount of information could be incorporated, the details provided follow patterns associated with other smaller-sized appeals. Plan's supplement titled 'Futures Valued' in the *Guardian* of 19 November 2005 is a case in point. It contained a large amount of apparently detailed but in fact rather superficial information in the form of stories about individuals pictured; for example pointing out how emaciated the child was, how the child improved over days and the reaction of the mother and villagers. In short, the symptoms of the problem were described in detail with the causes, when mentioned, shown to be natural such as locusts or a lack of purchasing power to buy food. This is a truism that merely paraphrases the problem and the excessive details hide some of the context. Readers also tend to scan quickly through long articles, a factor that is closely linked to creating (or suppressing) a receptive environment for the audience. Moreover, visual images that tend to 'stop the traffic', i.e. catch attention, are only about food distribution, emaciated children being weighed, and mothers and children in this supplement.

In sum, the use of naturalisation and technicalisation in INGOs' messages tends to de-politicise and de-historicise poverty.

Development as easy solutions

A theme-based review of INGOs' messages in UK national newspapers during 2005/6 shows that 'development' is the most dominant theme in INGOs' messages followed by disasters. Portrayals of disasters, discussed in the previous section, also show that 'underdevelopment' is conceptualised by INGOs as absolute poverty without any macro-level spatial or historical links with the rest of the world. So, the appropriate model of development becomes (a) short-term 'band aid' through urgent medical and food aid, as discussed earlier under 'medicalisation' of crises, and (b) long-term small-scale activities and projects. 'Third World difference' here is produced indirectly by showing the solutions to poverty as 'development' at a micro level, de-linked from macro-level realities and hence as simplified, small-scale, easy, consumable and, occasionally, as an 'investment'. These messages also reflect many contradictions. For instance, the overall narrative suggests that while 'our' little is a lot for them, it is also made clear that they are 'doing it themselves', as shown through the images of MW people engaged in an activity.

Development is usually shown by way of small projects mainly to meet basic needs such as livelihoods, health, water and education. The logic of the lowest common denominator (LCD) of basic needs that *everyone* wants, and cannot be argued against, legitimises development to be understood and shown in simplified welfare terms. Labels, names and postures have a considerable role in such projections and positioning. This 'performative character of naming' is also a 'precondition for all hegemony and politics' (Leclau, 1989: xiv). Labelling is a mechanism that is used to concretise power relations, categorise and determine access to resources (Wood, 1985). Labels or client categories such as 'peasants' and 'small farmers' are commonly deployed in these portrayals and reduce the complex lives of people to show them as categories across the three continents of Asia, Africa and South America that can be addressed in a homogenised way (Ferguson, 1990; Escobar, 1995).

Use of 'conversions' is another common strategy in INGOs' fund-raising appeals to show 'value for money'. These conversions show a specific amount in pounds sterling and what that amount can buy in terms of an item of 'help'. For example 'x' pounds will buy 'y' amount of medicines, seed or food. On the one hand, they show that 'our little is so much for them'; on the other hand, these conversions position the DW and MW across a more/superior versus less/ inferior status. This may be especially true when seen in the context of 'what we have' and its connection to our self-image of 'who we are', particularly in con-temporary consumerist societies. The messages connote the inability of the MW to do even small things on its own. While it is emphasised that this inability is not due to a lack of knowledge or effort but a lack of financial resources, the sheer smallness of these developmental activities without a macro-level structural context merely emphasises the importance of little donations. It simultaneously reinforces the ease and low cost of donations to the donor and implicitly underpins the relative status of the DW and MW. Moreover, the difference in purchasing parity always appears mysterious. Why 50 pence 'here' is worth so much elsewhere is never explained and the disparity remains unconnected to past or present global links, implying that it is just the way things are – the poor are poor because they are poor.

These messages do partially attempt to deal with the 'complex interplay of structure and agency' (Fox, 1998: 289) by showing various activities being performed by the global poor. In this way they dispel the notion of 'lazy' recipients and suggest that the money is going to the 'deserving poor' who 'work for themselves', which locates the mes-sage in both postcolonial and social policy debates. The distinction between the 'deserving' and the 'undeserving' poor is a classic one both historically and in contemporary welfare discussions. One school attributes poverty to behavioural characteristics such as laziness and dishonesty of poor people and, thereby, labels them undeserving of help (Golding and Middleton, 1982; Alcock, 2006). Cultural gener-alisations of people from non-European parts of the world, especially 'Africa', as 'lazy' were also common in colonial discourses (Hall, 2002). INGOs' messages until the 1980s, especially related to disasters, also faced criticism for their depictions of the MW as passive and 'negative', leading to changes in their policies towards showing 'positive' images of activity (Benthall, 1993).

INGOs' current messages work to dispel the idea of the global poor as passive and lazy and show that they 'work for themselves', which makes them deserving of help. It can also be argued that these messages reflect alternative development in terms of small community-based projects (Fox, 1998). However, the action on the part of the MW people almost always remains at an individual, not macro, level. So while this reassures that development is doable, its small scale also implies that the work will have to continue, a subliminal theme justifying the perpetuation of NGOs.

Parallel to projecting the inability of the MW to do small things, there is a Eurocentric hierarchy of 'need', aspiration and achievement that creeps in as illustrated by one of the images in an Oxfam Christmas Gifts catalogue (Direct mail, 2005, page 24). It shows the 'gift' of a greenhouse in Albania which is clearly a 'superior', more sophisticated, gift compared to the 'basic needs'-related gifts recommended for the MW people – a case of small gifts for small people?

Apart from development being shown as small-scale and for basic needs, it is also shown to be easy and consumerist by further simplifying it, as in INGOs' gifts catalogues. These messages are situated in the Western 'Christian' seasonal gifts culture of Christmas or Easter. One should know what the receivers of the gifts like; for instance, whether they would prefer a goat to a camel. The catalogue format gives a sense of choice, and the association of fun linked to shopping and catalogue browsing.

These catalogues also have feel-good connotations of gifting a needy person or community. 'Community' is a commonly used word in INGOs' messages. Raymond Williams calls it a 'warmly persuasive word' which 'unlike all other terms of social organisation (state, nation, society, etc.) . . . seems never to be used unfavourably, and never to be given any positive opposing or distinguishing term' (1976: 76). It also hides the 'complexity of community differences' to suggest a 'mythical notion of community cohesion' (Guijt and Shah, 1998:1).[7] This fuzziness and 'positivity' of the term might explain its popular use as against the problematic nature of terms such as 'Third World'.

Image 4.3   Oxfam 'How on earth do you wrap a donkey?'

The catalogues are firmly located within a consumerist culture that involves marketing techniques which tell you what you get and how you help, with a price for everything. At the same time, they eliminate the 'stress' of Christmas shopping.[8] They also involve a suspension of disbelief – one doubts if a goat will actually be bought for this needy person in this poor country but one goes along with it in the Christmas spirit. The seasonal spirit and the format of shopping catalogue also lowers the prospect of including deeper issues such as the structural causes of poverty. These messages, thus, preclude the inclusion of advocacy content. On the whole, 'the image of the blissful unification of society through consumption suspends disbelief with regard to the reality of division' (Debord, 1994: 45).

From the NGOs' point of view, the catalogue format removes one level or layer of operation by bringing together the donor and the INGO's final action. The field activities or actions of the NGO are listed in the form of products which the individual donor can choose from. The NGOs' activities are, thus, catalogued in a simplified format and made accessible to the public. The entire complexity of development is converted into solutions in the shape of products. The range of products on offer, too, is limited, in tune with the simple things required to 'do' development in the MW. These include tools to meet basic needs and livelihood such as livestock, mosquito nets, fishing nets, water taps and seeds.

This simplification and reduction of the complex issue of development then also makes the public legitimate 'experts' on development, as they choose what is best for the MW in terms of their personal preferences. It also lends a personal touch, a sense of closeness to the recipients and a superficial understanding of what's wrong and what can be done. This process is similar to child sponsorship schemes – instead of 'choosing' a child to sponsor one can choose an animal, product or activity.

On the 'positive' side, this marketing style is guilt-free and does not evoke a sense of responsibility amongst DW readers. It is also a 'novel' style that keeps the messages interesting, unlike the 'old' style of charity fundraising with its sense of *déjà vu* of distress and disasters. It also gives the reassurance that development is 'doable' and possible. The 'positivity' of these messages delves into the negative/positive debate on INGO imagery and raises an important question – positive for whom? Quite clearly, the messages are meant to evoke positive feelings amongst the viewers in the DW. The tone of the messages is such that harsh images of abject disasters are not common in these messages and the paramount aim is to make the individual donors 'here' feel good.

For INGOs, gift catalogues are a marketing triumph for all these reasons, in addition to the fact that they dig into the popular belief that British people love animals (Fox, 2004).[9] The cuddly livestock also has a special appeal for children. Though the animals remain different and 'exotic' – goats, camels, donkeys – they look cute and cuddly even when they stand alone and are not being held by an equally, if not more, cute MW child. Christmas gifts can be classified under the category of outwardly hyper-positive fundraising. The notion of 'happy natives'[10] (Hall, 1997: 245) is extended to the animals of MW, who are also seen to smile!

Another increasingly common depiction of development as livelihood is through economic stories that make good sense. Such messages show livelihood as an 'investment' with potential for growth where small investments yield big results. The variations in these utilitarian narratives include the rural success story – INGO helps farmers grow food and they go on to help other farmers. Another form is the small-scale trade success story, often of women, who become self-sufficient, proving that such help is a good investment. Such messages project a neo-liberal logic of sound economics and attempt to frame the story not in terms of charity but investment. However, the stories, yet again, remain within the usual epistemological frame – at a micro, individual level without incorporating any macro-level context which keeps them circumscribed within a 'charity' mode, charitable individual donation being a good investment for someone in the MW.

Conclusion

This chapter has critically analysed key INGO representations related to global poverty to show that, in a variety of ways, the causes of poverty are explained either as 'internal' features of the MW such as corruption, overpopulation and violence or as 'external' factors caused by natural or medical reasons which deny any connections and continuities between the MW and the DW. The consequent dehistoricisation and depoliticisation of issues subtly constructs the MW as 'different' and 'distant' from the developed world. Solutions to global poverty take the form of 'band aid' and simple and easy developmental activities. The varied discursive framing messages also heighten the MW's helplessness and dependence on the DW, thereby justifying small aid solutions.

INGOs' messages examined in chapters 2, 3 and 4 show how an overall construction of 'othering' – 'us' and 'them' – is established through projecting, and exaggerating, difference and distance in terms of knowledge and positioning realised through discursive strategies of infantilisation; feminisation; decontextualisation; binaries of active/passive, giver/receiver and rural/urban settings; and dehistoricisation. This naturally raises the question: how, then, do INGOs' messages connect the DW and MW? This is the focus of the next chapter.

PART II

ONENESS

Introduction

This book argues that INGOs' public messages are characterised by a dualism of 'difference' and 'oneness'. The first aspect of difference was the focus of Part I of the book. Part II focuses on oneness, exploring it first across the representations and then inside the INGOs.

Chapter 5 takes forward, and concludes, the 'representation' component of the representational field. It shows that difference is nested in a dehistoricised oneness of universal humanism in INGOs' messages. However, there are exceptions to this logic and some messages diverge from the dualism. These deviant INGO messages historicise the lives of the global poor by focusing attention on shared histories and structures that shape current global inequalities. Such messages are significant because they show both the existence and potential *within* INGOs' messages to contest their dominant myths. The chapter finally sums up the key elements of the visual analyses with some reflections on dualism and fetishism.

Chapter 6 begins to unravel the factors behind INGOs' messages. Based on interviews with INGO staff, it shows that oversimplification and decontextualisation in INGOs' messages stem from institutional and societal factors. 'Oneness' is reflected among INGOs through varied elements of institutional isomorphism that characterise them as well as their consideration of the DW, particularly British, publics as uniform and mono-cultural.

CHAPTER 5

ONE HUMANITY

INGOs' messages, examined in the first part of this book, project the MW as 'different' and 'distant' from the DW in many specific ways and across several axes. This chapter examines how INGOs' messages actually connect the DW and MW. I argue that this connection is made through the use of an ideology of universal humanism which brings together DW and MW into a 'family of mankind'. The constructions of difference and distance are woven in a thread of humanity that is historically unconnected, as shown in the first section. However, there are some crucial messages which are deviant and divergent as they attempt to highlight the historical and structural connections between MW and DW, thereby countering the difference that is prevalent in the bulk of INGO messages. The second section undertakes a critical analysis of these messages to show their strengths and limitations in resisting the overall INGO representations. In the final section, the findings and analyses of the 'representation' part of the book (chapters 2, 3, 4 and 5) are collated. The chapter ends with a summary of dualism and its implications.

Humanism and cosmopolitanism

This section explores how INGOs use 'universal humanism', nesting the dominant portrayals of difference of the MW within this ideology and seeking support from the readers for the same 'different' and 'distant' MW while connecting DW and MW on the whole. The humanism deployed works as a fuzzy, sentimental unifier and a discourse that is devoid of historicity in order to place human beings in a universal, dehistoricised space. It is linked to, and conflated with, an analogous notion of cosmopolitanism that similarly echoes a humanist idea of 'one family of man' and 'world citizens'.

A vast and contested concept, Enlightenment humanism is associated with 'the human', often in the sense of secular as opposed to other-worldly, but more generally in terms of the primacy and dignity of man and the notion of core humanity; namely the essential features that can define human beings (Soper, 1986; Burke, 1990). It also assumes history to be a product of human thought and action.[1] On the other hand, 'anti-humanism' emphasises the ideological status of humanism to argue that it is ideological and produced in specific historical processes (Soper, 1986).[2] The centrality of ideology is also generally reflected in cultural studies and postcolonial literature, which critique the lack of historicity in the notion of Enlightenment humanism that places humans outside ideology in a universal space.

Following this, Barthes' distinction between 'classic humanism' and 'progressive humanism' is invaluable here. According to Barthes, the former relies on 'the solid rock of universal nature' while the latter accommodates historicity (1993: 101). In his famous critique of a photographic exhibition titled 'The Family of Man',[3] Barthes showed how it projected the 'myth' of a global human community in two stages – first by emphasising difference in the form of the exotic diversity of daily lives, and second, by taking it away to show that underneath there is but one human nature and a common human essence (Young, 1990: 122). Barthes does not deny that birth and death are 'facts of nature, universal facts', but shows that removing history makes any comment about them 'purely tautological' (1993: 101). He illustrates the unfairness of 'classic humanism' through the following example (Barthes 1993: 102):

It will never be fair to confuse in a purely gestural identity the colonial and the Western worker (let us also ask the North African workers of the Goutte d'Or district in Paris what they think of *The Great Family of Man*).

Frantz Fanon, too, objects strongly to the duplicitous use of the ideology of classic humanism for colonial exploitations (1990: 251):

> Leave this Europe where they are never done talking of Man, yet murder men everywhere they find them ... in all corners of the globe ... That same Europe where they were never done talking of Man, and where they never stopped proclaiming that they were only anxious for the welfare of Man: today we know with what sufferings humanity has paid for every one of their triumphs of the mind.

Following Fanon's revelations of its association with the violence of Western history, the category of 'the human' has gradually come to be regarded with suspicion by many scholars and 'as a conflictual concept, divided against itself' (Young, 1990: 125).

The notion of universal humanism (Barthes' 'classic humanism') is spread across INGOs' messages in many forms. These include the 'one to one' or individual to individual connections that are best exemplified in child sponsorship messages. A child sponsorship insert used by Plan through the year was titled 'See for yourself the difference sponsorship makes'. The word 'see' here shows the importance of sight or seeing for oneself as evidence. The insert contained six images, a world map with Plan's project areas marked out, a table about finances and the text 'Sponsorship is about real people helping real people'. The use of adjectives and qualifiers is common in INGO appeals. The word 'real' here connotes not a fictitious world 'out there', but actual people. The term 'real people' is also used for both the sponsors and the beneficiaries, linking them into a chain or circle of humanity.

Universal humanism is also illustrated by stories about visits to sponsored children by their sponsors, both ordinary DW people and celebrities. These stories work within the frame of individuals connecting with individuals.

Plan's Supplement 'Look and Learn' in the *Guardian*, for instance, contains a story titled 'Take one sponsor', about a sponsor's visit with her son Robbie to Kenya to meet the girl she has sponsored. The images show the sponsored girl Kanini wearing a frock and smiling

Image 5.1   Plan, P-7/14 and P-7/15 A Sponsor's visit to Kenya

at the camera in front of a thatched hut; Kanini playing football with
Robbie; Kanini and Robbie petting a black lamb while another little
girl in a nice cream frock looks on with lush green trees in the background; and the sponsor, Harriet Griffey, at a health centre holding a
chubby black baby wearing a shiny blue satin frilly frock.

There is 'deliberate positivism' in the images, with smiling children and an idyllic background. The story talks about sponsorship,
Robbie's impressions of Africa based on television shows about wild-
life, the friendship he strikes up with Kanini, Kanini's family details
and Harriet's visit to a health centre, all of which evoke 'human' connections among individuals. The story briefly disrupts the dehistoricised version of humanism to move towards 'progressive humanism'
by including a slice of history when it mentions the comfortable life,
servants and large house of the British expatriates that the visitors stay
with in Nairobi. These 'ex-pats' had arrived prior to Kenya's independ-
ence from Britain in 1963. The text states that while life is comfortable for the whites ('mzungus'), 56% of Kenya's population lives on
less than a dollar a day and Kenya has high national debt. This part of

the text certainly fits into a deviant and rare category of INGO messages but it remains a part of the smaller print, which implies that it is likely to be missed by most readers who tend to scan through messages and only notice the images and the captions.

Another evocation of universal humanism can be found in the Asian Tsunami update story in Plan's Supplement where a celebrity actor, Shobna Gulati, is shown visiting a Plan Project in Tamil Nadu, India and holding the child she has sponsored – a picture that projects an individual, and individualised, connection as human beings.

Yet another illustration of universal humanism is found in Oxfam's myth-busting series, three messages of which were analysed in chapter 4. The fourth, and final, myth-busting appeal of Oxfam during 2005 (O-10, *Independent*, 28 July 2005, page 4) titled 'African Myth #4' has this statement in bold letters on the left side: 'CHARITY BEGINS AT HOME'. The right side contains an image of a globe followed by text in smaller letters: 'the world is rich in resources. There is enough to go around for everyone. Poverty is indefensible. If you have ever meant to do something to help end poverty, please join Oxfam today.' The message then goes on to ask for 'regular gifts' or for readers to visit Oxfam's website.

A carefully worded appeal, it uses terms such as 'world' and 'resources' with ambivalent and open-ended meanings. The sentences are carefully constructed to make their meanings ambiguous, leading to vague interpretations suggesting some higher 'universal' morals. For instance, the first sentence is a well-known phrase where 'home' can connote an individual's home, nation or even the world as one home. Then the world which is also our home is said to be rich in resources, implying natural resources. The next sentence, however, states that there are enough resources – presumably financial – to go around. This is then translated into monetary terms and the action sought is regular donation to Oxfam.

Although the appeal is somewhat unclear, this ad does employ the theme of universal humanism. Using the logic of the 'family of mankind', it asks for funds that can be used in the MW, which is also a part of 'our' home, namely the earth. It therefore asks the readers to look beyond their immediate surroundings of nation and region to think, like a 'cosmopolitan', of the globe as their home. However, this 'home' is without history and the divisions within this 'one world', rooted in history, are glossed over.

Universal humanism results in similar narratives for people across the globe without taking into account the differences among them.[4] The common narrative is that of poverty, which is the same everywhere and all the differences in dress and landscape, albeit rural, merely work to show that we are all the same beneath the skin with an underlying 'identical "nature"' (Barthes, 1993: 100). Barthes calls it 'the reign of gnomic truths' where humanity meets 'at the most neutral point of [its] nature' (1993: 101).

'Oneness' is also depicted through 'sameness' arguments. Plan's supplement titled 'Futures Valued' (P-10) mentions a sponsor's surprised comment after her visit to Tanzania that the people are 'much the same', with similar dreams to those that parents have in the UK. The sponsor also states that a lot can be learned from them, such as being happy and polite, and less materialistic. These comments also fall into well-meaning but romanticised notions that list the advantages and 'positives' found in the MW.

Further, the 'Futures Valued' supplement (P-10) portrays 'African children' as 'friends' to connote a sense of 'oneness' and positivity. The narrative also includes another way of 'distancing' – of 'us' from 'us'. The Tanzania story mentions at the end that 'many of us see children in Africa through images on the television as objects of pity and often as victims', but the sponsors returned thinking they had made good friends. These lines transfer the blame of the 'image of Africa' onto the television and detach themselves from it even though, ironically, the same supplement contains many images objectifying and victimising 'Africans'.

Another relevant concept is 'cosmopolitanism', which has become popular in recent years in discussions across a range of topics including NGOs and citizenship. Chouliaraki suggests that international NGOs' public messages have a key role in creating cosmopolitan sensibilities of helping others among DW citizens (2006). The fuzziness of the concept and its usage very often suggests a conflation of the term with humanism. Specific meanings and deployment of cosmopolitanism that echo the humanist idea of 'one family of man' can be criticised on the same grounds as above.[5] Such limited visions include what Peter Gowan calls the 'new liberal cosmopolitanism' that is 'based on the vision of a single human race peacefully united by free trade and common legal norms' (2003: 51). It is often 'presented simply as global citizenship' (Calhoun, 2003). While cosmopolitanism is attentive to the multiplicity of people's connections, it remains close to its Enlightenment roots of ethical universalism, which is suspicious of religion and entrenched traditions and uses the language of rights without recognising that individuals are also embedded in culture and social relations. In its responses to international conflicts and crises, it offers an attractive sense of shared responsibility; but the kind that takes the form of ethical obligation, not political action against social order rooted in history. It also takes the easier form of 'consumerist cosmopolitanism' to merely incorporate food, clothes, music, tourism and literature without any hard test for politics and relations between the 'local' and 'global' (Calhoun, 2003).[6] This implies that an uncritical application of cosmopolitanism as a 'good thing' with regard to INGOs and their messages can be problematic.

'Oneness' and solidarity are also manifested in some appeals through the use of a notion of a cosmopolitan club of world citizens. Oxfam's 'I'm in' campaign is a case in point. Launched in January 2006,[7] these appeals seemed to address young people to consolidate the gains of the MPH coalition campaign of 2005. The MPH connection is made clear in the formal stated purpose of 'I'm in' as elaborated in Oxfam's 'the little book of communications' (Oxfam, 2006b: 20) – 'Building on Make Poverty History, I'm in is founded on Oxfam's belief that poverty is a moral injustice that must be overcome'. Poverty here is clearly seen as a moral rather than a historical issue. The series showed individual young men and women from DW who had presumably joined or wanted to join the campaign. For instance, an ad (O-26, *Guardian*, 16 January 2006, page 14) showed a young man wearing a shirt, a sweater, a pair of trousers and a white band on his wrist. The facial features of the man suggest that he is a 'British Asian' who has joined the MPH campaign, as can be seen from the white MPH band that he wears.[8]

Another ad in January 2006 showed a young white man sitting on a chair holding a small boy. Both are well dressed and the child looks up to the man evoking the capability, strength and caring nature of the DW youth. A bottle of milk can be seen on the floor near the chair. This appeal of a young DW male looking after a child is also suggestive of a 'new man' cosmopolitan modernity. This is in marked contrast to the near-total absence of MW males in nurturing roles in INGOs' messages, which again projects difference.

Image 5.2   Oxfam, O-29 'I'm in'

The 'I'm in' campaign continued to show similar ads and posters in the tube (London underground) and trains and in the press with images of various young people, connoting a multi-ethnic and aware Britain. All images showed the people in a flattering light: well dressed, young and smart. These messages deployed a humanistic, cosmopolitan framework to appeal to individuals to join a 'club' of global citizens, once again without addressing any historical connections outside of 'human' links. The savvy cosmopolitan discourse in these messages carefully avoids messy geopolitics and history and subsumes material global relations under it.

Human rights

Universality is expressed through the concepts of 'rights' as well as 'needs'; occasionally used together as a phrase – 'rights and needs' of children, for instance by WV – thereby equating the two words. Similarly, a Plan insert highlights 'Plan's work with communities to promote children's needs and rights'. The word 'right' is generally used in this sense to suggest that all children have the right to basic needs. The term 'right' is also used independently, for example by AA in several messages, where it implies universal rights of all human beings to have access to, say, health and education. A direct mail brochure from AA (ActionAid, AA-direct mail, 2005), with details of child sponsorship, illustrates the use of 'rights-based' language:

> Why become a sponsor? Because you believe every child has a right to the fundamentals of life.

The connotations of 'justice' in the use of the term 'rights' employ a humanistic moral logic which argues that *all* human beings have the right to basic needs. In addition to this specific understanding of the concept of human rights, conviction in its effectiveness, as expressed on the website of AA during October 2005 under the caption 'please give a gift to ActionAid', is noteworthy. The text mentions that it is important for MW people to acquire knowledge of their basic rights in order to change their lives themselves. There is a certain naiveté in such expressions that implies not just faith in 'rights' but that if 'they' know their rights 'they' would do something about it themselves and in this sense it connotes 'their' ignorance. It is useful here to compare the works of authors such as John Rawls and Charles Beitz on the ethics of international aid, global justice and human rights and their counter-criticisms from scholars such as Thomas Pogge.

Comparing charitable donations with foreign aid, Beitz states that aid has been regarded as a kind of international charity, and hence understood as morally discretionary, but it should be considered as a part of global redistributive obligations founded on justice (1999). His notion of justice is based on what he terms 'cosmopolitan liberalism', which looks beyond the nation state to give primacy to each human no matter where they may be. Discussing political imperialism and economic dependence, that is, the issue of causality, Beitz adds that 'it make[s] little moral difference whether the regime is imposed by other members of their own community or by foreign agents' (1999: 119). Beitz finds it necessary to undervalue both historical and current, and domestic and foreign, factors to place the concept of 'justice' (as in justice for individual human beings) as the core issue.[9] Rawls, similarly, adopts a universal human principle when he insists that 'peoples have a duty to assist other peoples living under unfavourable conditions that prevent their having a just or decent political and social regime' (1999: 37). This is commendable but it overlooks something crucial. Pogge challenges Rawls' suggestion of 'duty of assistance' to the global poor by objecting to the very notion of 'assistance' because it is based on the assumption that the causes of severe poverty are internal to poor countries and not due to foreign influences such as historical processes of enslavement and colonialism and their legacies (Pogge, 2004).

This debate over charity or assistance versus justice resonates in the human rights discourse in INGOs' messages. 'Human rights' is a composite term – 'rights' is a legal category and 'human' a moral one. When placed together they stand for 'moral rights or claims by individuals' that entitle people to certain minimum standards of treatment by various institutions (Douzinas, 2007: 9). To be sure, the notion of poverty as a violation of human rights is a step in the right direction for the purpose of practice. By endorsing the connections of basic social and economic rights with civil and political rights, it makes the state and non-state actors legally obliged to uphold the right of poor people not to live in poverty. However, this is only one of the approaches to human rights and is based primarily on the notion of duties of humanity. The other approach, based on the notion of justice, looks at poverty as a violation of human rights caused by the culpable conduct of others. 'Human rights' is not a magic mantra containing an intrinsic notion of justice, but justice should form an integral element of the term. As Tom Campbell states, '[it] is the failure to alleviate poverty as well as complicity in or actually causing poverty that should be regarded as violating poverty-related human rights' (2007: 62).

I do not suggest that these two approaches are inherently contradictory. Accommodating both approaches within the notion of 'human rights' is likely to optimise both the theoretical and practical potential of the term as both humanity and justice can (and must) work against poverty. The case of a natural disaster may require a humanitarian reaction based on the notion of 'one' humanity, but a similar explanation in the case of global poverty caused by deep historical factors tends to make 'human rights' an abstract notion that merely avoids the issue of justice and causality.

The use of the phrase 'human rights' in INGOs' messages suggests the first approach of a universal moral basis for individuals who are a part of humanity but not historically located within it, in a specific place (country/region) that is linked to the rest of the world, notably the DW. In other words, the notion of rights is based on a dehistoricised notion of mankind as 'one' which does not accommodate any context of past and present macro-level connections of the specific set of people. The complete absence of a relational aspect, thus, keeps it located within a broadly charitable discourse and does not let it rise to the discourse of justice, despite the use of the language of rights.

In February 2005, Plan took out a full-page advertisement in major daily newspapers on 'The Campaign for Universal Birth Registration' (P-1). Captioned 'Write me down, make me real', it showed a small black boy in a t-shirt and a crumpled pair of shorts standing in the midst of four smiling DW leaders including George W. Bush and Tony Blair, who can be seen most clearly. The digitally manipulated

Image 5.3   Plan, P-1 'Write me down, make me real'

image shows one of the heads of state pointing his fingers towards the child who stares upwards at him.

The accompanying text indicates that millions do not possess a legal identity because their births were not registered, and this bars them from their rights to healthcare and education. The text adds, 'They will always be vulnerable, easy prey to the unscrupulous – the most likely child prostitutes and boy soldiers'. It goes on to mention that the right to a name and nationality is enshrined in the UN Convention on the Rights of a Child and endorsed by 192 nations but not yet realised, resulting in poverty and disadvantage. The text also states that Plan has been at the forefront of this campaign and has already helped millions of children, and then asks the readers to join the campaign.

It is a complex and contradictory message. The image attempts an overall positivity but also perpetuates a power myth. The power inequality, folded hands of the child, his crumpled clothes in comparison to the formal dress of the DW leaders – all heighten the distance between the two sides. While all four 'world leaders' are wearing suits, the child wears casual clothes. The smiling leaders also look pleased with themselves while the child's expression is neutral and questioning as if he is appealing to them. It could also be interpreted as a look of awe.

It is an interesting ad which can be read in many ways. Given that the child is black, the connotations, through a chain of semiosis, would lead his image to mean an African child, Africa and MW in general. However, the child, unlike many 'charity children', not only looks healthy but is seen to demand his rights from DW leaders. This is a refreshing stance. He stands in the middle, looking upwards to the left at one leader as if talking to him and does not stare straight ahead at the camera (and, thus, the viewers) in appeal.[10] On the other hand, he is dwarfed in size by the taller grown men whose relative height also symbolises power inequalities. This has been famously argued by Erving Goffman in the case of gender advertisements 'where social weight – power, authority, rank, office, renown – is echoed through relative size' (1979: 28).

The image thus uses a binary opposition. Three of these leaders also look amused as they talk to each other, which could be read as indulgent amusement at the child or lack of concern. Only one leader is shown to point his fingers (digitally manipulated when examined carefully) at the child and pay some attention to him. The metaphor of David and Goliath is quite clearly used in this image. However, the binary is deliberately invoked to convey the supposedly 'direct' voice of MW children. Curiously, the MW leaders who have to actually implement this child's right to legal identity, which their countries' governments have already ratified, are missing. In terms of its content, the message takes up a specific and important macro-level issue but locates it within a universal rights framework that is carefully legal, neutral, apolitical and ahistorical.

In sum, the humanistic approach in INGOs' messages that, following Benetton's slogan, I call 'united colours of humanity',[11] projects a sanitised, fuzzy and non-conflictual realm where humanity is shared but not its history. Humanism and human rights portrayed in INGOs' messages tend to gloss over the chapters of global history that contributed significantly, and still contribute, to current global poverty and disparities. Yet, among the plethora of such hegemonic messages, there are a few which attempt to counter the dominant myths. These deviant messages which resist the overall INGO representations, albeit within limits, are discussed below.

Contesting myths – shared histories and structures

This section shows that INGOs' messages, while often crude and oversimplified, are not closed and uncontested. These rare and varied messages attempt to contest the dualism of difference and oneness. Some of them tend to rupture the overall humanistic logic. However, others remain within the broad discourse of universal humanism.

The first series of messages negate universal humanism by introducing history into the representations. During March 2005, CA carried a fully text-based message in all major newspapers (CA-3, *The Sunday Times*, 13 March 2005, page 1). Against a mustard yellow background, it had the following headline:

Dirty, low down spongers.
We really should be ashamed of living off Africans.

It is the only ad by any INGO which makes a mention of Western history, not restricting it to a few decades but going back many centuries to highlight the continuities between MW poverty and DW prosperity. By far the boldest message in many ways, it mentions that

> Much of the suffering and poverty in the third world is man-made. For centuries, we've plundered natural resources and enforced trade and debt policies that are stacked in our favour. Africa desperately needs more aid and debt cancellation, but it also needs to be free of unfair burden of policies imposed by rich countries.

It then asks readers to give their opinion on CA's website – 'make yourself heard. And please do it today. By tomorrow, another 12,000 children's lives will be lost.'

The message also reflects a balancing act. It combines a bold and unusual statement with the traditional and common message of saving the lives of children and using the term 'Africa' in a generalised sense to signify MW. Again, while a longer history is mentioned the word 'colonialism' is carefully avoided and any responsibility of rich countries is categorised as 'manmade'. Nonetheless, the message ruptures the commonly used version of universal humanism to incorporate real, material historicity without placing itself outside it.

The terms *studium* and *punctum* from Semiotics are useful here (Barthes, 2000). *Studium* is the average effect of a photograph on us based on its general and cultural connotations. *Punctum* is the element which breaks or punctuates the *studium* by pricking us or by its unexpectedness (Barthes, 2000: 26–27). Barthes adds that '[t]he *studium* is always coded, the *punctum* is not' (2000: 51). The word 'we' in the message acts as the *punctum* as it locates 'us' into (and so breaks) the common code of the language of 'sponger' as distant from us – welfare benefit recipients, migrants and undeserving 'Others'. These are the categories of poor people whose poverty is blamed, by the right-wing media[12] and the behavioural academic literature, on their own characteristics, behaviour and 'culture of dependency', not on broader structures (Golding and Middleton, 1982; Dean and Taylor-Gooby,

1992; Dean and Melrose, 1999).[13] The use of 'we' in CA's message encompasses, and implicates, the entire DW. While the message uses the binary of 'us' and 'them', it is used to implicate 'we' and to show how closely both sides are intertwined, rather than showing 'them' as separate from 'us'.

Another message (CA-4, *The Times*, 9 April 2005, page 11) used a grey background to highlight the title, 'It's not called slavery nowadays. It's called "free' trade"'. The sarcastic title is supported by the small text which mentions how 'free' trade is 'a system where poor countries are not allowed to protect their farmers', making them lose their livelihoods and become 'enslaved by poverty'. The message goes on to call for trade justice where poor countries have the 'freedom to protect their farmers and infant industries'. This appeal uses the theme of slavery, which was also topical in view of upcoming events in 2007 across the UK to commemorate 200 years of its abolition.[14] Another departure is the mention of infant industries in addition to agriculture that moves beyond the difference of a rural MW.

Another appeal titled 'There's nothing free about free trade' (CA-16, *Guardian*, 26 September 2005, page 8), and shown repeatedly in all newspapers in colour and black and white versions during September and October 2005, contained a simple image of a pair of dark hands tied with a thick metallic chain and a lock with 'FREE TRADE' written on it. The colour of the hands and the short nails suggest that they belong to a manual worker. The colour version of the ad shows that the hands belong to a black person, thereby connoting it as someone from the African continent. It is obviously symbolic of the MW and the text does say so in the last sentence. The image occupies nearly half the space in the ad and thus makes one focus strongly on it. The text mentions that

> free trade is forced onto poor countries through trade agreements and as a condition of aid and debt relief. This means that growers and producers are overwhelmed by powerful international competitors and unprotected fledgling industries are destroyed. Trade Justice is a better way. (Christian Aid, CA-16)

After mentioning its petition to the UK government in this regard, it goes on to state 'There can never be justice without Trade Justice. Poverty will never be made history. And the developing world's hands will remain tied.' This message brings in issues of 'justice', linked to the relation between DW and MW that affect the industries of the latter.

These appeals break out of the universally humanistic concepts of rights and justice (i.e. each human being has a right to basic needs or justice requires that nobody goes hungry) to locate them within global connectivities and thus contribute to countering the dominant discourses of INGO messages. In this sense, they attempt to 'reverse the gaze' by rethinking the 'normal' markers of our boundaries *vis-à-vis* 'Others'.

A message from WOW subverts the myth of individual-level, rural, 'natural' hard work as the solution to global poverty found in many INGO public messages. WOW's insert titled 'She is working herself out of poverty ... yeah, right' contains on its cover a black and white photograph of a woman digging into dry earth with a shovel.[15]

The cover image has an almost gothic look with the woman's long flowing garment and her looming shadow clearly visible. The photograph has been taken from below and the camera angle makes her look larger. However, it is the accompanying text which gives a new meaning to the image. On the top of the image is the line 'she's working herself out of poverty' while at the bottom the message is subverted by the disbelieving and sarcastic text 'yeah, right', with the second word on a red border.

The cover catches attention and invites the viewer to unfold the insert and see the inside pages where it states 'No she isn't (working herself out of poverty)'. The remaining text talks about the unfair current world order, need for change, WOW taking the struggle against poverty into factories and fields as well as the corridors of power, highlighting exploitation and injustice and calling for policy changes on behalf of poor communities. The last page of the insert details the work of WOW: 'fight[ing] the things that cause poverty, like unfair trading systems and exploitative business practices', as well as enabling poor people to help themselves, followed by specific examples of

Image 5.4   War on Want 'She's working herself out of poverty'

WOW projects in different parts of the world. The choice of black and white images enframed within WOW's typical 'brand' colours: red, black and white, lends a timeless and eternal quality as well as a starkness to the images. Combined with the opening lines these suggest the futility of small efforts and lead the readers to WOW's campaigns, which are the 'real' work on the root causes of poverty.

While the message does not include any historicity, it negates many of the ideas dominant in the messages studied earlier. These include small-scale, individual-level hard work, such as tilling land, being the solution to MW poverty. It also uses a typically 'charity-ish' image of nature in the form of arid land and a farmer to challenge common INGO frames of rural, 'natural' work without the macro-level context.[16]

The issues of *current* global connections have been used in a few INGO messages. For instance, a leaflet of AA included the frequently used image of Nelson Mandela at London's Trafalgar Square, protestors in various MW regions and an inflated rubber dummy symbolising corporate muscle outside a branch of Tesco Metro supermarket. The 'muscle man' image signifying corporate muscle appeared repeatedly in AA's newsletters and leaflets on 'Stop corporate abuse' along with images of various MW labourers in a plantation carrying loads on their backs, and one of local protests against Coca-Cola in Southern India, a rare image of MW campaigners. Another leaflet titled 'Tesco's record profits hit £2 Billion but every little hurts' shows the image of a hut made of wooden logs and a black person wearing a black dress and cap standing in the yard in front of the hut, hand covering the face as if wiping tears. There is no caption for the image. The accompanying text carries quotes from various people in South Africa who work in fruit export farms for low wages, Tesco being the largest buyer of these fruits in the UK. The text also calls for tougher international and national laws on human rights for multinational corporations.

There is another instance of MW people shown as campaigners. An SCF leaflet contained a rare image of African children campaigning as an attempt to show a rights-based approach.

SCF also questioned the 'child sponsorship' approach adopted by other INGOs, an uncommon instance of an NGO raising doubts over a specific approach adopted by other NGOs.[17] However, there were no details to explain how SCF's child link scheme is more effective than child sponsorship schemes.

The amusement and indifference of DW leaders is an oft-repeated theme of INGOs. At one level, this is laudable as it brings attention to DW governments and their wider, unfair policies. At another level, however, it also conveniently transfers the blame to the 'world leaders' while subtly echoing the sentiment that 'we', INGOs and the larger DW populace, are the good guys – neutral, and not responsible. This repeated oppositional positioning also hides the close, albeit varying, links between INGOs and DW governments in terms such as the funding they receive and the staff who cross over from NGOs to government bodies (the 'revolving door', as it is referred to in development circles).

AA produced a 'rock music' poster called 'Ruff Trade; Third World Sell-out Tour 2005' jointly with the National Union of Students (NUS). The poster attracted enough attention to feature in an *Observer* news feature with the headline 'ActionAid takes fight to students' (AA-5). Clearly aimed at young people and students, it was captioned 'NMH', a reference to the UK's popular music magazine *NME* (New Musical Express). The message shows leaders from the UK, USA and Japan as well as the European Union Trade Commissioner Peter Mandelson as rock stars with punk hair, nose rings, black leather jackets, sunglasses and cigarettes with names such as 'Toni Blur' and 'George Tush' on their sell-out tour of developing countries 'forcing open new markets for their aggressive brand of rock'n'roll with its final super-gig in Hong Kong on 13th December 2005'. It goes on to label the 'tour' as 'BIGGER THAN THE BEATLES. EVEN BIGGER THAN GELDOF AND BONO' (ActionAid, AA-5).

Using digitally manipulated images of 'world leaders', the ad caricatures them as careless rock stars 'selling out' the MW through unfair trade practices. It thus highlights the wider, structural causes of poverty through representation of world leaders as punk stars and world trade systems as their 'aggressive' music.[18] The power of these world leaders is signified by projecting them as bigger than the Beatles, Geldof and Bono. There is also an interesting role reversal with the

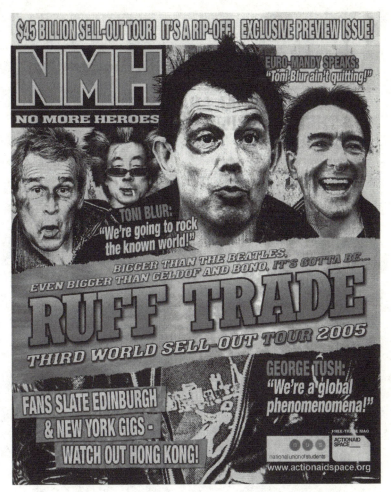

Image 5.5   ActionAid, AA-5 'Ruff Trade: Third World Sell-out
Tour 2005'

real rock stars appearing as the 'good leaders' while world leaders are transformed into 'bad rock stars'. A diverse repertoire of visual, textual and musical language is used here to communicate some of the deeper and wider issues around current global trade and its relation to global poverty and inequalities. The limited information content does not take away from the impact of the colourful, eye-catching and humorous ad with strong sarcastic lines, which serves its primary aim of generating interest among students and directing them to AA's website to learn more about the issues.

These messages incorporate some rare features, for example MW people campaigning for themselves in their own countries, which are not found in the dominant representations by INGOs. The macro-level global connections are also shown in terms of the policies and practices of DW leaders who are lampooned as punk stars as well as private multinational companies, such as Tesco, that do not pay fair prices to MW producers. However, unlike the CA message – 'Dirty, low down spongers' – these messages look only at current macro-level issues detached from historical connections and continuities. The messages also generally locate specific macro-level issues within a universal rubric of rights and justice. They also attribute the current problems only to DW leaders and multinational corporations who are labelled as 'bad guys', carefully separating them from 'Self'.

Distancing themselves from the prevailing situation, which is shown to have an independent existence not connected to the institutions representing it, is a common feature of many INGO appeals. This allows the messages, and INGOs, to position themselves as neutral outsiders. It also adds to the strength of the issues 'out there' which the INGOs then try to counter. Secondly, it allows NGOs to keep the focus away from the record of their own ineffectiveness in tackling the same problems, which continue to persist despite the long and established history of the INGOs that is clearly mentioned in many fundraising adverts.

The language and imagery of INGO messages tend to divide the actors into different categories – those who are responsible for the problems, those who suffer from the problems, and those who find solutions to these problems. Roughly, these respective categories pertain to DW leaders and multinationals as well as the MW with its distinctive 'internal' characteristics that create problems; MW and its people who face these problems and need aid; and NGOs which challenge the problems (and the actors who create them) and help the MW. While these categories are fluid, the overall templates remain fairly stable. Such messages have an inbuilt duality of advocating change while maintaining distance as actors somehow *outside* the broader systems and institutions, including those they get funds from.

Another way of maintaining distance is through use of 'direct' pseudo voices of MW 'beneficiaries' in the messages. These tend to show the INGOs as distant from the wider DW context and closer to MW ground realities, thereby adding to their legitimacy as the true voices from the 'field' of MW. This is exemplified in a WV leaflet titled 'Make my poverty history' that shows a small boy wearing WV's trademark bright orange coloured clothes and staring at the camera. The vulnerability and 'need' quotient here is enhanced through a wooden/bamboo pole serving as a 'participation shield' that the child leans against as if trying to shelter from the viewing eyes (Goffman, 1979: 70). Putting words in the mouth of a child is a strategy of appeal and an attempt to bring in voices from the field; voices that are the same across the entire MW. Such testimonies use the logic of the lowest common denominator (LCD) of basic needs that *everyone* wants. Such 'LCD messages' are also echoed by adults in many INGO messages. In the process, these enhance the legitimacy of the representation and those representing, namely the INGOs, as the 'true' voice of MW. Such testimonies work also as 'ascriptions' of 'real' and free voices of MW which the INGO merely publicises. All these strategies ensure that the NGO *stands for* the voices of MW as if it were *outside* the system of general exploitation in which it is implicated in many ways, including as an institution of knowledge and representation. The pseudo voices assume that allowing 'the subaltern to speak' (Spivak, 1988: 271, 294) within the same discourse makes it the true voice of the subaltern.[19] It does not consider that who is speaking *is* important but what is being said and within which discourse is even more important.

To sum up, while many of the rare and deviant INGO messages work as counter-discourses, others remain partially within the dominant discourses of INGOs' messages. In terms of numbers, the proportion of the deviant messages is also quite low, which implies that the overall INGO representations remain within the double logic of difference and oneness.

Distancing humanity – the power of dualism and fetishism

This section reflects on the significance of the dualism of difference and oneness inherent in INGOs' messages by bringing together its theoretical and empirical implications. The 'representation' component concludes with a discussion on the application of the conceptual framework and the findings of the entire visual analyses of chapters 2 to 5.

The analysis brings out the diverse ways in which specific discourses are constructed by INGO messages about global poverty and MW and their connections (or lack thereof) to the DW, reflecting the many 'ways of seeing' of colonialism, Orientalism, Africanism and development as summarised in my 'postcolonial lens', the conceptual framework set out in the introductory chapter. Given how intricately these are connected to each other, it is no surprise that many messages reflect overlapping ways of seeing. Both the fluidity and fixity of discourses are maintained through what Hall calls a 'system of representation' (1992a: 277). Various forms of representations also do not stand alone but work with other images and ideas, as a set, clustering to mean similar things through their associated meanings. Many such illustrations, as forwarded by Hall, echo in INGOs' messages, for instance, 'western = urban = developed' or 'non-western = non-industrial = rural = agricultural = underdeveloped' (1992a: 277). Furthermore, representations are not obvious caricatures. The strength of stereotypes is that they do not exist in pure form and it is their flexibility and variations which keeps them naturalised, alive and resilient (Dyer, 1993: 144).

The application of this conceptual framework to such a wide range of INGOs' annual messages of 2005/6 shows both its strengths and limitations. While its usefulness as a rough guide is invaluable, the operationalisation also clearly reveals that it cannot be applied strictly or mechanically and works best only when its porosity is kept in mind. The overlaps also stem from the polysemy and intertextuality of messages, both within themselves – that is, in terms of international charity or the 'NGO-ish' genre of messages – and in relation to the broader context of viewing that encompasses the wider society including media and education. For analytical clarity, I have disaggregated various categories and shown them one at a time, for example, development as small-scale and as rural. However, given the richness and polysemy of images, these are inter-related and work together to form meanings and understandings. Similarly, each message intertextually derives its meaning from other messages – by the same NGO, by other NGOs and in the wider media in general. And this is also valid across historical experiences of viewing or the earlier messages in a society that make up the palimpsest effect.

The categorisations facilitate easier understanding of the dominant representations by this subsector of INGOs in a given period; they do not erase the variations or essentialise the messages as monolithic. While the analysis reveals dominant discourses, it also shows the complexities and fluidity of representations and how these play against each other.

The analysis of INGOs' representations shows that while there are instances of counter-hegemonic messages, most INGO messages project the MW as 'different' and 'separate' from the DW. Simultaneously, and ironically, the messages exclude the role of the big, historical stories of DW colonialism and imperialism in current MW poverty and continuities thereof. A dominant theme of difference and distance in INGOs' messages is realised, in manifold, intricate and paradoxical ways, through portrayals of characters that infantilise and feminise MW and show it as a passive recipient of an active and giving DW (chapter 2), the use of space to divide the globe visually into an extremely vulnerable, poor and rural MW as against, and unconnected to, a rich, urban and modern DW (chapter 3), and decontextualised framing of poverty through either 'natural' or 'internal' causes, oversimplification of development and a general dehistoricisation and depoliticisation of issues (chapter 4). This remote and different MW is, then, brought together with the DW as a part of a common humanity, although a few deviant messages do rupture the dominant myths (chapter 5).

If conceptualised in terms of global cultural flows, as in Arjun Appadurai's notion of 'scapes' – flows of people, technology, finance, information and images, and ideologies (1990) – the fluidity and multiplicity of such flows is largely missing from INGOs' public messages. What come across are mainly one-way projections. With regard to people, the messages show a one-way flow of DW people (INGO staff, celebrities, sponsors) going to MW. Similarly, 'help' in terms of technology and finance is transferred from 'here' to 'there'. The information and images from 'there' are shown selectively without making historical connections.

The primary mode of making connections in INGOs' messages is through the notion of 'one' universal humanity. Oneness is evoked through certain ideas, foremost being universal humanism which claims that all human beings are one. This oneness does not have any place for historicity. It is, thus, a sanitised, ahistorical version that absolves the DW/Self from any role in the current state. Other concepts used to evoke oneness are those of rights and justice which claim, for example, that it is not 'just' for any human being to go hungry, or it is the 'right' of every human being to have food. The concepts of justice and rights are used to support a bottom line argument where 'facts' are stated about the current problems but *not* about how this situation came about historically. The situation is then labelled unfair with the declaration that something must be done about it. The end result of these concepts is the loss of continuities and lessons embedded in history. This projects the myth of an MW 'out there'. It is *another* world, historically unconnected to 'us' except in a universally humanistic way where good DW human beings help good MW human beings. As Barthes eloquently states, 'myth deprives the object of which it speaks of all History. In it history evaporates' (1993: 151). Oneness, thus, works as the overall space within which the difference of MW is nested in INGOs' messages. It is also the humanistic logic which connects DW and MW.

Such messages, thus, follow a subtle doublespeak, an 'inside-outside' strategy, which espouses humanism and difference at the same time. Humanism implies 'we are one' as human beings and excludes any real, geo-political or historical connections, such as slavery, colonialism and imperialism, that have played a significant role in shaping today's global inequalities. While this humanism imagines itself as 'one', it does contain subtle 'rules of admittance'. Only 'good' and history-less individuals are admitted to 'humanity' as free-floating and 'innocent' human beings whose current state has nothing to do with their belonging to an MW that is intricately connected to the DW. Only the idea that it has nothing to do with 'us' bestows upon these individuals the 'deservingness' of aid from fellow human beings. Through this logic MW people are brought 'inside' humanity. At the same time, the same people are constructed as the 'Others', different from 'us' with problems unique to them, such as corruption and over-population, which cause their poverty. This logic again puts the MW people 'outside' humanity as 'we' know it in the DW. INGO portray-als set up a hierarchy of subjects – 'good' and 'bad' – as well as rules of inclusion and exclusion that decide who/what gets counted and who/what omitted.

INGOs' messages find it very difficult to assign multiple identities to MW individuals who are also part of a continuum – a specific com-munity, a region, a nation and the MW which, in turn, is influenced by a much larger and connected globe. The insistence on categorising an individual either as an individual delinked from a greater history and national/regional collectivity or as a 'human', namely a part of the largest global collectivity or 'family of man', but never in-between is striking. In contrast, however, when it comes to assigning values to label large chunks of MW populations, the middle ground of collec-tivity is re-discovered and people are uniformly labelled as culturally fixed – corrupt, lazy, religious – in an inescapably frozen and unchang-ing way. They belong to a 'culture' (nation/region) that is unable to change, but paradoxically the very same people do not share in the collective history of their nation(s) in relation to the DW. In sum (and to put it crudely) the two worlds – DW and MW – are first stretched and placed on two extreme ends and then they are connected or brought together on, and through, the common and universal ground of humanity. The messages suggest that 'Others' can be engaged with only on the basis of a shared humanity, not a shared history.

In the agency and structure interplay within INGOs' messages, the individual-level agency of some poor MW people is privileged, as seen in their depictions as active workers. Although this is important, the broad narratives remain at a micro and ahistorical level. While the material history of MW poverty is sidestepped, the ways of seeing stemming from the same history paradoxically reveal themselves in

INGOs' messages through the palimpsest effect. Just like in a palimpsest, a parchment or manuscript which has been erased and inscribed over, traces of previous inscriptions emerge in INGOs' messages to show how 'the past' constitutes 'the present'. Put differently, while most INGOs' messages ignore, and thereby indirectly erase, 'the past', they ironically reveal it through the ways of seeing that are rooted in the same past.

Yet another problem with individual stories that are presented without a mention of their place in global history is that they implicitly project a 'centre–margin' vision in which the two remain unconnected and free-standing, the centre having become so completely on its own and similarly the margin remaining marginal entirely due to its own fault. What it obscures is that they are a part of the same whole and the 'margins' are integral to the 'centre' as both have been intricately connected and shaped by a common and connected history. When we talk about global poverty, no one is unconnected. There is no child, male, female, farmer, factory labourer in MW and no consumer, worker, welfare recipient or charitable sponsor in DW who is not integrated with the world economy and society. An individual can be a conduit and medium to show a larger, more accessible picture but without the wider context of the life of this individual the story is just that – a fetish, a means to feel good and finally a cruel reflection of power asymmetry through visual violence.

The postcolonial lens contains the modality of fetishism projected through displays of decontextualised body parts, such as eyes, which has been the most common way of understanding fetishism including within the INGOs' imagery debate. This is undeniably a valid interpretation but is a narrow understanding of Marx's highly complex notion of commodity fetishism. While a detailed discussion is beyond the scope of this book, it helps to apply it to the overall messages of INGOs. Sut Jhally (1987) provides a particularly useful account of fetishism with regard to communications and advertising. Commodity fetishism occurs when there is a split between 'appearance' (of things in the market place) and 'essence' (real social relations). In its simplest sense, fetishism is decontextualisation; for instance, a body part detached from the body as shown through, say, the big 'needy' eyes of a child. At a broader level, it is the appearance of goods, for instance in communications, which 'masks the story of who fashioned them, and under what conditions' (Jhally, 1987: 50). Fetishism, thus, empties commodities of their meaning by hiding the real social relations behind them. In this sense, by disguising the material social relations of the lives of MW people, which are rooted in history and inextricably connected to DW, the overall messages of INGOs, I contend, collectively amount to fetishism. Marx argued that profit on capital that originates in labour presents itself as 'capital-interest' so that not only is the 'memory of [its] origins' obliterated but it is 'actually placed in a form diametrically opposed to this origin' (1981: 968). This resonates in INGOs' messages where not only are the origins of social relations between MW and DW obliterated but they are couched in a way that is diametrically opposed to these origins, as 'aid' and 'help' towards DW.

The lack of a historical context which includes a connection to 'Self' serves as a receptive vacuum in which the knowledge about MW without any relation to 'Self' is produced and reiterated by INGOs' messages. This lack of knowledge, thus, itself becomes a kind of knowledge. Roger Silverstone highlights that 'mediated communication must be understood as both producer and product of hierarchy, and as such fundamentally implicated in the exercise of, and resistance to, power in modern societies' (2005: 190). The carefully neutral, dehistoricised and apolitical tone of most INGO messages does not take away from the fact that all messages are inherently political as they seek to define, enframe, exclude and persuade. While the double logic of 'difference' and 'oneness' enables ahistorical and depoliticised narrations, it can also be argued that the sheer depoliticisation itself is a highly politicised act. Humanism works as ether – an amorphous sphere that allows INGOs to place their messages within it while sidestepping the issues of power, namely the unequal power relations that are a product of history. The issue of power does, however, still creep in through questions such as what gives the capacity to the DW to be benevolent towards 'Others'? What gives DW the right (and the power) to say we are all human? Who decides the terms of representation and action?

It is puzzling that INGOs, as 'cusp' organisations that connect the DW and MW through their work, tend to show messages that are limited and disconnected with few interstitial, liminal spaces. Why do the messages of institutions placed at the centre of an interconnected world fail to show the fluidity of global connections? The possible factors that underlie INGOs' messages are explored in chapters 6 and 7. Based on interviews with INGO staff and members of the British public, these chapters seek to explain and contextualise INGOs' messages.

CHAPTER 6

UNIFORM FIRST WORLD –
NGO PERSPECTIVES

You photograph with all your ideology.
>   (Sebastião Salgado cited in Ritchin, 1990: 147)

Drawing on interviews conducted with key INGO staff working
in communications, fundraising and advocacy,[1] this chapter demonstrates why INGOs communicate the way they do. It also shows
that the theme of 'oneness' remains relevant to the production side
of INGOs' communications in two ways. The first of these relates
to the specific characteristics of institutional isomorphism such as
branding, commercialisation and professionalisation that are making
INGOs increasingly similar to each other and the hectic commercial
environment in which they operate. The second way in which 'oneness'
affects INGOs' communication is through their ideas about audiences,
who are assumed to be characterised by a homogeneous and mono-
cultural Eurocentric 'Britishness' that precludes any real engagement
on their part with their imperial past and the wider links to the MW.
Both these sets of factors influence the communication strategies of
INGOs.

This chapter is divided into four interconnected sections. The
first section concerns INGOs' policies of visual communication and
the role of different 'voices' within and outside the organisations. It
demonstrates that INGOs' current understandings and practices are

overpoweringly driven by the Ethiopian imagery debate which limits the ways of thinking about public messages across a narrow and simplistic range of 'negative' and 'positive' imagery. The second and third sections discuss the institutional reasons for the simplification, decontextualisation and dehistoricisation of these messages. The final section focuses on audiences and shows that essentialised Britishness of audiences is assumed by INGOs.

A limited debate – the 'negative'/'positive' divide

The immense importance of images was mentioned by all informants. Broadly speaking, imagery was recognised as very 'powerful' and seen to be significant in itself, implying the great responsibility INGOs have in communicating with audiences visually. It was also seen as an instrument to generate interest and get into the media. Put differently, the importance of images ranged from being accepted *per se* as being powerful in shaping perceptions, to being instrumental in igniting interest in a story or being helpful in building the INGO's 'brand'. However, most informants viewed the messages in terms of low expectations or narrow aims. There was also a lack of independent assessment of INGOs' messages and restricted MW feedback on these public messages.

Based on the recognition of this importance of images, several organisational actions have been taken within INGOs to ensure a level of what can be called 'flexible control' or 'controlled flexibility' in practices of visual communication. This means that these organisations have internal processes and systems that control the flow and use of visual communications while permitting a degree of flexibility to the specific staff members who actually use them. Some of these measures include attempts to ensure that pictures come from one source such as a picture library to ensure checks. In the case of all the INGOs, most images come from the picture library but a few may arrive directly from the field to a specific desk, such as advocacy, which then sends it to the picture library before or after using it for a campaign. Some INGOs have also created specific posts for visual communication to ensure a filtration process. As a result, images are checked and monitored by a Picture Editor or Creative Director before use.

INGOs also have guidelines and policies on visual communication that are linked to the NGO's brand and values. These guidelines incorporate a basic bottom line of requirement that no 'needy African child' is represented in the messages (Oxfam, 2006b: 58) and pictures which could be construed as 'presenting people as passive and helpless or people being presented as victims out of context' are avoided (ActionAid, 2006: 23). These guidelines also highlight other issues including how to show 'need with dignity' and comparisons of posed versus realistic images.

The setting up by INGOs of mechanisms to ensure overall standards and procedures for visual communications, which are also revised periodically, is also related to the issue of internal coherence, that is, the relations among different departments and their messages. The need for all relevant departments to speak 'in the same tone of voice' (informant, INGO 7) was expressed by every INGO. Informants also recognised the importance of other departments such as Communications in contributing towards the profile and brand awareness of the organisation and their indirect effects on the success of fundraising and advocacy messages.

The importance of images was acknowledged by all INGOs. Yet, it was surprising to see that no specific studies or evaluation had been carried out by any INGO on the influence of their images on public perceptions. The informants indicated that marketing studies were done periodically to judge the success or failure of specific appeals and campaigns, especially fundraising campaigns, but there was no specific component of imagery in these studies to explore their unintended effects.[2] One informant indicated that his organisation had questioned a limited number of members of a targeted young audience in educational institutions about a specific campaign and the feedback had been positive (INGO 4). Another informant indicated that the INGO tests out school posters and development education material at the design stage before a full launch of the material (INGO 5). One INGO planned to conduct an audit every six months to take an overview of the images used by the organisation to see if they 'speak in one voice' or not (INGO 3). However, this proposal did not include any consideration of how these messages feed into public perceptions and understandings.

Secondly, each message was seen in isolation. While other INGOs were observed, particularly to see if they were using any 'negative' imagery or had introduced a new or innovative communication campaign, there was no assessment of the collective influence of their messages on the public. Regular collective evaluations of even the messages of an individual INGO in terms of how they informed public perceptions were not carried out.

Thirdly, incorporating MW voices, for example through the feedback of Southern partner organisations, was also rare. The most common response to the partners' role was in terms of logistics, not feedback on or input into the messages. For a given story, the partner NGOs in the MW usually provide support such as transportation and other arrangements for the photo shoots. The limited role of MW partners was ascribed to practical reasons – constraints of time or lack of need in view of the expertise within the INGO. The informant of an INGO emphasised that it was important for them to listen to their partners' voices for programme formulation to know what local people need but it was not practical in communications:

> We listen to them a lot but there's enough knowledge within this building and within communications and the programme and NGO 3 values for us to be able to approve material. (informant, INGO 3)

The overall procedure of creating a story can be a bottom-up approach where a field staff member or MW partner can suggest a story which is then approved by the INGO Head Office. However the final product, i.e. the public message, does not usually incorporate any MW feedback. The ways in which the voices of MW partners can filter up are usually indirect, from other interactions between the INGO and the partner in specific wings of the INGO. Whether these voices are heard depends on how open the NGO staff are to the voices of their MW partners. There is also the critical issue of power asymmetry between the INGOs and their partners who depend on them for funds, an element that was missed in most discussions except one where the informant raised the near-impossibility of getting any

meaningful MW input into communications from the partners even
if asked for:

> I think it could probably potentially put them in a very difficult
> situation – they wouldn't want to be critical but, on the other
> hand, we do want as honest a feedback as we can get. (inform-
> ant, INGO 5)

To summarise, INGO informants mainly considered the importance
of visual communications for narrow, organisational aims with little assessment of their wider impact on public perceptions. Further,
selective issues from the imagery debate of the late 1980s and early
1990s across a distinctive axis of 'negative' and 'positive' imagery were
also seen to drive the current understandings and practices within the
INGOs, which drastically limited the ways of thinking. A frequent
comment made by the informants, when asked about their policy
on visual communications and the actual practices, pertained to the
appropriateness/rightness, or otherwise, of images shown. This was
expressed through a range or cluster of terms. I gradually found these
expressions to be common across the INGOs though the informants
varied in their understandings of these terms.

All INGO informants said that they tried not to show certain types
of negative messages at all. Images of starving children were illustrated as the minimum baseline they would not cross. Clearly drawing
again on the immense criticism of the 'pornography' of such images,
there was now self-policing by INGOs. I was also told that they were
surprised to see such images used occasionally in the media or by
another INGO as they seemed to be from another era:

> Somebody used a picture in today's *Guardian*. It is basically a child
> crying next to a grave and I was quite shocked, it's quite a shock-
> ing image, black and white, really like it should have been taken
> in 1975. And it was being used today. (informant, INGO 4)

Thus, there was agreement among INGO informants over the policy of
not showing images of extreme starvation. However, as already shown

by the visual data, there were many examples of such images originating from these NGOs in the public domain during the given period. A clear and open unease was expressed about these specific images. Talking about the image of a starving child, the informant stated:

> It breaks a lot of rules that we like to impose for ourselves. You know we wouldn't really want to be showing a child who is naked ... I think it was just a mix-up and it ended up getting used and we've had internal analysis of what had happened and that a general consensus that actually it was a mistake and shouldn't have been used. (informant, INGO 7)

While the above INGO attempted to distance itself from the image by stating that it was used as a result of a 'mix-up', the informant from another INGO denied that it was one of its images, and argued instead that its publication must have been the result of a decision by the media, in this case the specific newspaper. The messages in the form of features or news stories which also seek donations do tend to be an ambiguous area. It is difficult to attribute such images to a clear source – INGO or media – as the messages range from paid features to free space from the media and the final selection of each image is based on negotiations between the INGO and media staff. Nevertheless, readers do associate the message with the INGO in view of the appearance of the INGO's name, logo, web link or donation form. INGOs' guidelines also highlight the importance, and consistent use, of INGO's name and logo due to the 'brand' associations the viewers make with them. For instance, Oxfam's brand booklet mentions the importance of Oxfam logo for Oxfam's 'Visual identity' (Oxfam, 2006c: 57).

So, all INGOs claimed that their images were governed by what they saw as a 'post-starving child' state. Not showing images of starvation, it was emphasised, was indicative of 'positive' images. The INGOs who had shown such images argued that they were either not responsible for it or the images were a 'mistake'. Other INGOs, proud of not having shown 'negative' images, pointed fingers at other INGOs that had shown such images, albeit without providing any specific names. These discussions indicate an open, though rather narrow, consensus on the 'don'ts' of imagery within the INGOs.

The other side of the debate, namely 'positivism', was indicated through the emphasis on INGOs' values, policies and practices to show only the images they considered appropriate or right. One common, central idea was 'need with dignity', a term used to describe the INGO's core messaging in normative terms, namely what should and should not be shown. The idea of showing 'need with dignity' also combined the two ends of imagery – negative and positive – where the negativity of need could be balanced by showing it in a dignified, somewhat positive, way that minimised negativity.

> And we always want to make sure that we show people who are strong, dignified people like you and me but just happen to be in a very unfortunate situation. That's key for us and we also don't want to perpetuate the perception of the countries that INGO 3 works in as being basket cases, unable to help themselves and therefore worthy of our help. (informant, INGO 3)

This statement reflects a strong sense of humanistic empathy – 'dignified people like you and me'. It also responds to the anti-welfare argument to emphasise the 'deservedness' of the individuals who try to 'help themselves' and the countries whose situations are not completely 'negative' and beyond help but who have the potential to come out of the 'very unfortunate situation' they 'just happen to be' in. This is also the bad press argument that was a core of the imagery debate on Ethiopia and one which INGOs still respond to through their sporadic efforts to show that 'Africa' is not a 'basket case'.

Showing 'need with dignity' was encouraged at least in rhetoric and policy. Translating it into practice was a more complex endeavour. For some, this was because their understanding of the concept of 'dignity' was relative and abstract and hence hard to operationalise. For others, 'dignity' was a workable concept but still difficult to translate into practice.

The informant from INGO 6 argued that her organisation preferred to use terms such as 'victimising' or 'not victimising' which were clearer, stronger and easier to implement than 'dignity'. The INGO 4 informant opined that showing what is right and what is not was subjective and ultimately related to the 'look in the eyes'. The importance of eye contact to make the 'human' connection was also mentioned by INGO 2 informant. During 2005, this INGO had a policy of not showing people looking at the camera but it found that this had made images 'distant' from the viewers. Hence, it was revising this aspect of its visual communication policy. Barthes expresses the connecting power of eye contact and frontal pose (2000). Specifically discussing 'emergency' reportage, he finds himself unable to say anything about deaths and wounds and goes on to lament dramatically: 'Oh, if there were only a look, a subject's look, if only someone in the photographs were looking at me!' (Barthes, 2000: 111).

The issue of eye-contact with the camera (and thus the audience) is a debatable subject. Conveying 'need' through the eyes, it has been argued, places the photographed in an inferior position compared to the viewer and thus connotes availability (Nederveen Pieterse, 1992: 131). On the other hand, Comaroff and Comaroff argue that it can suggest the ease and trust that the photographed subjects show in their photographer (2007). Clearly, there is no given, generalised answer to this issue. The meaning of the 'look' can only be case-specific and read with regard to the entire message, who shows it, where, to whom and how. If seen in isolation, it risks becoming a generalised and mechanical issue instead of forming a part of the complex ways of understanding a message. Sight and photography are complex and situated acts that can only be understood through deconstructing not just what is within the frame of an image but what is excluded and how intricately it is enmeshed with the wider context of its production and reception.

Some informants argued that it was possible to translate 'dignity' visually. This was described by them through broad humanistic values, as the quotes below show.

I don't think it is that abstract ... if you would feel uncomfortable yourself of being portrayed in a particular way then that's a good way of testing it. (informant, INGO 5)

I mean you get a fairly good, instinctive idea, it's really just put yourself in those shoes and if you were, ill and dying in a refugee camp somewhere, would you want to be photographed? Probably not. (informant, INGO 3)

These views echoed a humanistic ethos, mere articulation of which was considered adequate to effect it. This was aided in policy terms, specifically by some INGOs, through 'real-life' examples in their guidelines and relevant booklets for staff to be used as examples of dignified, positive images. However, what appears as a simple test of human values, with or without illustrations of images that echoed these values, was hard to apply – as revealed by the many 'mix-ups' during 2005 which even the respondents found hard to justify.

A common way of illustrating 'dignity' was in terms of 'empowerment' which, in turn, was shown through activities or active people. One of the many such examples shown to me as evidence in practice was an image of women grinding something with long poles:

We wanted strong and *empowering* images, we wanted, you know, this one in particular, people doing things for themselves. You know, moving away from the old style imagery of people being helped, if you like. (informant, INGO 7)

A policy of using depictions of 'active' people was also explicitly shown to challenge myths about Africa as a lazy continent:

I think there is a perception that people in African countries and struggling countries that they are actually not doing much, you know, they're kind of sitting there waiting for aid to be delivered. And it was clear from these pictures that that simply wasn't the case, you know they had active lives, they might have had to go for a long time to take their cattle to go to wherever but then you know they lead very active lives. And so yeah I think that would be certainly quite a number of the comments where people went to the website that's the kind of thing that they would say – *it's just like us,* isn't it? (informant, INGO 5, emphasis added)

INGOs also believe that such myths hinder the effectiveness of their messages. Oxfam, for instance, has tried to counter them through its 'myth-busting' appeals. CAFOD has undertaken a participatory photography project called 'EthiopiaLives' to show the daily lives and activities of Ethiopians, as photographed by them, and counter the association of Ethiopia with famine and passivity.

The positive aspects of messages that INGOs strive to show were also indicated in terms of 'hope'. It was described in a variety of ways such as a suspension of belief, or an optimism that makes people believe 'something good can happen. So it's about hope' (INGO 1). Hope was a term used by INGOs to indicate that a message of hope was a positive one.

Another informant mentioned the practice of not cropping the image to include the 'context' as a way of showing dignity:

> I think one way of maintaining people's dignity is not, some-times cropping, you know, cutting out the context can take away that dignity. I think if you show people in the context of their lives, show what's going on around them, the people they have there to support them, it just helps tell the story more and helps explain the context. (informant, INGO 2)

The idea of positive images being progressive has its origins in the imagery debate of the late 1980s and early 1990s. The debates strongly criticised the negative depiction of MW by the media and INGOs through images and stories of starvation and the abject poverty of nameless MW, particularly African, masses. As a reaction to these criticisms, INGOs moved towards policies and practices of 'deliberate positivism' (Lidchi, 1999) that included images of happy, active MW people who were also given names to individualise them. Benthall's (1993) apprehension that this could well become a 'dogma' of positive images replacing the earlier negative images seems to have come true. Both INGOs' messages and interviews suggest an unquestioning faith in a narrow view of 'positive' images among INGO staff instead of questioning the very meaning of 'positive' images, their relation with other images and the place of 'context' in INGOs' messages. Why are 'positive' messages defined only as happy, active images of MW individuals? Do they reflect, or mask, the continuities and complexities of MW poverty and development and their relation with DW? Or do they show a 'post-intervention' scenario of an INGO project? After all, what does the image of, say, a smiling MW child say? There was scanty evidence to suggest any comprehensive engagement with these questions, although one informant did mention it when discussing photographs of 'cheesy, smiling, grinning children ... we wouldn't use those kind of images, it's fair to say that they don't really say anything' (informant, INGO 2).

At a broad level, a simplified and limited understanding of 'negative' and 'positive' can be attributed to the tendency within policy processes to rely on overly simple narratives and motifs. Martin Minogue argues that policy processes encompass such a range of complex dimensions of environment and interactions that they require the generation of simplified models and grand theories in the form of short and simple narratives in order to gain support for adoption and implementation (1997).[3] This provides only a partial explanation as further analyses, in the following sections, demonstrate.

Institutional isomorphism – professionalisation, marketisation and branding

The tendency to think within a restricted 'negative'/'positive' approach to communications is increasingly leaning towards excessive focus on 'positivity'. This is also reflected in the growing tendency to oversimplify messages, best exemplified in the gift catalogues, which further avoids messy content. These oversimplifications are due to the intertwined forces of increased competition, commercialisation, marketisation and institutional isomorphism, namely, the tendency for organisations within an institutional context to become alike. Each of these factors requires elaboration.

The idea of the 'simplification' of messages reflects a general tendency to oversimplify or 'dumb down' messages. It is important to state that simplification *per se* is not necessarily a bad thing. The visual analysis has shown several examples of contextualised messages represented in simplified styles that resist the dominant myths in INGOs' messages (see chapter 5). That a complex message has to be simplified to make audiences understand it is self-evident. It is, in fact, part of the job of the communications staff 'to enlist wider support by conveying complex messages in a straightforward way' (Edwards, 2002: 92). However, the style or form of simplification can sometimes pre-empt the incorporation of complexity, as in the case of gift catalogues where the consumerist, 'feel-good' and 'hyper-positive' aspects of the messages deter messy contextual issues and further depoliticise messages.

Discussing the organisational structures of international NGOs, Helmut Anheier argues that 'despite the remarkable diversity that characterizes INGOs we also observe common characteristics and patterns of similarity' (2005: 350). These isomorphisms are also true of INGOs' messages as seen in the visual analyses and echoed by INGO staff, as in the following quote:

> at the moment you can look at the imagery from NGO 1, NGO 2 and NGO 3 and it's all mixed up, you won't be able to tell what belongs where, would you? (informant INGO 2)

Apart from the use of similar images, there is a growing trend across INGOs to oversimplify the content in messages. At one level, this is in view of the perceived complexity and dullness of developmental topics. I was frequently told that 'root causes' of MW issues are not 'sexy enough' to capture readers' imagination. Assumptions about audiences played a big role in these arguments. During a discussion on various MW issues pioneered by an INGO and later taken up by others, the informant thought that, while the INGO would itself not opt to simplify, the simplification of messages was indeed a reason why other INGOs were able to reach wider audiences:

> Yeah, I think we are kind of half-jealous that they can make it work on a larger scale than we can but I think they can only because they are dumbing-down and they are simplifying it. (informant INGO 6)

Similarly, the marketing success of Christmas gifts was explained in terms of its simplicity and the way audiences feel about the messages, as the following quote shows:

> I think the way this kind of scheme works, people almost in a sense feel as though they are buying something tangible. And helping people, you know, get on with their lives and there's something specific that's going to be life-changing for them. And I think although the world is never as simple as that, we all know that, that's the trouble, but for a lot of people this is a very easy way into development, people can see we do a whole range of things. (informant INGO 1)

Simplification of messages was deemed important to make the audiences understand the messages quickly, clearly and easily especially in 'the communication environment [that] is just so increasingly hectic and quick and busy' (informant, INGO 3). A corollary of this increasingly hectic and competitive environment of INGOs has been the growing professionalisation and commercialisation of INGOs. Professional marketing staff and strategies such as 'branding' are now common in these organisations and this, in turn, contributes to the 'hectic' environment and simplification of messages. The commercialisation and branding of INGOs, however, are not wholeheartedly approved of by many within the INGOs:

> The word brand is a word which makes lots of people in this building shudder because it's seen as a marketing, commercial word. In fact what we mean by brand is, you know, a short cut for the public or consumers and something which will have values associated with INGO 3. (informant INGO 3)

Slick ways of professional marketing to reach audiences, in an increasingly competitive sector, include use of 'novel', more simplified ('dumbed-down') and better 'packaged' schemes such as the gift catalogues that show development as easy, doable, consumable and 'feel-good'. These trends are also likely to grow in the current institutional climate of INGOs.

The few INGOs that had not adopted the gift catalogues were quite critical of the approach of 'buy a goat, person happy', but added that such schemes 'fill a need' (informant, INGO 6). This means that the schemes are delving into an already existing 'market' of gifts which also indirectly echoes an *a priori* understanding and acceptance of the consumers/audiences/public. They also thought, and hoped, that these messages were a fad that would fade away soon. Responses of those who have adopted these schemes were largely pragmatic, ranging from slight unease to complete acceptance.

A general awareness of the limitations and implications of the oversimplified format and consumerist elements of these messages for the INGO's overall messages was expressed but it was not considered strong enough to stop the use of these immensely successful new schemes:

> I mean this particular product in a sense, if you look at the goat there, [*shows the photograph of a young girl with her goat in a pasture in a non-gift message*] obviously there you are talking about a person, a real person, and you are talking about their life and the way the goats work, here [gifts' catalogue] it's an image about effectively buying goats. So in some ways you could say it's slightly depersonalised, you think more of the end product but as an entry level, fundraising scheme, it does work. And I think you then hope that you can build more information into the communications further on down the line. (informant, INGO 1)

Other INGOs expressed a wholehearted acceptance of the gift schemes without any hint of awkwardness about the pure consumerist aspects of these public messages. The informants claimed that these schemes were based on different motivations of the audience and that they were trying to incorporate more details and information into them but in the final analysis they were gift catalogues:

> but ultimately what it rests on is people don't come to it because they want to end poverty, they come to it because they want to buy gifts. (informant, INGO 3)

Incorporation of gift schemes into the INGOs' communications and brand was done either by looking at them as a new 'product' or as a 'sub-brand'. While a product is a fundraising strategy, a sub-brand has a broader scope aimed to move into a new area or address a new audience.[4] It is relevant that the issue of internal coherence with the need to speak in one voice and have consistency between different messages was raised frequently by INGO informants. While all INGOs were concerned about internal coherence, the ways to achieve it differed. Some were against compromising while others found concepts such as 'sub-brand' to accommodate an overly simplified message within their overall brand and values.

Such INGO strategies indicate a coming to terms with the fiercely competitive marketing environment (to which they also contribute) and making a space that allows and justifies those strategies. This is not just about the competition among INGOs, but the near-morphing of these third sector organisations into private sector corporations drawing upon the wider marketing environment. The fierce competition among INGOs for 'market share' implies finding new market segments or audiences as well as attracting existing audiences with more appealing messages in tune with their wider, consumer culture. Strategies to achieve this include ambitious marketing targets and greater use of marketing professionals and private sector advertising agencies. These invariably increase the pressure to achieve fundraising targets at any cost as well as bring marketing elements from corporate sector advertising into the INGOs' messages, leading to hybridity in both organisational and management matters as well as the messages. As one informant commented about the effectiveness of the organisation's images:

> We want those images to operate not just within the charity communications environment but we want them to stand up in a general communications, marketing magazine, press environment. So I think just being aware of the wider environment. (informant, INGO 3)

The works of institutional theorists provide some useful explanations here. Institutional isomorphism promotes the survival and success of organisations. In order to become isomorphic with institutional environments, organisations adopt similar structures, strategies and processes to gain legitimacy and resources for survival (Meyer and Rowan, 1991: 49–53). DiMaggio and Powell (1991: 67) identify three mechanisms of isomorphic change:

> (1) *coercive* isomorphism that stems from political influence and the problem of legitimacy; (2) *mimetic* isomorphism resulting from standard responses to uncertainty; and (3) *normative* isomorphism, associated with professionalization.

The marketisation and corporatisation of INGOs' public messages, in particular, reflect mimetic and normative processes of isomorphism. As dynamic actors in a volatile, increasingly competitive and uncertain environment, INGOs respond to the increasing professionalisation and marketing orientation of their peers and other private organisations by mimicking them. But this is only a part of the story. A fuller understanding requires a wider contextual analysis of INGOs that investigates their relationships with their environment which, in addition to the institutional context, also encompass the macro socio-economic setting and legal structures.[5] In terms of isomorphism, this is described through the first mechanism, namely coercive isomorphism, which is caused by 'cultural expectations' (DiMaggio and Powell 1991: 68). The wider environment of INGOs is particularly germane in understanding why messages include or exclude specific contents.

Decontextualisation and dehistoricisation of messages

Decontextualisation in INGOs' messages can be partially explained by the way many NGOs define and operate 'context' within their public messages. 'Context' was a term often mentioned by INGO staff. While there was general agreement that the context should be shown in the messages, the concept was understood and defined in varying ways. These divergent views were, nevertheless, located within a range or gradient. A diagrammatic depiction of the gradient of 'context' shown within INGOs' messages is given in Figure 6.1.

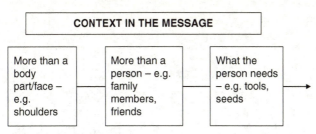

Figure 6.1   Gradient of 'context' shown visually in INGOs' messages

A key level of this gradient consists of defining 'context' as more than a body part, such as a face, and more than a single individual. For example, in the case of messages with children, focusing on more than the close-up of a child's face was considered to be a step towards incorporating context and an improvement on the imagery used in previous years, as one informant stated:

> [...]new set of ads which give actually the context in the frame of the image. So it's not head and shoulders anymore, they are moving away from that and we are using a child in a community. So you can see, you know, where the child is, where they need that sort of thing. (informant, INGO 4)

Similarly, in disaster situations, the presence of help, such as feeding or medical treatment, was shown as the 'context':

> in this image you can see that the child is malnourished but you can see the inspection and the help being shown there. So again you know there is some sense of relationship there. We wouldn't use a sort of cut-out shot of a starving child looking at the camera because that shows well, it [*pauses*] incites from the viewers sort of pity and it's just you know begging type image from the whole situation of images coming out of the 1980s and Ethiopia. We try not to use that kind of imagery. (informant, INGO 2)

One of the meanings of 'context' was the immediate environment of the characters shown. The informant from an INGO emphasised the importance of showing the day-to-day activities and the people in the lives of MW children.

> When you are choosing pictures [you look for] different types of images, different distances from the subject, relationships of the child ... with family members or friends or whatever, you know, maybe helping out around the house or maybe playing with friends or at school. (informant, INGO 2)

Another way in which context was understood was through 'need'. This took the form of what MW people need, such as toolkits. Once this was identified, attempts were made to include this 'context' in the message in the shape of farm implements, seeds and other things.

As these illustrations show, views differed among the INGO informants but only within a limited range or gradient, reflecting a degree of isomorphism. The context in developmental messages was defined in a fairly narrow sense focusing on the immediate lives of MW people that could be shown spatially in an image.

The immediate lives of MW people are also connected to their broader and historicised location within X country in MW and the globe, the temporal and spatial connections that can be included in a message through the written text. During further discussions on the INGO informants' views on incorporating the 'context' of global poverty or 'root causes of poverty' with a 'sense of history' into it, informants argued that the incorporation of historical background into their messages was problematic. While some thought that excluding history would make the message more agreeable and 'positive', others thought it diluted the issues and yet others argued that it was too complex for audiences. Figure 6.2 summarises some of the reasons that were forwarded by INGO informants for not bringing history into the public messages.

Public messages were deliberately defined in terms of the 'current global situation', de-linked from the past for reasons such as keeping the messages simple, understandable and 'positive'. The 'past' was also

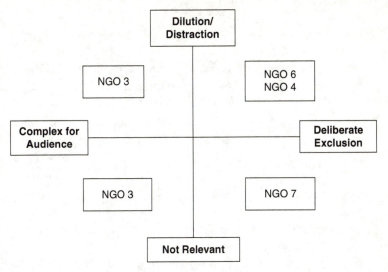

Figure 6.2   Historical context in INGOs' messages

considered to be a distraction from current purposes, as expressed in this statement:

> I don't think we're trying to hide anything, it's just, you know, this is the way the world is, this is what we could do to make it better – that's what we need to try and get out there. Even that is complicated enough, you know, and on the campaigning runs, fundraising, there's just so many messages even just within that – this is what the world is, this is how we can make it better … anything beyond that we just don't really have (anything) to say. (informant, INGO 3)

Exclusion of history was also a deliberate attempt to avoid evoking guilt complex and to be 'positive'.

> But as someone who really put things out in the public arena, I think I have to say that we restrict our talk quite significantly about the historical aspects because then, of course, you get to the name-calling, you get to the guilt-complexes, you

get to – look what the British did. You know you get into that whole quagmire, and instead what we are trying to be is a little more positive in that way. I guess in that way I would say what's more interesting is finding solutions instead of talking about the problem all the time. (informant, INGO 6)

The 'negative' connotations of history, as reflected in the above statement, assume that their exclusion works as a component of a 'positive' message for audiences in the UK, which are also taken to be homogeneous. This shows that INGOs cater first and foremost to their understanding of the Northern public and their sensibilities and any historical reality or MW views in this regard is secondary. This also raises the question: for whom do the messages have to be positive – people in DW or MW?

Decontextualised and dehistoricised messages of INGOs also stem from other factors that include legal norms and managerialism. A legal requirement demanded of INGOs is their 'neutrality'. The English Charity Law considers only a purpose that is for the public good or the relief of poverty as charitable and excludes political activities such as campaigning (Lever, 1997). The ambiguity of the term 'political' has resulted in Oxfam and CA occasionally coming up against the limits of charity laws, but the UK Charity Commission has never gone beyond mildly rebuking these NGOs (Black, 1992; Benthall, 1993). This legal constraint often implies that INGOs operate within a statutory regime that forces them to avoid 'political' issues such as historical context. But this has not fettered a few INGOs from presenting deviant and critical messages, as illustrated earlier. Further, given the mixed message style of most INGO communications, slipping in 'political' context, albeit in a subliminal manner, is clearly possible.

The downplaying and exclusion of history within INGOs' messages can also be explained as an outcome of managerialism, with its emphasis on rationality, which considers management as 'good' and politics as 'bad'. Its naive view of policy processes and neglect of politics also leads to an inordinate focus on the future and too little focus on the past or present. As Minogue states, '[t]he answer to "bad management now" is "better management tomorrow"' (1997: 22). The persistent emphasis on novelty and change by development organisations (Lewis, 2007) is also understandable because it allows these organisations to look forward rather than backwards and gives a sense of 'hope'; an idea the INGO informants also mentioned as a conscious component of their messages. Rachel Wrangham illustrates how 'historical amnesia' was produced in a Department for International Development (DFID) rural development project in Mozambique (2005).[6] Scant attention was paid to important historical factors in either the project document or the dominant views of the project staff, who prioritised an imagined future that had no continuity with the past even though historical perspectives were available to them. Kothari and Minogue call it the 'futuristic approach to development' (2002: 12) which avoids the messy present and moves on to future policies and projects.

One market – cultural or institutional denial?

The importance of audiences was a frequent theme in the interviews. There were many presumptions and ideas of 'oneness' and commonality about audiences. I call it 'Britishness'; a Eurocentric stock of knowledge and value systems assumed valid across almost all segments of British publics notwithstanding their differences of age, class and ethnicity. With some exceptions, audiences were taken to be monolithic, uniform and homogeneous, treated as an *a priori* entity and largely accepted pragmatically as they are. INGOs operated on the assumption that certain issues would be acceptable to such an audience while others would not.

The dominant concern was with the need to 'link the message with the audience' or 'meet the audiences where they are', as reflected in the following statement:

It is quite a paradox, isn't it? Because you can wait till everybody in your country understands the dynamics of poverty and how it's caused. Or you can start to talk to people where they are at and what moves them and how they can be affected. And so I mean if you want the ideal then [*laughs*] nothing will change ...

you got to engage people where they are at and not be in your
NGO insulated ivory tower. (informant, INGO 4)

The above statement is not only based on assumptions about the stock
of knowledge of audiences but also, by and large, accepts audiences
pragmatically and realistically. It also implies that any initial 'side
effects' of campaigns, such as reinforcing myths, would necessarily be
considered collateral damage; a price one has to pay to engage people
in the first place. This 'pragmatic' school of practitioners also looks
at the audiences as an *a priori* entity, a mass of people who are pre-
existent without ever having been influenced by INGOs. This belief
was also reinforced by the following response to my question on how
MW myths have arisen in the first place:

> I think a lot of it, I mean some of it is understandable because
> there is massive corruption in the developing world and people are
> naturally wary of giving money ending up in the wrong place. I
> think also a lot of the myths are very convenient to people, they
> excuse themselves from having to care about developing countries
> or having to give because they can put up all these reasons – oh
> you know NGO X is a massive organisation, they spend all their
> money on admin, I'm not giving them any money or if I give
> up money to Africa it'll end up in people's pockets. (informant,
> INGO 3)

Some INGOs did ask more searching questions about their audiences. One respondent pondered why certain messages, such as
those with smiling children, continued to have such great appeal
for people:

> It could be a positive image, yes. I think we should as a society
> have moved on from the 'aah factor' of poor little children but
> it is something that connects people, people have children you
> know all over the world. So I can understand it but then if it's
> the only thing that motivates people, that's a little bit worrying.
> (informant, INGO 5)

The informant of another INGO was also critical of the 'aah factor':

> One big concern of ours is to make sure that our partners are not portrayed as these poor little poor people, they are so dumb, we need to support them! What we are trying to do is [say] these people know what to do but we just need to help them out a bit basically. So along the whole thing that we work in solidarity and together, I think that's where we are trying to differentiate ourselves from the 'buy a goat, person happy'! (informant, INGO 6)

While disapproving of such 'buy a goat' messages, the same informant nonetheless admitted that such schemes have their place and the INGOs that use them 'fill a need', thereby indirectly echoing an *a priori* understanding of audiences and market scenario.

Diversity of audiences and potential to change their attitudes was also seen across time. I was informed that it was possible to transform a set of audience into another 'type' of audience over time. Comparing fundraising messages with a specific advocacy campaign, an informant stated:

> there is a lot of work being done in moving this audience to coming for campaigns. There's that shift. So maybe somebody starts off with (fundraising) because that's the way they think that they can engage with the subject but then when they learn more about INGO 4 they start thinking about the possibilities of campaigning, writing to the MPs. So there is a move. (informant, INGO 4)

Yet, the same audience was considered homogeneous, uniform and monolithic when it came to showing the macro historical context and root causes of poverty because INGO informants thought these would be completely unacceptable to this audience. There was a broad social consensus that historical context could not be mentioned:

> history is still 'kings and queens of England' and I think we do shy away somewhat from our colonial legacy. (informant, INGO 4)

However, no empirical evidence was provided to justify this view, or to demonstrate the audiences' lack of acceptance of INGOs' rare and deviant messages. One such message, I was informed, had received 'good responses' from the audience. I was also told by one of the INGOs concerned that 'criticism is actually a good thing' because it shows that the messages are having an impact and also exposing their critics' ideologies, for instance, their 'pro-free trade' stance.

Imperial history is not the only problematic issue that is avoided in INGOs' messages. The tendency to avoid messy issues is also exemplified with regard to the subject of 'race', which is not addressed directly. This was brought home during a discussion about how people connect 'with another face' (informant, INGO 6). I was informed that people in the UK do not respond to images of people from South America in fundraising messages.

> Every time I do an appeal on Asia or Africa, it's gonna do *better* than anything I do on Latin and South America ... With fundraising I wish we did talk about this – if it's the racial background of the person in the image, it's what is crucial to make a difference then ... So *yes,* I don't know, much of that actual history is racial background. We always try to make sure that we have a cultural mix, or racial mix in there, because we *do* work with all different people. (informant, INGO 6)

The above informant did wonder if the racial background of the person, which makes Asians and Africans *look* different from most Europeans, is a crucial factor in eliciting response. Effective fundraising requires that MW people do not look like 'us' outwardly. This point is emphasised in other development studies research on issues of 'race' and colour. For example, Andrea Cornwall observes the absence of fair-skinned Brazilian children in the UK adverts of ActionAid because they 'don't fit the image of what the deserving poor or the innocent child ought to look like' (2005: 19). Skin tone is the easiest signifier of 'difference' that is apparently 'demanded' by British audiences but this latent issue of race does not appear to be engaged with directly or adequately by INGOs, as the above quote demonstrates. Sarah White writes of the '"colour-blind" stance of development which both marks and masks its centrality to the development project' (2002: 407). INGOs' avoidance of race issues seems to be a part of a 'code' of hiding it within a liberal humanist perspective that seeks to deny difference and in so doing normalises it (White, 2002). Instead of engaging with this issue the audiences were once again assumed to be homogeneous and accepted *per se* by the INGOs.

A common way to circumvent problematic and conflictual issues, such as those of race and history, is the humanist way that appears to be a recurring theme across INGOs' messages. Universal humanism here works, on the one hand, to project a genuinely empathetic response towards 'Other' human beings and, on the other, as a post-race and history-less humanism. The humanism reflected in conversations with INGO informants seemed to straddle two sub-streams of this discourse, which Barthes calls 'classic humanism' (1993). The first showed 'one' humanity. Talking about the constraints INGOs face from the audiences' apathy, one informant stated:

A lot of people think oh we shouldn't help other people until we've sorted our own problems out and we would like to point out that we don't believe in national boundaries in that way, we're working together globally as a humanity and you know the earth is our home, we're all on it. (informant, INGO 3)

The idea of being 'together globally as a humanity' shows a vision of 'one' humanity without 'national boundaries' that also falls within the rubric of cosmopolitanism or 'global citizenship' (Calhoun, 2003).

A second sub-stream portrayed humanity as 'just like us' with the 'good' and the 'bad' facets:

It is a fact that ... of Africa we mostly see sort of poverty and the tough issues that people have to deal with in their daily life. What we don't see so much of, you know, the fun and the good things that go on and I quite like looking at, you know, looking at some of the good moments in people's lives, in Africa. And

the things that Africans do to help themselves as well. (informant, INGO 2)

The above statement specifically mentions the good (and bad)
moments in the lives of African individuals that are 'universal' to
all human beings. The balancing of negative imagery with positive imagery is also accommodated by this organising principle of
humanism to show a universal human life with its ups and (mostly)
downs but it again does not allow a deeper, macro-level understanding and projection of how the negative state came about, and why it
persists. INGOs consider it necessary to highlight such micro-level
good personal moments but not the macro-level success stories of specific countries and their leaders. Are they unconsciously trying to
reflect, and counter, a generalised belief that 'Africans' *are* somehow
sub-human, incapable of any positive moments, unless such moments
are explicitly shown?

Both these streams of humanism are generously used by INGOs to
connect MW with DW but most messages do not attempt to explain
the deeper, macro-level background, carefully circumventing the
genealogy of MW poverty and remaining unselfconscious of their own
connections to the current geopolitical structures.

To explain the pragmatic acceptance of a perceived homogeneous
audience requires the bringing together of organisational and institutional factors including notions of culture, 'Britishness', denial, and
the legitimacy and accountability of NGOs. Multiple accountabilities
of NGOs include accountability 'upwards' to their donors, trustees and
governments and 'downwards' to their partners, beneficiaries, staff and
supporters.[7] NGOs' accountabilities to their 'beneficiaries' and contributors are paramount morally because of their values of participation and empowerment and their claims of legitimacy (Edwards and
Hulme, 2002). INGOs' messages reflect the complex ways in which
they reconcile and prioritise their accountabilities to different consti-
uencies. Being accountable to MW 'beneficiaries' takes the form of
showing them with 'dignity' but not as historicised subjects as this
could clash with their legitimacy with Western audiences, which form
part of the wider environment. There is, thus, a clear tendency within

INGOs to prioritise away from their MW constituencies towards their British audiences.

Furthermore, INGOs' assumption of this Eurocentric 'Britishness', as in disengagement with imperial past and history, across a collective consciousness of audiences, leads to an isomorphic response of avoiding any inclusion of historical background in INGOs' messages. This mechanism of isomorphism is a form of 'coercive isomorphism' that results from 'cultural expectations in the society within which organisations function' (DiMaggio and Powell 1991: 68). Cultural expectations here are of a Eurocentric Britishness that includes cultural denial, ambivalence towards empire and 'postimperial melancholia' (Gilroy, 2004: 98), which is presumed to be fixed, overpowering and *a priori*, something that is best left alone. This presumption does not consider that INGOs' messages themselves can, and do, contribute to or resist Britishness. It also raises an important question whether this is a case of cultural denial on the part of an entire society, or institutional denial by INGOs, or both, as INGOs too are constituted by their society and 'Britishness'.

Cultures are neither monolithic nor closed or static. Their dynamism and ever-changing nature has been famously illustrated by Appadurai (1990) across five 'scapes' of flows of people, technology, finance, information and ideologies. The assumption that British audiences uniformly possess this Britishness also takes the view of British culture as fixed and 'white' with little reflection on, for example, its diasporas, and the general fluidity and ever-changing nature of culture.

Conclusion

This chapter has presented and analysed the production-side data collected from INGOs based on interviews conducted with their staff members related to specific fundraising and advocacy campaigns of 2005/6 and visual communications in general. It shows that INGOs' messages are broadly viewed across narrow, organisational aims with little assessment of their impact on public perceptions. These are not merely technical or organisational-level issues but moral discourses that carry a range of assumptions.

There is considerable emphasis by INGOs on showing MW individuals with dignity but their depictions are at micro level, detached from their place in the world and history. This rests on a limited, and specific, understanding of 'negative' and 'positive', with the former considered an objectionable and the latter a desirable portrayal in INGOs' messages. The inordinate emphasis on crude categories of 'negative', particularly seen in the representations of starving babies, and 'positive', exemplified through images of 'activity' and happiness, restrict the scope of a message, and neglect its potential to connect people differently and change the discourse from 'charity' to 'justice'.

The centring on oversimplified categorisations epitomises a lack of visual literacy which ignores both the 'hybridity' and the power positioning of those involved – the haves and the have-nots; those who represent and those who are represented. Homi Bhabha uses the term 'hybridity' to explain the mutuality of relationship between the coloniser and the colonised and the inauthenticity of the 'Third World' (1994). Given the long history of material and cultural flows, particularly colonialism and resistances to it, authentic and discrete societal categories are non-existent. At the same time the power asymmetries that determine who controls the terms of representation are very real. The focus on crude categories does not permit greater nuance and epistemic change in the understandings and projections of 'Self' and 'Others'. It fails to recognise either the inauthenticity of the material separation of these categories or the disparities in the position of 'Self' and 'Others'.

The exclusion of broader context appears to stem from INGO informants' desire to evade messy issues such as those of race and history; an attitude stemming in part from managerialism, namely, a general preference for management over politics and future over past or present; and the INGOs' institutional context of commercialisation and isomorphism. These are also based on assumptions about the acceptance (or lack of it) of such information by the audiences. This, when seen in the context of the relative importance of various 'stakeholders', clearly shows a privileging of DW audiences over MW views. Moreover, a fixed and 'mono-cultural "Britishness"' (Hall, 2007: 7) of audiences is also assumed by INGOs. How true are such assumptions about the homogeneity of audiences? Can INGOs assume that Britain, as a whole, is Eurocentric and disengaged from its history? And are not INGOs themselves drawing from and contributing to it by silencing the historical continuities of MW poverty and its links to DW in their messages, which reinforces this Britishness? To what extent are INGOs' messages a result of cultural denial, institutional denial or both? These are important questions that underpin the entire debate about the legitimacy of INGOs as institutions of representation. Part III probes these questions by exploring the responses of some members of the British audience to INGOs' messages in chapter 7.

PART III

REFLEXIVITY

Introduction

Parts I and II of this book discussed the themes of 'difference' and 'oneness' by investigating the first two components of the representational field of INGOs' public messages – representation and production. Part III examines the third aspect – reception – and also brings together the three components of the representational cycle

Chapter 7 is based on in-depth interviews with some members of the British public regarding specific INGO messages on disasters, long-term development and structural aspects of global poverty. It adds to the understanding of the ways in which INGOs' messages are received and finds clear links between knowledge and emotions, and the personal and collective. The responses of many audience members to the exceptional messages challenge INGOs' assumptions of a fixed notion of Eurocentric Britishness. The deviant INGO messages were quite influential and led to nuanced understandings and reflexivity among many interviewees. These responses underline the possibility of change and suggest new ways to foster reflexive understandings of global poverty and development amongst Western publics. The multiplicity and commonalities found in the audience responses both question the generalised form of Britishness and expose its resilience.

Chapter 8 draws together the threads of difference, oneness and reflexivity. It sums up the arguments of the book and connects the themes and components of the representational field to highlight their significance for INGOs and our understandings of global inequalities.

CHAPTER 7

LIVES OF OTHERS – AUDIENCE RESPONSES

ME2 (Male, elderly respondent 2)[1] – They eat dogs in India, don't they?

[*I remain silent*]

ME2 – Dogs **and** cats.

[*I can no longer hold my silence. I say in a deliberately calm tone, trying to maintain my status as a neutral interviewer*]

ND – Most Indians are vegetarians.

[*We look at each other. He takes another sip of beer and adds*]

ME2 – In China then [*pauses*]. China **and** India.

[*He looks away and I begin talking about other issues. The crisis is over and the conversation can continue . . .*]

The above extract of conversation with a British white, male, elderly person (ME2) forms a part of the interviews I conducted with an indicative small group of members of the British public or audience. Such examples of prejudice and ignorance (in this case of the generalised 'barbarianism' and 'backwardness' of 'Others') were uncommon but an essential slice of the diverse mix of complex, ambivalent, inconsistent and circumlocutory responses of those interviewed. These are also part of the reception environment the INGOs deal with and address. A caveat is in order here. The chapter makes no claims of empirical breadth or representativeness but aims primarily to challenge assumptions of homogeneity of audiences as well as provide a glimpse of the receiving context of INGOs' messages, a 'market' which is neither uniform nor static but no less challenging.

Based on twelve in-depth interviews with members of British public, this chapter examines the responses of these viewers to a range of INGOs' messages of 2005/6,[2] their understandings of issues raised in the messages and triggered by the messages, as well as the intertextual ways in which they received the messages. This not only helps to explain the ways in which messages are received but also to judge the responses against the assumptions made about the audiences by INGO staff about their 'Britishness'. I keep in mind that messages are read in divergent ways by individuals based on their identity and life experiences which make up their 'stock of knowledge'. While there may be a 'preferred', 'dominant' or 'hegemonic' reading which is intended by the producer or reinforces a prevailing ideology, 'oppositional readings' can be made of the same text which contest the dominant meanings of the image. A third reading may be a 'negotiated' one where the viewer interprets something from the image and its dominant meaning (Hall, 1993).

Each interview lasted between one and two hours. Detailed analysis of all interviews involved looking for patterns and themes, commonalities and divergences across gender and age as well as individuals. I placed small ads in council libraries and colleges across Greater London to seek respondents and randomly selected the first twelve volunteers, drawing in equal numbers of each gender from three age groups – young (18–29 years), middle-aged (30–59 years) and elderly (60 and above).[3] Those who volunteered turned out to be middle-class, fairly diverse with respect to their educational qualifications and vocations and with a single common 'ethnic' denominator – they were all 'white British'.[4] While these members of audiences do not exhaust the entire range of INGOs' target audiences, it is noteworthy that most fall in the category of 'warm supporters'. This means that they were interested in charities, concerned about varied causes and had a history of charitable activities such as donation of money and old clothes, voluntary work, child sponsorship and shopping at charity stores.

Eight messages were shown. These were Concern (CW-1{CW-1/1 to 1/4}) – 'Food Crisis in Sub-Saharan Africa', Oxfam (O-11{O-11/1 to

11/15}) – 'How Oxfam is Helping Around the World', WOW Insert – 'She is working herself out of Poverty. Yeah Right', Plan (P-4) – 'Sponsor a child with Plan', Oxfam Christmas Gifts' Insert – 'Oxfam Unwrapped', CA Christmas Gifts' Leaflet – 'Present Aid, Oxfam (0–29) – 'I'm in' and CA (CA-3) – 'Dirty low down spongers'.

The chapter is organised in four parts. The first section gives an overview of the general responses of the interviewees to the work of international charities and their messages. The second section explores the respondents' specific responses to three types of messages – disaster ('negative'), development ('positive') and advocacy. The third section examines in detail further responses triggered by the advocacy message of CA (CA-3) that contained historical information.[5] The fourth section looks at the main literature on audience responses, particularly to images of atrocities and 'Others', in the light of the interviews and the effects of INGOs' messages including the changed views of some respondents. The diversity of responses, along with several commonalities, amply challenges the 'mono-cultural character of "Britishness"' (Hall, 2007: 7) assumed, and fostered, by INGOs while also revealing its deep structures and durability.

INGOs and the genre of charity messages

INGOs' messages were seen both as advertisement and documentary by all audience respondents. To the extent that they were seen as advertisement there was a sense of mistrust about the message, the level of which varied depending on the viewer's perception of both the contents of the message and the INGO. The respondents' opinions about INGOs ranged from cynicism and doubt to a very high level of trust. In this regard, some of the responses triggered by the messages about the INGOs included comments on the Asian Tsunami which had recently mustered massive donations and raised the profile and income of INGOs. Many raised doubts about the utilisation of funds and distribution of aid and wondered if it was going to the right people. The cost of providing aid, i.e. the administration costs of NGOs was another issue raised frequently.[6]

The variations in the levels of trust in the message, as reflected in the viewers' responses, ranged from ads *per se* not being trustworthy, as they had an ulterior motive or agenda, to INGOs being untrustworthy for reasons such as doubts about funds' utilisation and distribution. Persuasive communication is 'typically unwanted communication' (Dahl, 1993 cited in Messaris, 1997: 5) and people tend to avoid advertising, a fact some of my respondents also expressed. But an overarching belief in the message did dominate because it came from the INGOs that were ultimately considered highly credible. Viewers expressed their faith in charities through statements such as 'we have to trust them' (MM1) or 'And then you recognise the logo from Christian Aid. So people would be trusting it' (FY2).

Another dominant theme that emerged could be called 'the Oxfam effect'. It was common to hear the comment 'Everybody has heard of Oxfam' (MM2) or 'by giving to Oxfam you are giving to a secure charity' (FE2). Oxfam is a 'household name' and has been rated as one of the top five brands in the UK, commanding a very high level of public trust as is revealed through these interviews.[7] This trust in Oxfam and other INGOs was made evident also by many comments by respondents about their personal travels across MW where they had not come across any starvation. They still did not doubt the images because they had faith in the charities.

Another way of understanding these responses is through the 'truth claim' of the photograph. This is the documentary-like or evidence effect especially of a photographic image that suggests that it is real and 'attest[s] to the instantiation of the moment ("it happened")' (Radley and Kennedy, 1997: 438). A photographer had to be present to capture the event that had to have happened. I contend that the trust in the message was a result of a combination of the 'Oxfam effect' and the 'truth claim'. It stemmed from belief in the photograph as a piece of documented evidence as well as the reputation of the organisations showing the image.

There were many general reactions about INGOs. One of these was the view about the importance and value of the INGOs in 'saving lives'.

FY1 – It shows that not enough is being done and I think if it wasn't for charities these people would be wiped off the places.

Nearly all respondents unhesitatingly accepted the charities' presence in MW countries. Their reservations were about specific messages or the feelings evoked, such as individual-level guilt, but not about the role of charities. The unquestioning acceptance of INGOs reflects the importance of the actions or mandate of the INGOs as publicised through their messages about the work they do in the MW. This has also been demonstrated in large surveys such as the 'Public Attitudes towards Development' 2006 survey where 78% of respondents considered international charities to be the main contributors to the reduction of poverty (ONS [Office for National Statistics] for DFID, 2007). This was reaffirmed in the case of the Oxfam-*Metro* two-page spread (O-11) where most respondents thought that it clearly showed the distribution of poverty across the globe and that the MW was 'eager for help' (ME1).[8]

In addition, the importance of INGOs as media institutions was also commented on by most respondents who stated that they relied on charity messages for long-term information on disasters and crises.[9] One elderly male respondent also considered that it was a tough job for charities as 'developed countries are isolated from developing countries' (ME1). This is quite a significant statement and touches upon 'isolation' and 'distance', which appears 'real' but is, in fact, a combination of perception as circulating in wider discourses and real as signified by the power asymmetries between DW and MW which 'isolate' the former from the latter but not vice versa. The same respondent reverted to this issue to compare mass media with INGOs:

ME1 – I think I was speaking earlier about … the developed world being insulated from the non-developed world … well, I am one of those individuals who rather thinks that the *perceptions* of the developed world are very much in the hands of those who control the mass media and that is why it is only occasionally that perceptions of the non-developed world filter through and reach the populace in the developed country. And this is why this is also a hard job for international aid agencies to raise awareness and more equally, or more importantly, to actually, to call for some *action* to be taken, not mere passive awareness but *action* on the part of the populace.

The messages also made the individual respondents position themselves in specific ways. One way of 'subject-positioning' was expressing a personal or family background that made them 'giving' or 'aware'. Almost all of them tried to project themselves as 'good guys' through their actions and knowledge. Most respondents did indeed have a history of charitable activities, reflecting the truth of their claims. However, such statements were also evoked by the entire context of viewing charity messages that expected a response of some kind from them. Further, the respondents also talked about their charitable ways and views to counter-balance statements they made that could be perceived as non-charitable. For instance, the interviewees would say they were good people who bought greeting cards from Oxfam but were being honest in saying that the MW was corrupt or lazy. And quite often they would later contradict or extend their statements or react differently to the same issue.

Positioning was also expressed through the logic of 'big effect of small effort' through statements such as 'the big effect a small donation can have' (ME1) or 'you don't need to give a lot for it to make a difference to someone … that has nothing' (FM2) or 'smallest things make the biggest difference' (FY1). This positioning, which is also common in the INGO messages in their use of 'conversions' (£x can buy y amount of a,b,c), reflected what can be called a 'combined positioning' as it expressed faith in both the value of a small donation and the effort of the INGO that would have a large effect in MW. It did not permit questioning why the relative positions were so disparate in the first place but took for granted a given state of extreme inequality.

There was also a widespread knowledge about a 'typical' charity message and the respondents recognised this instantaneously. It is apt to call this a charity genre or 'box' of charity messages. For example, viewers could easily recognise different 'stages' of charity – a pre-intervention image in the form of a disaster image of, say, barren land or starvation and a post-intervention image of a happy child, as illustrated below.

MY2 [*On the WOW insert cover image*] – It's the barren land and the aridity of the land, the lack of water and the person that you can tell is poverty-stricken because of the clothes that they are wearing and the posture they are in – bending down to work as opposed to standing up tall.

FY1 [*On the image of a child in a disaster message*] – I think using children as imagery and I know, it's not like exploiting them because these poor children are in desperate need. I think that really hits home to people and people kind of, it pulls on your heart strings most definitely.

MM2 [*On the image of a happy child in Plan's appeal*] – Yes it's good. You see a child there, seems quite happy … So yeah it's like a positive, positive thing that this charity could be *working*.

This evidently stems from the familiarity of the viewers with the 'charity genre'; something many also mentioned – seeing such images, especially disaster images, 'all the time' on television. This suggests a certain level of 'literacy' or knowledge about a charity message that the viewers of all ages possessed based on their exposure to such messages over a long period of time. Talking about child sponsorship, for example, a young male respondent stated:

MY1 – I remember my father used to make jokes – maybe this is part of Western culture but he'd say, you know, I sent 10 pounds for two of these children and they still haven't arrived yet [*smiles*], you know, he'd make these jokes. So this kind of joke shows you that we are not too bothered, we live in our happy Western world, it's just a joke. At the same time the joke says again how long this has been going on, you know, I'm talking about the joke which has been 15 years old. So this has been going on for a long time.

An associated issue relates to the expectations from a charity message. For example, people shown were expected to *look* a certain way as associated with the MW and charity recipients and skin colour was an important aspect of this look. The image of a white, young male with a baby shown in Oxfam's 'I'm in' campaign surprised most readers, who could not fit it into the charity genre.

> FY2 – I wouldn't associate it with Oxfam. I'd think it's something to do with parenting group or something [*both laugh!*].

On the other hand, the child in Plan's child sponsorship appeal fitted the bill even though, unlike a 'charity child', she was smiling and looked healthy, which some said could imply that the 'need' was less – 'It's quite clearly ethnically different to the British. The Plan one the child is in a distinctly African dress making it clear that they are not from here' (ME1). The child in question was a dark girl in a frock and this description could easily fit a British child. The fact that she was clearly seen as 'different to the British' was due to a host of factors – her dark (non-white) skin, her colourful dress which could not be seen clearly but suggested that it was an 'African' dress, and her appearance in an overseas charity ad – which led to a quick chain of expected or dominant readings.

In addition to their literacy about charity messages *per se*, the interviewees showed an understanding of messages within an intertextual stock of knowledge. This wider knowledge was based on related events such as Live Aid (1985) among the older respondents and Live 8 (2005) among the younger respondents. Geldof and Bono were mentioned very often, particularly by the younger respondents. Knowledge of right-wing press and tabloids with their distinctive language, as used by CA in the 'dirty low down spongers' appeal (CA-3), was another illustration, even though the respondents had mentioned that they regularly read other newspapers such as the *Guardian* or *The Times*.

Thirdly, there are special features of the real-life reading experience that influence the way a message is read. This was illustrated by the way the WOW message was read by all viewers at first glance, and most at second and many more careful readings. The common reaction to the message was that it was a 'classic image' (MM2). The message was invariably read without the accompanying text, which states 'Yeah Right' and changes the meaning of the pictorial image by subverting it to show the futility of the act of tilling land in isolation. I was struck by this reading by all respondents even when I asked them to return to the image. The real-life reading experience of audiences is such that they tend to skim through newspapers and decide to read the details only if their imagination is captured by the image and the caption. Even under different reading conditions of the interview where the audiences had more time to look at a message, it was remarkable that most missed out even on the caption or anchor, observing only the image to read it in a dominant manner as a classic disaster, charity image.

This observation feeds into the image-text debate by raising questions about the significance of the accompanying text. Should a message be analysed based on the image or with its text? Barthes discusses two types of relations between image and text. In the first, termed 'relay', the text extends the image to add a new meaning to the image (1977). In the second relation, which is also the most common, the text elaborates the meaning of the image and it thus 'anchors' the image. However, Kress and van Leeuwen rightly argue that Barthes' account fails to see that 'the visual component of a text is an independently organised and structured message – connected with the verbal text, but in no way dependent on it: and similarly the other way around' (1996: 16–17). The extra factor of the condition or situation of reading is extremely helpful here. Image and text do appear to be connected but not dependent on each other. The respondents predominantly reflected the primacy of the visual over the text even when the two elements coexisted in the same message. When they did notice the text, it certainly worked as a 'relay' and changed the meaning of the image but the image also worked independently as a 'classic' disaster image. Thus, it is most likely that the relation between the image and text is case-specific and depends on the real-life reading situation of the readers.

Connecting 'self' with 'others'

The respondents showed a broad understanding of the genre of charity appeals. This resulted in dominant readings of many messages, especially the 'classic' ones of disasters and suffering as shown by the responses to Concern's image of a starving child, Oxfam-Metro spread and WOW's image of a woman tilling barren land. Similarly, the image of a smiling child carrying books, as shown in Plan's appeal for child sponsorship, was seen as a 'happy' image after the INGO had intervened and helped. However, as we have already seen, INGOs' public messages also contain 'non-classic' messages. I now discuss how respondents read these images *per se* as well as in relation to other images.

In order to tease out important similarities and differences among the responses, I compare and focus on three different types of images – a) 'negative': disaster (Concern, CW-1 – Emergency Appeal on Food Crisis in Sub-Saharan Africa showing a starving child named 'Halima' and Oxfam, O-11 – 'How Oxfam is helping around the world'); b) 'positive': development (Plan child sponsorship) and Christmas Gifts (Oxfam and CA), and, c) 'deviant': advocacy (Christian Aid [CA-3] – 'Dirty low down spongers').

Reactions to the disaster images of starvation and suffering were fairly similar across all respondents. Expressions such as 'distressing … familiar' (ME1), 'tasteless in a way but powerful' (MM1) and 'shocking' (FE2) were common. While there was a dominant or hegemonic reading of these images based, in part, on their familiarity, there were other reactions that can be termed 'oppositional' in their effects. While similar comments were used to describe the image, the *action* to be taken by some respondents or the *feeling* they evoked were found to be against their dominant purpose of generating sympathy through shock. A few respondents stated that they felt they were being manipulated by the INGO, which they resented.

> MY2 – Whichever way you look at it, the image of child in some sort of distress and clearly quite malnourished. It invites sympathy but it also invites the cynical response … one feels that it's manufactured to tug on my heartstrings and get me to start donating money to the appeal and it does sound cynical but it happens with a lot of these appeals.

On the other hand, many also indicated that they did not consider the images 'stark enough' and they could 'shock a little bit more with the

images' (FM2). Women respondents from the middle-aged group particularly argued that they were not shocked by the images and it was
important for their children to see such images to know how lucky
they themselves were.

> FM1 – I think these images could be a bit more hard-hitting
> because a lot needs to be done.

> FM2 [*On the image of the woman holding the child in Oxfam and
> Metro feature (O-11)*] – She actually *looks incredibly healthy*, doesn't
> she? (*laughs*) I was thinking. And then I literally looked at that,
> I didn't think of her as this child's mother as she looked too
> wealthy and too well-posed. I assume she is perhaps an aid
> worker.

> FM2 [*On Concern appeal*] – The image isn't too stark. The image
> is *good* ... even down to the fact that this child actually isn't
> being held. This child is being held in a restraining way, isn't
> she? Not lovingly.

One young man (MY1) said that he would have had a stronger response
to the image of starving 'Halima' (Concern appeal) had she been 'a
white baby' as the society had taught them to value a 'white Western'
more than any other. This respondent, nevertheless, expressed ambivalence as he contrasted his rational and emotional thinking and wondered at the role of 'compassion fatigue' (Burnell, 1993; Moeller, 1999)
and 'cultural upbringing' in shaping such values.

> MY1 – I don't get too emotional from seeing this image, to be
> honest. It doesn't upset me that much probably because I'm used
> to seeing this image. We see it so often that it doesn't have any
> impact on me. With honesty I could say that if this was a British
> child I would feel differently.

> ND – But even a black child can be British.

> MY1 – If you look at the bed, you can see that it's made up ... of
> maybe handmade from bits of leaf or ... if that was blankets, if

this baby was white I would see that it was a Western picture. So this was Scotland or France I'd probably give more money with all honesty, I would be more likely to give money and that's to do with some of the probably of prejudice that I have as a Western person but I would probably, and again I am being totally honest, I'd probably, it's just something that's brought into me that white Westerners are somehow more important than other countries, people in other countries. On a rational level, I'd argue this life is as important as mine but I am being honest on the image that I see and what would upset me more emotionally I would say I would more likely give money if this was a Western country and this baby was white than it was, you know, black and from a Third World country. And I don't know whether that's to do with the fact that this image is common or whether that's just to do with the cultural upbringing that I've had.[10]

Unlike the disaster images, the Christmas gift messages were not familiar to all respondents but they still had similar, dominant readings of the messages. The only minor exceptions were some responses on the lack of details in the catalogues and doubts over whether the particular 'gift' will be bought by the INGO or not. Common terms expressed for Christmas gifts included 'fun', 'funny', 'cute', 'animals', as well as the option to choose from a catalogue. Thus, the respondents reaffirmed the appeal of gift catalogues that evidently combine a consumerist culture with their love for animals – 'We are a nation of animal lovers' (MM2). In addition, many mentioned that it filled their desire to be 'seen as giving' (FM2), because the scheme involves buying 'gifts' for friends and family though they are ultimately 'given' to MW recipients. The younger and middle-aged respondents self-consciously expressed their awareness of it as a fashion or a fad but said it had a feel-good factor that they would go for.

MY1 – So this appeals to my Western life. So I can, you know, I am having a coffee or a drink with someone and I can say – guess what I bought? Some worms for someone in India or you know farmers in Bolivia or whatever. It can be like a feel-good factor

I suppose. In that sense it's doing its job, it's appealing to me because it is giving me the buzz of Western feel-good factor.

The elderly respondents echoed these views. One respondent (ME1) also conveyed it in terms of 'sacrifice' he would be willing to make by having a 'relatively austere' Christmas so that someone else could have a 'happier life and a merry Christmas'.

In marked contrast to the messages of disasters and gifts, the reactions to CA's advocacy message cannot be categorised under any specific reading and contained a range of responses. After many stages of analysis, patterns gradually emerged and these were clearly linked to each age group. While there were few common reactions across ages, there were several commonalities within each age group.

The first group of elderly respondents had two broad sets of reactions. One was a denial of its core message – 'we have lived off Africans (for centuries)'. Some openly refuted this view as untrue. One respondent added that Britain had suffered heavily in the Second World War and 'no one came to help us' (FE1), thus evading the issue of colonialism to label Britain as the 'victim' or the wronged one.

FE1 – We didn't have communications that we have nowadays.[11] It was only after the Second World War really where we ourselves suffered greatly and were not helped by others.

The second form of response was made through expressions of lack of understanding of the issues and an open sense of unease. Some said they were not good at Economics and hence did not understand the effects of colonialism. They also tried to question me about the views of Indians on colonialism. Others described the lack of awareness for reasons such as weak communication technologies and media before the 1980s and getting to know about MW starvation only through Live Aid of 1985. They still refused to link MW starvation and poverty to history but emphasised only the 'help' they had provided, and continue to offer.

One of the dominant reactions from the middle-aged group was similar to the first group of elderly respondents where all but one said it was not true. However, there were slight variations when compared to the first group. This group changed its opinion or qualified it by saying it was true but 'not nice' or 'negative' (FM2) or 'offensive' (FM1) to say so, especially by an INGO and particularly by Christian Aid with the emphasis on 'Christian' (FM1). One respondent, however, said, smilingly, that it made him 'feel guilty but in a nice way' (MM1).

The third group of young respondents did not take any offence at the message. They thought it was a 'good approach' as it goes 'straight to the idea' (MY2) and 'play[s] a lot on prejudice' (FY1) about immigrants as spongers.

> FY1 – I agree with it. I think it's disgraceful. I think it's a good use of words really. People say in this country, I think maybe that's what they are focusing on, you know you get these ignorant people in this country that say oh, these asylum seekers come over and they take our jobs and they take our benefit money and they are just here for a free council house and they are sponging on us. I think it's a way on words to people in this country like we're the spongers really of these Third World countries – people come here for a safe haven and probably wouldn't want to be in this country if they didn't have to be. I think most people would rather be in their home country with their family and not fleeing persecution. So I think that's very good definitely.

They also found the informal and 'friendly' (FY2) language to be part of the appeal of the message. Regarding the content, the chain of signification led them to comments on supermarkets, fair trade and 'links to our lives', as the following conversation shows:

> MY1 – maybe [the one] I like the best is the Christian Aid one … dirty low down spongers. We really should be ashamed of living off Africans and you think – what, what? I mean even myself, and I am well aware of the issues, when I first saw it I said what, living off Africans, I don't get it.
>
> ND – Were you offended by it?

MY1 – I was inspired more than anything else, not offended because I like to think our nation, Britain as a nation, is an independent nation. It's not really, is it? It never has been. It's always been dependent, we talk about globalisation, you know, in the last 20–30 years but critics have said no, this is no different from what's been going on for hundreds and hundreds of years.

So, CA's advocacy message had different readings and there was no common reaction across ages. However, there were several commonalities *within* each age group. The overall reactions, however, led to many further reactions that are discussed in the next section.

History, knowledge and emotions

The CA message triggered many other reactions from all respondents on colonialism and its role in MW poverty that were based on their knowledge of history. What emerged from these fascinating discussions shows clear and strong links between knowledge and emotions. It also uncovers a specific Britishness, analogous to Eurocentrism, based in specific versions of history.

Group 1 of elderly respondents in the age group 60 plus were quite uneasy about it and had many strong reactions to colonial history and its link to MW poverty.[12] They echoed many common versions of Eurocentric histories that explain Europe's current prosperity due primarily to its unique and superior climate, demography, technology, state, family and mentality (Blaut, 2000). The reactions ranged from awareness about colonialism expressed through its refutation and denial; evasiveness in terms of not understanding economic details or transferring the blame to the MW; claims that it was in the past and now more was 'given' by the DW to MW; to the acknowledgement of colonialism as a reality but one that was true of all DW nations, carried on with the help of the MW elites and even being beneficial to the colonies or what Ferguson (2004) calls a 'good thing'.

FE1 – But then again we were not the only ones because there were people in the higher ranks of India who were also doing the

same. I mean we couldn't have done it alone. So this is humanity, this is a human experience that we have. That is why I say
that we could not be aware, some people were certainly, but as
nations as social groups we were not aware.

While the dominant version of the acceptance of colonialism reflected
unease and evasion, there were also open views, for example, expressed
by a male elderly respondent as the following interview extract
shows:

ME2 – People *know* where all our wealth comes from. Go down to
the British Museum and look what they've got – everything from
other countries. The main thing is these massive great houses ...
sugar plantations ... We became wealthy off the rest of the world.
But we also took civilisation to the rest of the world at the same
time. So there is a counter balance. We are the fifth richest country in the world and we are only a tiny little island – how did that
happen?

ND – You tell me [*smiles*].

ME2 – We sailed seas and explored.

ND – So how would you react to this particular message?
[CA – Dirty low down spongers]

ME2 [*laughs*] – We are *not* living off Africans.

ND – If you read the small print, they explain it. Do you agree
with that?

ME2 – No. The South Africans are living off the Africans. I
agree to a certain extent but I think we put more than we take
out now. What would those countries be like if we'd never gone
there? Never gone to Africa. Or India. If the British had never
gone to India what would India be like? Have you ever thought
about it?

ND – Yes I have.

ME2 – They had their own civilisation but would it still be like the civilisation they had or would they've changed or would they be watching television these days? Would the poverty still be there? And I think it would be the same with Africa. If we had never visited Africa, poverty would still be there. Also in these countries, there is of course long poverty, long war. It's not because we took the diamonds out of Africa a few hundreds years ago and all the wealth and everything else.

Another respondent (FE1) also argued that the British deserved their wealth, even going on to say that 'Others', including the Mediterranean people of Southern Europe, are lazy.

FE1 – We just simply happened to develop in more practical ways. The countries that developed in Europe in practical ways were in the Northern part of Europe which is the influence I always think of climate – it's cold. In a hot country you just climb a tree, bring a coconut if you are thirsty, crack it, drink it … What's the point of striving and for *what*? … You know we are entrepreneurs, why not? And even by being entrepreneurs they did a lot of good in the sense that they gave people the opportunity to live a better life, people who worked for them … they certainly lived a better life than they, if not they wouldn't have gone to work for them. Let's face it.

ND – Are you talking about those in the colonies?

FE1 – Yes.

That the climate of northwest Europe uniquely favoured its histori-cal achievements is a common slice of Eurocentrism as highlighted by Blaut (2000) in 'Thirty Reasons Why Europeans Are Better Than Everyone Else (A Checklist)'. Another view expressed was that the British were tired of being made to feel guilty for something which was 'such a long time ago' (FE2). This is an occasional but not uncom-mon expression in many sections of the UK media. Discussing how to deal with 'national shame' that haunts generations of white South

Africans, author, academic and Nobel Laureate J.M. Coetzee wryly advises:

> Such people might learn a trick or two from the British about managing collective guilt. The British have simply declared their independence from their imperial forebears. The Empire was long ago abolished, they say, so what is there for us to feel responsible for? And anyway, the people who ran the Empire were Victorians, dour, stiff folk in dark clothes, nothing like us. (Coetzee, 2007: 44)

Priyamvada Gopal exposes the sheer self-absorption and narcissism of the very idea of 'guilt' when she argues, '[the] point isn't for Europeans to feel guilt, but a serious consideration of historical responsibility isn't the same thing as blame game. Forgetting history is tempting but undermines a society's capacity for change' (2006: 2).

The second group of respondents, all of whom were in their late 30s and 40s, expressed their awareness about colonialism but with some unease, variation and contradiction.

> MM2 – I mean, really, whoever is responsible or whatever is responsible for poverty is immaterial.

They also echoed the views of the elderly respondents by opposing or being ambivalent about any personal gains that Britain and its people, as a whole, had made from their empire, as suggested by the CA message. Women, in particular, also said it was 'not the right way to appeal to people' (FM2) and mentioning history was 'negative' (FM2) and 'offensive' (FM1). At the same time, they said that they were surprised to observe how few of their friends knew about colonial history.

The level of awareness and knowledge about colonial history among the young respondents from the third group was very low compared to the other groups. With the exception of one male respondent, who is in academia, they had little idea about colonialism. History to them, as taught in schools, was about Hitler, the Second World War and the Victorians.

FY1 – [with the] Victorians it was just lifestyle: Victorian life in
Britain, architecture. I did history at A level – World War, it was
very kind of Hitler and Stalin.

Disengaging with or erasing history has been a long process spread
across many institutions including media and education. Shohat and
Stam mention that '[s]tandard core courses in universities stress the
history of "Western" civilisation, with the more liberal universities
insisting on token study of "other" civilisations. And even "Western"
civilisation is usually taught without reference to the central role of
European colonialism within capitalist modernity' (1994: 1). This was
also reflected in the responses of the young persons I interviewed. They
knew that Britain had 'the biggest empire in the world' (FY1) but could
not react further than that it [empire] meant 'tea trade with India'.

FY2 – They don't give you very much the nasty side that Britain
had in colonialism. It's like we had all these countries and we
don't have them any more, slightly not really saying what it was
like under British rule and how the people were treated. You
know, they can't sound Britain as too bad because the country
we are living in you are meant to see it in a slightly more [*laughs*]
patriotic light.

The young respondents, thus, came across like a clean, blank slate
and the answer to the effect the CA message had on them perhaps lies
in this space. It is because they lacked knowledge about colonialism
that its mention in the message did not offend them since it did not
evoke any strong feeling in them. Instead, it gave them the opportunity to dispassionately appreciate global poverty as their responsibility,
which they described mainly in terms of current institutions such as
supermarkets and multinationals. The disconnect from history in their
case arguably appears to be a 'positive' as it is a temporal space that
allows them to receive a message about self-incriminatory history with
a sense of detachment unlike the other groups, particularly the elderly
respondents, whose knowledge of history was intertwined with their
emotions and reactions.

Despite the small number of respondents, it is striking that some interviews echo many observations of sociologists such as Gilroy (2004) on the (dis)engagement of British society from its history; a disengagement that, I would argue, in turn contributes to and is an integral part of its Britishness. The pages that show the links and continuities among different parts of the world and their histories are missing from Western textbooks (Shohat and Stam, 1994; Davis, 2001).[13] These erasures work in varying ways as the 'invisible empire' (Wemyss, 2008: 23)[14] or 'the amnesia of empire' (Hall, 2002: 5); selective history, ambivalences and melancholia about Britain's imperial past that forms the wider context of the ways in which 'Others' are shown, seen and understood. The lack of engagement with the deep-rooted and longstanding connections between the MW and DW within British society across the domains of education systems, media, governments, popular culture and official accounts has resulted in a deep ambivalence among British people about their history that Gilroy calls 'post-imperial melancholia' (2004:98). He argues that the inability of British people to work through their history has resulted in a silence that affects their responses to 'Others'. This dis-engagement with the colonial history has resulted in losing sight of their collective and shared history to think of post-colonial immigrants, for instance, as intruders, and causes of MW poverty as 'internal' to the MW.[15] Norman Davies, too, argues that the Empire had an enormous impact on a complex and diverse perception, 'the layer of consciousness that historians now call "Britishness"', and includes 'feelings of xenophobia and superiority' (1999: 815, 911).[16]

Of the variety of reactions of the respondents to British history, the most surprising finding for me was the total lack of knowledge among the youth. History to them, as taught in schools, was Celts, Hitler, tea trade with India and Victorian lifestyles.[17] I later looked into literature on British education to find that there already exists a term – 'Hitlerisation'[18] – to describe this obsession. Educationists are extremely concerned about this aspect but unable to agree on what should constitute the curriculum in schools.[19]

Although Eurocentric Britishness was found across many respondents, it was not clear cut or uniform. While the young respondents' lack of knowledge meant they did not take offence at the mention of colonialism, they too occasionally reflected the cultural legacies of colonialism and its knowledge production, as in the case of the respondent (MY1) who saw 'Others' in terms of colour, which led him to devalue their lives. This valuation was, however, ambivalent and backed by his awareness of 'cultural upbringing'. The reactions of even such a small number of these white British respondents were, thus, far from homogeneous, challenging the very idea of an essentialised Britishness. Further, these responses underwent changes as 'new' knowledge was encountered, as elaborated in the next section, which again questions the fixed and unchangeable nature of Britishness.

Porous boundaries of personal and collective

While there are no up-to-date studies specifically on INGOs' messages, two recent empirical studies on how the British see the MW form a backdrop of the predominance of negative discourses about MW that prevail in the DW.[20] The first detailed three-part study on the portrayal of the developing world by television, commissioned by the UK's DFID (2000), found that MW is largely viewed in a negative light by British public. The content study of news and feature programmes found unbalanced coverage limited to disasters, wars, terrorism, bizarre events or visits by prominent DW individuals. Another study by the INGO Voluntary Services Overseas (VSO) on how the British see the developing world was based on interviews with the British public, visitors from developing countries and expert commentators. It shows that they have a uni-dimensional but well-entrenched view of the MW driven by negative stereotypes of poverty, famine, war and oppression (VSO, 2002). Such tropes also showed up in the audience interviews conducted for this book, echoing wider discourses about MW prevalent in British society that circulate through various institutions.

The 'root causes of poverty' the respondents mentioned during the interviews, scattered across and triggered by different messages as they viewed them, ranged from factors outside anyone's control such as natural causes and famines to MW's 'internal' problems such as wars, corruption and overpopulation, as the following quotes demonstrate:

FE2 – I think natural causes and the other main cause is aggression, wars and conflicts. They seem to be the two main causes of most of the difficulties.

FE1 – I have lived in South America, I know what corruption is. It's tremendous.

adding later –

FE1 – They are brought up being dishonest. In Argentina particularly they are brought up being arrogant, thinking that Argentina is the best country in the world etc., etc. So they have a lot of social background which makes it very difficult to come out of the state they were always in.

MM2 – Because of the corruption of the governments. That's clear. Everybody knows that.

FY1 – It's all very corrupt I think over there.

MM2 – How can you allow people to continue having, you know, tons and tons of kids and allowing them to starve to death? Doesn't make sense, does it? ... we've given *billions*, nothing is ever done, it carries on year in, year out. They keep on having famines, they keep on having kids and the kids die [*Angry silence!*]

FY2 – It only gives you – *civil war*, well I don't know about that and so why that started? Something building up I mean 14 years it wouldn't have just happened. So what's that background [emphasis added].

While they echoed wider discourses, the explanations of many respondents underwent changes. This was because of the overall range of information they received from the messages, which either made them question their own explanations or seek more information, as the last quote above shows. The respondent here mentioned civil war as a reason but began to ask more as she read further.[21]

These responses show that while individuals negotiated meanings based on their own stock of knowledge, resulting in variations in the ways in which some images were read, there were also dominant readings and understandings based on collective knowledge, symbolic maps and the tools available in society. As Wetherell and Potter (1992: 78) postulate, '[a] sense of identity and subjectivity is constructed from the interpretative resources – the stories and narratives of identity – which are available, in circulation, in our culture'. Berger states this more simply – '[t]he way we see things is affected by what we know or what we believe' (1972: 8).

The overall understandings of the respondents were based on individual and societal knowledge as well as other messages which they viewed; that is, the intertextual dynamics of different messages. Here, it is important to highlight the influence of the CA message. Several respondents shifted their positions over the course of their viewing experience. By the end of the interviews, many respondents who had objected to this message for being 'untrue' or 'not nice', began to use the language of this message – 'we're responsible', we 'plundered'.

> FM1 – I have heard, not within our immediate group of friends but we do have members of families and other people that we know who, you know, who don't give to charities maybe because they think – they are not getting themselves out of poverty and we are giving all this money and they don't have an understanding of what's gone on and *how we plundered*. It works all the way through, it works into Iraq now, doesn't it? And they think that what we are doing there is a good thing rather than a negative thing. And they are the people who don't want immigrants in our country, it's that kind of attitude and how you deal with that I don't know [emphasis added].

Similarly, some other reasons for MW poverty that began to crop up included the actions of 'rich countries' governments' in addition to multinationals. Thus, there was a discernible shift in the respondents' stock of knowledge.

> MM1 – Traditionally adverts about aid to developing countries are based on the fact that due to their geographical position, the natural elements within their country, factors outside of their control and outside of our control, has made them poor and because of that we should be giving to them. The charities tend to, like to use that message because it is softer on the conscience of the people that are giving the money.
>
> ND – Why do you say that?
>
> MM1 – Why? Because it's better or they may want to persuade people to give without pointing out that they are, at least partially, to blame for what is going on. So you don't insult the person that you are asking the money from where as this (the CA appeal) is taking the opposite view and trying to make us face up to, you know, saying that we have some responsibility here. So it is not just down to you to give because you feel sorry for these poor people and what has come to them but maybe you are partially to blame and maybe it is your duty to give some money.

The above respondent's observation that charities like to use a message that is 'softer on the conscience of the people that are giving the money' (MM1) illuminates why INGOs like to keep their messages simple and easy on the conscience. It also underlines that such soft-pedalling may not be warranted and gives too little credit to audiences. The viewers clearly came across as both 'charity-literate' and 'charity-loyal' and capable of negotiating meanings without all being offended by any message of historicised responsibility. The reactions of most middle-aged and young respondents to CA's message also show the transformative ability of contextualisation and historicisation to induce indignation and a discourse of justice.

The CA message seemed to have a huge impact, as reflected in the adoption of its language by some respondents, and the responses of many middle-aged and young interviewees who stated that it was one of the messages that would 'stay with them'. For many respondents, it created a 'liminal space' of understanding where change in

perspectives could occur. The message allowed them to re-contextu-
alise and redefine issues, thereby shifting the discourse from an indi-
vidualistic choice of charity to that of a broader social responsibility.
This clearly implies that there is potential to experiment and expand
the box of charity messages.

There has been very little academic research on audience responses
to the full range of international NGOs' messages. There are, however,
limited studies on responses to images of atrocities and suffering in
general. The two main themes around which these studies tend to
cluster are those of 'distance' and 'denial'.

Arguments about 'distance' take different forms. Physical or geographical distance from the site or personhood of suffering is one form
(Chouliaraki, 2006). Another stems from a vague notion of modernity,
where the modern life itself creates distance (Edkins, 2000). A similar
argument is based on the technologies of modern communication or
the act of mediation that create distance as one watches suffering on
television from the safe confines of one's living room and, thus, feels
remote from it. Silverstone, however, argues that media should be
thought of 'as a process of mediation ... involving producers and consumers of media in a more or less continuous activity of engagement
and disengagement with meaning' (1999: 13). If mediation is seen as
a constant engagement between texts and people, then it does not
explain any automatic creation of distance. 'Distance' is a limited and
a flawed argument. The argument of distance created by modernity
is abstract and essentialist and treats audiences as 'gullible zombies'
who passively and wholeheartedly accept messages. Sheer physical
(geographical) or 'modern', technological distance is over-ridden in
numerous instances when people respond to a crisis because they are
moved by what they see. Again, modern technologies themselves not
only convey news widely but also lend an urgency and immediacy, as
seen in the case of the Asian Tsunami in the media. Moreover, modern technologies also allow for faster travel, thereby reducing physical
distance. Finally, the notion of 'distance' itself is framed by the messages and wider discourses that project MW as 'distant' in the first
place, erasing the historical connections. As seen by the responses
to the CA message, when confronted with historicised connections,

the understanding of many respondents changed from the notion of charitable giving to that of inter-dependence and responsibility.

The second major theme is that of 'denial', suggested by Cohen, which broadly states that people deny the existence of atrocities for many reasons including psychological and social factors. Denial includes cognition, emotion and morality, which respectively mean denying facts, not feeling and not recognising wrongness or responsibility (Cohen and Seu, 2002: 189). Cohen uses 'denial' as a 'code word' (2001: 3) to organise scattered understandings of these phenomena across states, forms, content, levels, actors and types of denial and it is worth engaging with some of its useful aspects.

'Context' is important in, and to, our understandings and Cohen acknowledges the role of decontextualisation in denial. However, he suggests that a limited plot of crisis and saving in messages overlooks the fact that audiences' understanding is not just visual but captions and words play a big role. My interviews, however, challenge this. Nearly all respondents drew the meaning of the WOW message from the image, ignoring the caption. Secondly, Cohen assumes that the accompanying text will necessarily contextualise the image, but we have seen in the visual analyses that the mere presence of accompanying text means little. It is what is stated in that text which matters. Further, as the interviews of INGO staff show, what gets included in the text is, *inter alia*, informed by the ways in which 'context' is understood, and INGO respondents defined 'context' in a narrow and dehistoricised sense of 'immediate' environment.

'Denial' works as a useful tool to categorise audience responses but cannot by itself explain *why* denial takes place. Obviously, there are complex reasons behind denial which are context-dependent and vary across time, setting, people and the very specificity of the act. In the interviews conducted for this book there were many instances of denial by individuals who argued variously that solving poverty was impossible or hopeless or that there was poverty in Britain as well. These were all expressions of individual denial to engage with MW poverty. However, their overall view of global poverty being unconnected to their lives was based in, and underpinned by, the lack of historicity; a vacuum which did not permit engaging with it at a deeper and wider level. INGOs' messages are about specific issues and people and there is a history between who is shown and who does the seeing based on the material and cultural global history of the past few centuries. To ignore this is a mistake. In order to explain audience responses, it is essential to productively unite the links, and their multidirectionality, from the individual to the institutional and collective levels of knowledge and track corresponding levels of denial. Understanding the plurality and shifting positions of audience responses also requires engagement, not just with pre-existing scripts but with what happens when 'new' and contrarian knowledge is confronted. One need not deny what one does not know or claims not to know, but what is one's reaction when one is unexpectedly told that one is a 'sponger' who 'lives off Africa'?

Audience responses show that discourses can be modified, as has also been argued by many. Susan Sontag endorses the prospect of reversing the gaze when she discusses photographic representation – '[t]he force of photographic images comes from their being material realities in their own right, richly informative deposits left in the wake of whatever emitted them, potent means for turning the tables on reality – for turning it into a shadow' (1979: 180). Deacon et al. (1999: 138) take this further to argue:

> Ultimately, behind any conventional relations of signifiers and signifieds are decisions, however ingrained and 'natural' these may now appear, and these decisions can always be modified and reversed, with possible consequences for the ways in which public communications communicate, or for the ways in which particular sections of society are represented. If signs can change, so can cultural relations and social institutions.

Conclusion

This chapter has mapped how particular INGO messages were received by members of the British audience via a small indicative group of respondents interviewed. The interviews highlighted the importance of INGOs and their messages for the British public, thereby showing INGOs' enormous significance as institutions of representation. The interviews also showed the audiences' familiarity with the genre of charity messages and a clear privileging of images over text in terms of what the audiences noticed in a message.

While most audience members reflected a dominant reading of the messages of disaster and development, their responses to the advocacy message, which showed the responsibility of DW nations in MW poverty, differed across different age groups with the respondents from the older groups reacting strongly to it.

The audience interviews confirm some INGO assumptions. However, they raise many more questions. Many INGO informants had reasoned that audiences would react adversely to detailed contextual knowledge such as historical background in INGOs' messages. Such assumptions on the part of INGOs were confirmed only by some respondents from the elderly and middle-aged audience group. This is indicative, to a degree, of the durability of Eurocentric Britishness and suggests INGOs' task is not easy. The younger respondents did not show any unease about history, probably due to their lack of knowledge about it. In view of this finding, the overall diversity of responses and several cases of shift in the audiences' stock of knowledge, there is sufficient reason to doubt INGOs' assumptions which seemed to be based only on essentialised notions about audiences. And these assumptions are a crucial factor in drawing the boundaries of representations: the speak-able and the unspeakable.

In exploring people's responses to a range of charity messages, clear links were found between knowledge and emotions, and the personal and collective. So, the only way to fully grasp the responses is through combining the social with the psychological and the micro with the macro, the intersection of which explains the common understandings of MW issues as de-linked from the DW.

INGO messages work in a specific context of knowledge or lack of it. But INGOs and their messages are themselves integral parts of this discursive landscape that shapes notions of MW and global poverty. INGOs feed into and draw upon existing discourses about MW in the DW. This includes the knowledge (or lack of it) about history that gives specific meanings to the messages and plays a significant role in distance, denial and lack of understanding.

The small number of interviews does not permit generalisations but they clearly make a case *against* any generalisation about audiences. It is crucial for INGOs to explore how their messages can fill in the gaps in public knowledge, alter audiences' understandings and 'moral space', to use Silverstone's wonderful expression (2007: 5), and encourage actions backed by a sense of justice and responsibility.

CHAPTER 8

TOWARDS REFLEXIVE
UNDERSTANDINGS

In early 2011, as I was completing this book, I was struck by two seemingly contradictory events. While I was teaching a postgraduate class at the University of London, a student mentioned a 'silly and meaningless' INGO poster he had seen in a tube station which was asking him to 'be humankind'. During the same period, I was approaching the INGOs to seek permission to reproduce their messages in this book. The expected copyright issues did crop up but there were also instances of, dare I say, 'denial' of many messages especially the 'classic' old school disaster ones. 'We have moved on' was a common response. If the INGOs thought they had moved on, why was this, incidentally 'white British', young student not moved by their new messages? Although I am a regular follower of INGOs' campaigns, these comments prompted me to pay extra attention to the most recent messages of INGOs. Two of these messages, advertised in UK's newspapers during January and February 2011 are reproduced below-

Be humankind ...[1]

- *Oxfam*

I don't just give. I get. I get back all the time. And what a feeling![2]

- *Barbara, Supporter of ActionAid and the human spirit*

One word clearly stands out – *human*. This root word is a key component of the 'positive' side in the dichotomised debate on INGOs' messages. The sheer explosion in its usage clearly suggests the escalating trend of 'positivity' in INGOs' messages, in tune with wider institutional changes of corporatisation and marketisation. I analyse the acceleration of these developments in this concluding chapter in addition to bringing together the key arguments of the book and discussing their implications for the theories, policies and practices of INGOs.

Distant lives, still voices

The exploration of a 'representational field' of INGOs' public messages provides a fuller understanding of the range of INGOs' representations, how these messages engage with the DW public, how they are seen within the NGOs themselves and above all how they relate to, and constitute, each other.

The study points to the need for a comprehensive analysis of overall messages stemming from the subsector of INGOs if we are to understand the narratives they produce individually *and* collectively. The conceptual framework of the 'postcolonial lens' allows the individual messages to be analysed in isolation and also facilitates the analysis of a series of messages. This is particularly useful because the overall understanding of the messages is based not on a single message but the entire gamut of messages circulating in a society. In this connection it is useful to revisit two concepts – intertextuality and palimpsest. Messages are always situated in relation to other messages intertextually and to previous messages like a palimpsest with past traces. INGOs' messages maintain a careful silence over our common global history and thereby work as an erasure of the past. However, ironically, the 'past' reveals itself through traces of 'old' ways of seeing in the present texts. Thus, a comprehensive evaluation of public messages should take cognisance of the messages *around* them across both the current and older messages.

The visual analyses in chapters 2 to 5 show the presence of powerful colonial discourses in INGOs' messages, though there are some crucial, albeit sporadic, attempts to counter these hegemonic representations. These representations mythically project MW as 'different' and 'distant' from the DW and serve to erase the former's diversity, complexity and historicity. Difference is projected through discursive strategies of infantilisation, feminisation and binaries of an urban, dynamic and giving DW and a rural, stagnant and receiving MW that suppress liminal spaces of understandings. Simultaneously, the messages circumvent the context of our enmeshed histories and structures and connect the DW and MW through a dehistoricised 'oneness' of humanity. MW is conceptualised as 'distant lives, still voices'[3] — underdeveloped and without historical links with the DW; a distant empty space inhabited by 'still', history-less people to be 'developed' through small-scale activities and rid of poverty that has been caused by 'internal' or 'natural' factors.

It is a paradox that the messages of institutions placed at the centre of an interconnected world fail to show the deep roots and fluidity of global connections. Interviews with INGO staff (chapter 6) help us understand this puzzle. They demonstrate that public messages are viewed in terms of a limited debate of 'negative' and 'positive' where the former is equated with images of starving children and the latter with narratives of MW individuals shown 'helping themselves' and DW supporters 'feeling good'. There is inadequate engagement with contextual issues and the historicised location of both DW and MW individuals within wider structures. The exclusion of broader context appears to stem from INGOs' evasion of messy issues such as those of race and history, in part stemming from managerialism which prefers management to politics and gives priority to the future, neglecting both the past and the present. It is also linked to INGOs' institutional context of corporatisation, commercialisation and isomorphism where they tend to become similar to one another in order to survive and grow. This is also based on INGOs' assumptions of 'oneness' of audiences, a mono-cultural and fixed Eurocentric Britishness that precludes any acceptance on the part of these audiences of contextual and historical information.

Audience responses to INGOs' messages (chapter 7) demonstrate the immense credibility of INGOs as institutions of representation.

The interviews both confirm and challenge INGOs' assumptions about an essentialised notion of Britishness. That the readers would react adversely to detailed contextual knowledge of historical background in INGOs' messages was substantiated only by some respondents. While this may well suggest the durability of some forms of Britishness, the overall diversity of audience responses provides sufficient reason to doubt INGOs' assumptions of a homogeneous and unchanging audience. Discourses are not fixed but fluid and capable of change and the shifting positions of some respondents show the potential of contextualised messages to change public perceptions and alter discourses.

Implications for NGO management

It is useful to bring together and reiterate the key implications of messages for the policies and practices of INGOs. INGOs' public messages have significance across all aspects of NGO management. In terms of internal management, the messages relate to internal coherence through the tensions between fundraising and advocacy. There is a high incidence of hybrid messages with blurring of lines between disaster and developmental imagery and the inclusion of fundraising elements within advocacy appeals. The views in the literature that favour advocacy over fundraising (Lidchi, 1999) are challenged by some advocacy messages which validate myths about the MW instead of contesting them. Many advocacy appeals also seek funds, thereby making the very purpose of these messages ambivalent. So fundraising and advocacy messages are not easy to distinguish, and neither type can be lumped under a 'good' or 'bad' category and privileged *per se*. Further, advocacy messages form a very small proportion of the overall messages despite the many in-depth studies conducted by the INGOs' research and advocacy wings. There is considerable scope to make use of such research and publicise it through their public messages to educate and mobilise audiences.

INGOs' role as hugely influential media actors has paramount significance in a profoundly connected world. Seen from the perspective of the global flows of money from the DW to the MW that directly or indirectly act against poverty, for example migrant remittances or official bilateral and multilateral aid, INGOs' contribution is relatively small but their credibility among Western publics is very high. So the consequence of their messages in shaping perceptions and achieving tangible results through awareness and mobilisation may be far greater. Their media role can, and should, be more effective and there is a need for INGOs to pay more attention to this role in their policies and practices.

The third important aspect of NGO management concerns NGOs' relationships. INGOs' messages dualistically construct relations between the DW and MW that set the MW as 'distant Others', albeit a part of the same humanity. The public messages of INGOs appreciate, and reflect, the wider society. Indeed, INGOs are themselves both a part and a consequence of their environment, which includes the wider society they send out their messages to and the society they themselves come from. The embeddedness of INGOs in a Eurocentric 'Western' context must not be overlooked. The boundaries of INGOs' public messages are circumscribed by the broader societal context. This informs what they assume can (or cannot) be said to British audiences, leading to an institutionalised denial and silence over the contextual, historical background of global poverty and inequalities. This not only reveals the importance of their environment but the differential privileging of its various parts, with a clear preference for the perceived sensibilities and collective consciousness of British audiences. In terms of multiple accountabilities, despite the balancing acts of INGOs to be accountable towards both the MW 'beneficiaries' and the DW audiences, they end up being more accountable towards the DW.

The institutional legitimacy and power of INGOs are maintained, reproduced and enhanced through the public messages that meet the wider expectations of an assumed British society. At the same time, INGOs and their messages shape wider discourses and produce the audiences and British society. The multi-directional processes continuously constitute each other. The social context influences INGOs' policies and practices which in turn constitute the same context. So, denials at the different levels – individual, institutional and societal – feed off each other. Hence, the line of separation between the INGOs and the public is rather thin and porous. Neither the narrator nor the narrative is removed from the society.

Beyond 'the human'

Oversimplified and dichotomised understandings of 'negative' and 'positive' continue to drive INGOs' messages, with all INGOs striving towards the latter. After the backlash and introspection that followed the portrayals of the Ethiopian Crisis of 1984, the INGOs have been determined not to show any 'negativity' and the trend of 'positivity' has been escalating since the 1990s. The heavier leaning on 'positivity' is also in line with increasing corporatisation and marketisation of INGOs. Instead of the much-needed epistemic change that considers how messages can be contextualised, the trend seeks 'new' and easy options to achieve this through images such as those of idealised, happy and 'active' MW people. The desire to move away from the 'don'ts' and taboos of 'negative' messages has led to growing emphasis on 'safe' messages, even if they do not say much. If showing problems is 'negative' and is bound to invite criticism, show more of 'self' ('self' with a small 's' which focuses on 'me' both as an individual and as a 'human being') – what I get, how I feel. And 'the human', which always lay just beneath the surface, now emerges as a clear, grand word in the vocabulary of INGOs' messages that can be applied across the board.

What does 'the human' say and what does it leave unsaid? When Oxfam tells us to 'be humankind' it implicitly suggests that we are not being 'human' if we do not care for 'Others'. It also says that our humanity is *the* connector and we need not think beyond it. Being human should be enough for us to want to 'help' other human beings who are otherwise unrelated to us. It also becomes a mask of indeterminate humanity that covers our shared histories and deep connections. Not only does it camouflage but it positively encourages us not to think about our deep-rooted links to the perceived 'Others'. It asks us to buy into this narrative of 'oneness' which ignores its deep schisms we have created and continue to recreate. It gives us a tempting but superficial sense of morality. It also insults the intelligence of many such as the student mentioned at the start of this chapter, who is able to see the sheer emptiness of stating the obvious and the ability of 'the human' to hide what lies beneath this 'humankind'.

When AA addresses us through the 'voice' of 'Avis, Supporter of ActionAid and the human connection', who enthuses: 'What a feeling! I don't just inspire others. I feel inspired. Every day. And what a feeling!' (*Metro*, 2 February 2011, page 28), we understand what we, as individuals, will gain. We are invited to 'feel inspired', 'change the world' and 'myself', 'give' and 'get, get back all the time' and get the feel-good high – 'what a feeling!' The colourful sketches of stars, rainbows, birds and blooming flowers that surround 'Avis', 'Barbara' and others in the AA messages connote the feelings that can be mine too. These are the 'After' and 'Then' images, the latter half of 'Before-After' or 'Now-Then' and suggest that I too can be a part of this hyper-positive la la land. The focus on 'self' and interactivity is also in accordance with the new brand strategies which aim to enhance the organisation's brand value through 'my' participation and the focus on 'me', who is addressed individually. It constitutes me as a 'consumer' who is clearly informed about what I get when I 'buy into' AA.

Twin processes of decontextualisation and recontextualisation are in play here. Global poverty is dislocated from its historical and structural setting and recontextualised under the rubric of humankind. Both forms of humanity – collective and individual – are deployed in relation to the brand. 'The human' is collectivised and individualised to serve the brand. Humanity serves to create a consumer environment that is conducive to building up attachments with the brand. It is not an *a priori* entity that INGOs merely tap into but is actively carved and enhanced by INGOs. So catering to what apparently exists without any thought for INGOs' own contribution towards making it serves as yet another form of institutional denial.

'The human' is a powerful concept and a key connector when sudden natural disasters strike different parts of the globe, from the Asian Tsunami of 2004, the Haiti quake of 2010 to the Japanese earthquake and tsunami in 2011. The wide misuse of this context-specific concept as an all-encompassing term that can be applied to systemic, intricately connected global inequalities serves to ignore the historical structural connections and disguise their embeddedness and continuities.

INGOs need to ask if it is right on their part to consider messages from the narrow aims of organisational survival and brand building. Do they want to reveal less and less and hide more and more through their current tropes of 'positivity' or do they really want to 'move on'? Should their messages make consumers of citizens, even as the representations use a pseudo-cosmopolitan language to frame the very same consumers as global citizens – those who look beyond their borders and help other 'less fortunate' human beings – and carelessly (or is it carefully?) refuse to locate any of us within the wider context of our shared history and structures? Is it enough to reproduce the fairytale pretence of one happy planet of nice human beings helping others? Or are these lost opportunities that INGOs must tap into to 'reverse the gaze' and inculcate reflexivity among Northern audiences?

The importance of INGOs' messages cannot be emphasised enough. As media institutions and opinion-makers, INGOs should be creating the space for an understanding of global poverty within a historicised and connected perspective and not using their messages as burial grounds. Their messages should stimulate new thinking and a sense of justice and responsibility, not provide a narcissistic escape from it. INGOs can and must build up the potential space of audience understandings by projecting more contextualised explanations of current global poverty and inequalities. It is time for INGOs to decide if they would like to project deeper contexts of global poverty (and prosperity) and instil new attitudes or carry on with small, individual stories without the context of global realities. The former path would give them stronger legitimacy on behalf of MW and help build a better-educated constituency of British public that is able to engage with the issues with a greater understanding of justice. The latter option would maintain the status quo of inexplicable problems 'out there' which the 'good' British citizens can help mitigate through their self-congratulatory 'charitable' and feel-good gestures. This would also continue the processes of erasing history and numbing memory, and contribute to the projects of collective amnesia and even revisionist versions of history by highlighting only the 'charitable' aspect of the global reach of powerful DW institutions and individuals. INGOs need to ask themselves if they wish to mirror an assumed pre-existing society or show a mirror to it.

INGOs' right to define the MW stems from unequal power relations embedded in connected histories and structures, the very narratives they obscure in their messages. How they use this power is enormously significant in determining how global issues are understood and connections made between DW and MW. INGOs' messages should not be about 'othering' but about 'joining', and creating common reflexive spaces that make 'another knowledge possible'.[4] In conclusion, let me reappropriate and reapply the words of Mahatma Gandhi, currently being used by more than one INGO – 'Be the change (you) wish to see in the world'.

ANNEX I

COMPARISON OF METHODS OF TEXTUAL & VISUAL ANALYSIS

Method of analysis	Explanation and application	Advantage	Disadvantage
Content Analysis	Identification, classification and coding of major themes (Applied across UK newspaper data)	Reduces complex and large information into manageable categories	Erases detailed nuances within a text/image
Discourse Analysis	Identification of discourses in the messages (Used for overall visual and textual analyses)	Considers the patterns as well as the rare, absent and 'deviant' cases	Can be an abstract and difficult method which is also as good as the theoretical lens used
Compositional Visual Analysis	Study of formal elements and principles of an image-line, shape, colour, space, balance, texture, contrast etc. (Used for detailed study of important images)	Aids understanding of arrangement and elements of visual data	Predominantly formalist and useful mainly to *support* the analysis of the content of a message

Continued

Method of analysis	Explanation and application	Advantage	Disadvantage
Semiotics	Study of signs that allows us to interpret what images signify. (Used for all visual analyses and detailed study of important images)	Decodes data to reveal layers of meanings	Neglects context and discourses across the range of messages

NOTES

1 Introduction

1. The Asian Tsunami was an undersea earthquake that occurred on 26 December 2004 along the coasts of the Indian Ocean. It killed more than 225,000 people in eleven countries, especially in Indonesia, Thailand and Sri Lanka.
2. There is a curious dearth of studies specifically on the subsector of INGOs. The most recent baseline survey done for European NGOs is by Adèle Woods (2000) and is based on 1993 data. It is clearly 'symptomatic of a chronic lack of factual data' for this subsector of NGOs within the voluntary sector (Stubbs, 2003: 331). There is a tendency to either lump the subsector with the UK voluntary sector or to conduct micro-level studies on specific NGOs.
3. Based on data for Top 500 Charities.
4. The growing professionalisation of INGOs in a commercial and competitive environment is also closely associated with the importance of 'branding' for INGOs, and the language of brands is not uncommon amongst INGOs.
5. Some international NGOs were even accused of practising the 'capitalism of mercy' not out of a 'genuine concern for the wretched of the earth' but to 'boost their own size and prestige' (Hancock, 1991: 16).
6. Maggie Black writes specifically about Oxfam (1992). However, these issues were common to all INGOs.
7. Tensions between raising money and raising awareness are illustrated by Joy MacKeith (1992).
8. Hosea Jaffe shows that until the sixteenth century the current concept of 'race' did not exist. It was applied to animal breeds before this period and its application to human beings began during the 1600s and gained

strength with the rise of the idea of a 'European man' who was superior and separate (1985: 46). This argument is supported by many studies
(Rigby, 1996).

9. It is not uncommon to hear that colonialism is no longer relevant and is just
being used as an excuse by MW, particularly African, leadership. It is appropriate to stress here that the historical contextualisation of global inequalities is crucial in representations. It frames issues in terms of justice, not
charity, by showing the links with current structures and power asymmetry.
This is especially true in the environment of amnesia of empires that characterises the DW. Engagement with history does not mean playing a 'blame
game', evoking guilt or inverting the existing Manichaeism to project an
essentialised view of good/bad categories of MW/DW. Partha Chatterjee
states that people across the world *are* trying to forget legacies of colonialism
and get ahead but there are mixed successes and failures precisely because
of the continuities with the past and their embeddedness (2007: 87), which
makes it critical to engage with history.

10. These include Max Weber, Lynn White Jr., Robert Brenner, Eric L. Jones,
Michael Mann, John A. Hall, Jared Diamond and David Landes (Blaut,
2000).

11. Similar to the historians' narratives, sociological and economic theories of
'modernity' conceive it as a purely European idea and phenomenon that
assumes a break from both the past and other parts of the globe (Bhambra,
2007).

12. John Pilger observes that 'with each generation, it seems, come new mythol-
ogists' who project British imperialism as 'benign, wise and essentially
truthful, even a gift to humanity' (2003: x).

13. John Newsinger's book *The Blood Never Dried: A People's History of the British
Empire* is replete with evidence of the effects of Britain's brutal empire on the
lives and economies of people across the British Empire (2006).

14. Photographic images played an important role in the overall representations. Olu Oguibe shows that photography arrived in Africa in 1839, the
year of its invention, with Horace Vernet's pictures of Egypt (1998). The
camera soon became a permanent part of European explorations and colonial
projects (Oguibe, 1998: 566).

15. The use of Michel Foucault's notion of discourse as power/knowledge is also
common to authors such as Edward Said, Stuart Hall and Arturo Escobar
across postcolonial, cultural and development studies (Schech and Haggis,
2002: xx).

16. 'The stereotype can be defined as a collection of traits thought to characterise or typify a group, in its physical and mental aspects and in its behaviour

patterns' (Preiswerk and Perrot, 1978: 173). Stereotypes are a 'crude set of mental representations of the world' (Gilman, 1985: 17).

17. Cohn's analysis has wider applicability across many colonised regions. Andrew Apter, for example, shows how the identification of 'a stratified field of spectatorship that mediated colonial relations' in Nigeria drew upon the hierarchical arrangement of the native races in colonial India (2002: 564). This also provides one explanation of the homogenising effects of colonialism across the 'non-West' stemming from the application of perceived knowledge about one region to another.

18. The links between actual conquest and knowledge are valid for all colonising projects. In the case of British colonialism in India, Cohn clearly states that 'the conquest of India was a conquest of knowledge' (1996: 16).

19. The intricate and interrelated mechanisms which produced Orientalism and homogenised vast regions into limited stereotypes and binary portrayals, maintain their validity even today through similar ways of representation. An example is the representation of 'Islam' as a simplified, largely monolithic construct (Said, 1997; Mamdani, 2004). Steven Rosen also argues that Orientalism is an essential part of modern consciousness (2000).

20. Fanon argues that the notion of 'irrationality' is applied to 'the blacks' – 'the loathsome idea derived from Western culture that the black man is impervious to logic and sciences' (1990: 130).

21. Perceptions of certain classes of people, the 'undeserving' poor, as 'lazy' and 'irresponsible' have also been prevalent in the UK since Victorian times. Such 'images of welfare' feed into the view that behavioural characteristics of poor people cause their poverty and hence they are 'undeserving' of help, particularly welfare benefits (Golding and Middleton, 1982).

22. Ruth Mayer has analysed diverse recent images and narratives from American mass culture including films, novels, comic books and hip-hop culture to show the lingering presence of colonial discourses and what she calls the 'cultural stereotyping' of Africa, which includes both romantic notions of innocence and primitivism (2002).

23. Though these regimes of representation were predominantly European constructs and originated in colonialism and 'modernity', they have now been appropriated by a range of institutions and regions at all levels. This has also led to a paradox of reconceptualisation of 'the truths' about MW within DW paradigms and their return to and circulation in the MW (Escobar, 1995).

24. Development here includes a range of developmental sectors such as health, education, water and livelihoods in addition to disaster-related work and

advocacy. Hence NGOs, such as WaterAid, that specialise in a specific development sector, are not included in the book.

25. Newspapers searched include eight daily newspapers: *The Times, Guardian, Independent, Evening Standard, Daily Mirror, Daily Mail, Telegraph, Metro* and three weekend newspapers: *The Sunday Times, Sunday Telegraph* and *Observer.*

26. This mind map draws on issues that have emerged from the research, some of which have received greater attention in the book. It is an unfinished diagram to which many other issues can be added.

Part I – Difference and Distance

1. Therefore, they contain some inevitable repetitions and seemingly over-determined categorisations which are essential to understand the dominant themes and motifs in INGOs' representations. However, in chapter 5 I also explore the 'deviant' representations that contribute directly to countering dominant discourses.

2. The content analysis is based only on the appeals in the UK national press to gain an overview of the range of messages that appear in this public domain in a given period. A significant exercise, it gives a comprehensive idea about the volume as well as proportion of different types of INGO messages in a year. The overall visual analysis, however, also includes an approximate total of 7,000–8,000 still messages in other formats such as inserts, pamphlets, leaflets and direct mails.

3. The study classifies INGOs based on their annual income during 2005/6 as: large – above £50 million; medium – between £10 and £50 million; and small – less than £10 million. Action Against Hunger, Farm Africa and War on Want are small INGOs. The remainder are medium to large INGOs. Oxfam is the largest INGO with an approximate income of £290 million in 2005/6 (Charity Commission website).

4. Surprisingly, SCF had very few messages in the press though it is the second largest INGO. This may have been due to organisation-level changes in SCF in 2005 that included a change of CEO and 're-branding' of the organisation.

2   Cast of Characters

1. Further analysis in chapter 4 demonstrates that the categories of 'active'/ 'passive' do not show the complete picture because their *levels* vary across characters.

2. An AA insert makes this link clear by stating it 'never singles out individual children for special attention' but works with their community, though the images of single children contradict this assertion.

3. Matt Smith analysed sponsorship appeals of 2002. The same caption was still being used in 2005 by AA, which also demonstrates that many messages are used by INGOs over a long period and build up audiences' familiarity with the people shown and the INGO.

4. American photographer Lewis Hine (1874–1940) was a pioneer in documentary photography. He used his photographs of working children and working class families to campaign for legal and welfare reforms. These photographs reflect his genuine desire to improve working class conditions as well as the Reformist ideology of the time that worked within a Christian framework of fatherly care and authority (Clark, 1997).

5. *The Times*, 6 November 1972.

6. For example, Kabeer, 1994.

7. Oxfam Christmas gifts catalogue 2005, page 25.

8. *Daily Mirror*, 5 December 2005, pages 20–21.

9. *Metro*, 16 November 2005, page 49.

10. This categorisation was also not straightforward as messages were often mixed, containing both passive and active characters. In addition, the characterisation into 'active' or 'passive' itself was hard to capture. To take an example, a man sitting with a child could be considered passive as there was no movement or evident activity. On the other hand, it could mean he was looking after the child, making it an active image. Other elements within the image, such as a milk bottle, were used to decide if the image was active or passive (this was indicated in the coding guidance in the worksheets on the entire corpus of messages).

11. Similar implicit binaries are also evoked, often on INGOs' websites, for things shown through images of, say, helicopters of INGOs *vis-à-vis* basic tools of MW 'farmers'. Such images have connotations of the 'difference' of strength, skills, modernity and advancement.

12. It is interesting to note that while Oxfam's actual donation form does not include any appeal, the two-page spread contains five images. This again illustrates the hybrid nature of messages, making it hard to attribute any single image to either the media or the NGO.

3   Distant Spaces

1. The cover of David Arnold's book, *Famine – Social Crisis and Historical Change* (1988) shows the image of a group of local men unloading sacks of

grain. It is titled 'Unloading grain from a steamer on a wharf by the Volga, Sisran area, 1921'. While one can see some women sitting in the background as well as two steamers, the image is noteworthy for showing local men actively engaged in dealing with the situation in marked contrast to current depictions of famines in the MW.

2. The authority of SCF, with its long history and high reputation, is often deferred to by other INGOs when discussing children. This puts SCF at a higher level of expertise and specialisation, on a par with UN bodies in INGO messages.

3. 'Christian Aid Week' is the annual fundraising event of CA and is usually held in May each year.

4. The conceptual division of Europe during the Renaissance was between South and North (Wolff, 1994: 4).

5. These news stories-cum-appeals show both the popularity of the MPH campaigns and Oxfam's influence and connections within media. The *Daily Mirror* is a tabloid newspaper and I was unable to find any other NGO adverts during my extensive search of this newspaper over a period of eight months. Tabloids, in general, consider wealth to be more newsworthy than poverty (Dean and Melrose, 1999). These appeals are the only exception.

4   Global Poverty – Causes and Solutions

1. 'How to make friends', page 3, column 2, paragraph 2.

2. 'Call for Change' is a joint feature of Oxfam and *Metro*. The choice of every image and caption in this series cannot be attributed only to Oxfam. The selection of images is usually discussed and negotiated by the NGO and the media organisation concerned, which makes it their joint responsibility.

3. This framing is similar to the common representations of Sudan between the years 2003 and 2005 by the UK newspapers which, surprisingly, include items in the *Guardian* and the *Observer*, the UK newspapers which have an open empathy for African issues (Campbell, 2007).

4. Content analysis shows that 27% of the total INGO messages in UK's national papers during 2005/6 featured disasters – food crises, natural disasters or political conflict. However, several 'developmental' items also contain images of other crises such as medical ones (e.g. HIV/AIDS), which implies that the percentage of disaster images is much higher.

5. There is an important argument to be made about the historical responsibility of industrialised nations in current environmental crises. While detailed discussions are beyond the scope of this book, it would be pertinent to keep

this in mind as well as the fact that the poverty of developing countries also reduces their capacity to cope with such crises.

6. While the appeal did not contain any images, it appeared, for instance, in the *Independent* alongside and on the same page as the news feature on Niger's starving children. The feature carried the image of an emaciated child. INGOs' appeals often appear alongside the news item and images of crises and starvation in the newspapers. This means that, in a strict sense, the NGO is not responsible for showing a shocking or desperate image but gains from it. Such instances of symbiosis between NGOs and media are common. De Waal argues that disaster stories in the media are 'little more than commercials for relief agencies' (1997: 84).

7. Spivak critiques the concept, saying 'I don't want to use the word community because it is so often put in binary opposition with developed societies' (2007: 180). This shows the inextricable link between meanings and practices and shifting connotations of language – meaning is not necessarily inherent in the word (though many labels are evidently demeaning) but in its usage.

8. This was also mentioned by someone in the audience interviews who had earlier chosen to 'gift' from a WV catalogue.

9. I was told of the marketing success of this 'new product' by several INGO informants, which also explains its ongoing use by the INGOs.

10. This is a common idea in colonial discourses that showed 'Africans' as happy and joyful in their simplicity and closeness to nature, projected through smiles and singing. Stuart Hall shows this through a stereotype of the 'good negroes', black slaves in America who were entertainers and musicians (1997: 245). He cites the example of corresponding stereotypes in American films as shown by Donald Bogle's *Toms, Coons, Mulattos, Mammies and Bucks: an interpretative history of blacks in American films* (1973).

5 One Humanity

1. This is also linked to 'development'. The pre-Enlightenment understanding of development was as an immanent and cyclical process with decay and destruction as its integral parts. The eighteenth century European Enlightenment introduced the idea that progress through reason and science could increase human wellbeing. This idea proffered solutions to two conceptual problems posed by modernity – dealing with the different and diverse cultures faced by European explorers, and making sense of the radical changes and uncertainties of modern age. Enlightenment allowed development to be conceived as an intention that could be controlled by human

agency. Furthermore, by seeing history as linear and the promises inherent in progress, Europe could feel optimistic and also see itself at a higher level of achievement in relation to other societies (Shanin, 1997 cited in Schech and Haggis, 2000).

2. While the positive connotations of Enlightenment humanist doctrine linger, the works of both structuralist and post-structuralist scholars such as Louis Althusser, Michel Foucault, Friedrich Nietzsche and Roland Barthes have also underlined its negative associations (Soper, 1986).

3. The exhibition (curator Edward Steichen) was first held at The Museum of Modern Art in New York in 1955 and then travelled to many different cities including Paris, where it was reviewed by Barthes.

4. These also signify the INGOs' reach and evidence of their presence in different locations.

5. Craig Calhoun calls Enlightenment humanism 'a new cosmopolitanism' that 'involved relative elites without a responsibility for ruling' (2003: 89).

6. Cosmopolitanism has associations with Lidchi's term 'consumer aid', which she used to describe Live Aid (1994).

7. The 'I'm in' campaign continued to run during 2007, with some revisions in style.

8. This is the only advocacy appeal by Oxfam that does not seek donations.

9. Beitz reasserts this point when he explains that 'cosmopolitan liberalism' 'does not take societies as fundamental and aims to identify principles which are acceptable from a point of view in which each *person's* prospects, rather the prospects of each society or people, are equally represented. Because it accords no privilege to domestic societies or to national (or multinational or non-national) states, cosmopolitan liberalism extends to the world the criteria of distributive justice that apply within a single society' (Beitz, 1999: 215).

10. Gazing at the camera can contradictorily connote both the photographed subject's 'need' and subservience (Nederveen Pieterse, 1992) and the trust in the photographer (Comaroff and Comaroff, 2007).

11. The Italian clothing company Benetton is well known not just for the global reach of its clothing merchandise but its often controversial and provocative advertising strategies as well as its slogan 'United Colours of Benetton' (Kraidy, 2003).

12. For example, between 1962 and 1981 there was a spate of representations in the UK media of 'Asians flooding the country in their millions and scrounging off the state' (Parmar, 2003: 289).

13. See, for example, Julian Baggini's article titled 'Spongers' in *New Humanist*, March/April 2008. The connotation of the word 'sponger' (also used with or in place of 'scrounger') as an undeserving parasite is linked to the

longstanding debate on welfare dependency or 'dependency culture' in Britain, its roots going back to the 'residuum' poor of Victorian England who later acquired the label 'underclass' (Dean and Taylor-Gooby, 1992). As far back as 1978 there was a play called 'The Spongers', written by Jim Allen, which condemned public attitudes and opinions about state welfare and council beneficiaries as parasites.

14. Slavery was abolished in Britain in 1807 but outlawed only in 1833 and continued in modified form after that as 'indentured labour' (Ashcroft et al., 1998: 212–215).

15. Given WOW's size and budget, it is not surprising that WOW had no press advertisement during 2005.

16. The same image without the accompanying text was used by Oxfam as far back as 1992 (Source: Oxfam archives), which shows how similar, sometimes even the same, images keep circulating. Instances of the use of identical images by several INGOs and media were also found in newspapers, inserts and websites during 2005/6.

17. A few INGOs were critical of child sponsorship schemes, as indicated on their websites.

18. It is also reminiscent of the 1970s when punks subverted notions of 'Britishness' by transforming icons of British nationalism, for example, the cover of Sex Pistols' record 'God Save the Queen' had the image of the Queen's face transformed by safety pins (Gilroy, 1995: 123).

19. Spivak draws on Antonio Gramsci's term. Subaltern means 'of inferior rank', a term adopted by Gramsci to refer to those groups in society that are denied access to 'hegemonic' power and hence the means to control their own representations (Ashcroft et. al., 1998: 215–216).

6   Uniform First World – NGO Perspectives

1. The chapter draws on eight interviews conducted between October and December 2006 with staff members of seven INGOs. Each interview lasted up to two hours. Respondents included Head of Marketing, Picture Editors and Fundraising, Communications and Campaigns Managers.

2. Regrettably, the marketing studies were considered confidential internal documents that could not be shared with me.

3. A well known example is the 'broken windows' theory of Wilson and Kelling which argues that minor forms of disorder, if left unattended, result in an increase in more serious crime (1982). This hypothesis became highly influential, leading to 'order-maintenance' policing across the USA and UK even though subsequent decades have not provided any substantial empirical or

theoretical evidence of its validity (Harcourt, 2001). The simple logic and narrative of the broken windows idea was key to its appeal.

4. John P. Jones defines a large brand as one with a market share of 10% or more (2007: 108). Discussing commercial brands such as Coca-Cola, he argues that 'splintering' of 'large brands into groups of sub-brands to cover subcategories of users' is usually a response to new competitors but it can cause 'a break up of the user base' and enhance the vulnerability of the brand (Jones, 2007: 109).

5. Martin de Graaf (1987) also explains this in his strategic management framework, which shows the importance of environment for NGOs. He argues that NGOs can control, influence and appreciate different levels or parts of this wider environment.

6. Similarly, James Ferguson's study of a World Bank project in Lesotho showed how the institution's dominant discourse of development influenced the way the nation of Lesotho was conceptualised as an underdeveloped nation without any historical or spatial context of its links with South Africa, and accordingly provided with an appropriate model of development by the World Bank (1994). In a recent work on Egypt, Mitchell reiterates the power–knowledge link to show how 'expert knowledge works to format social relations, never simply to report or picture them' (2002: 118).

7. Sarabajaya Kumar depicts the complexity of accountability relationships through 'Relativity', a lithograph by Escher in which the reference point for what is above and below changes each time one looks at a different part of the picture (1996: 238).

7 Lives of Others – Audience Responses

1. Keys for abbreviations used in audience interviews: ND – Myself; M – Male; F – Female; E – Elderly (Group 1, Age 60 and above); M – Middle-aged (Group 2, 30 to 59); Y – Young (Group 3, 18 to 29); e.g. MM1 – *Male middle-aged respondent 1; FY2 – Female, young respondent 2.*

2. Eight messages containing a higher number of images were shown.

3. Much as I would have liked to conduct a large reception study combining a survey with interviews, I had to stay within the time and financial constraints of the research.

4. 'White British' was a term used by most respondents to describe themselves (all respondents were 'English' and middle-class). In the book I use the term 'British' to express nationality and citizenship, fully recognising its internal dynamics and distinctions such as English, Welsh, Irish or Scottish.

5. CA-3 Message main text: 'Dirty low down spongers. We should be ashamed of living off Africans.'

6. These issues are included in Oxfam's list of myths (Oxfam, 2006a).

7. The UK's Most Valuable Charity Brands (Intangible Business, 2006).

8. Most respondents also commented on the format, i.e. that an advertorial, especially spread across two pages, was a good idea as it was it more likely to be read. They also stated that seeing the Oxfam logo and donation form in the corner would indicate to them that it was an Oxfam appeal. This is relevant to the issue of unclear boundaries between media and INGO messages and confirms my view that readers are likely to associate such messages with the INGO because of its brand symbols such as name and logo as well as the appeal for donations contained in the items.

9. The media may be the chief source of information for DW publics but agenda-setting and quality of stories are also informed by NGOs because of the media's dependence on NGOs for access, particularly in view of the significant decline in foreign-based correspondents. In 2004 only four British newspapers had correspondents in Africa as against 20 in 1974 (Seaton, 2005: 149).

10. This statement is an example of what I described earlier as 'positioning'; namely the tendency to state that they were being honest before saying something politically incorrect. This respondent too was merely being frank, as he himself stated, and his comment must not be seen as a generalised projection of his overall views and personhood, for he otherwise showed a fair level of awareness and concern about issues including historical connections.

11. This respondent was not only highly educated but had also worked in the media. Her comments must also be seen in the light of studies which show that during the late nineteenth and early twentieth centuries various propaganda bodies across Britain publicised the colonial project as well as world views of Social Darwinism, i.e. evolutionary ideas of societies to project the British as uniquely superior in comparison with the rest of the world. This was done through a range of 'new visual culture' encompassing advertising, theatre, cinema, broadcasting, churches, youth organisations, literature and the education system (MacKenzie, 1984: 253). Similarly, exhibitions about colonies were common, for example, the representations of India and Egypt in Exhibitions in Europe (Breckenridge, 1989; Mitchell, 1989).

12. It is worth reiterating that all respondents from this group repeatedly probed me about India and what I (and Indians, in general) think about the British Raj, showing a keen awareness and desire to know about the Raj from an

ex-colonised. This was in marked contrast to the younger respondents who were curious only about my university, LSE, and my research.

13. Preiswerk and Perrot in their extensive study of Eurocentric myths prevalent in Western history textbooks show that even as the books acknowledge slavery as a 'particularly atrocious aspect of European colonial expansion' they try to minimise its impact by showing the positive benefits it brought to the colonies such as 'towns, with parks, churches, schools, hospitals and an ordered way of life'. Further, the textbooks also illustrate uneasiness and desperation through their attempts to rationalise slavery as 'an historical inevitability, as the product of deep, underlying forces and not of men acting on their own responsibility' (1978: 150–151). These mythical histories also demonstrate the ambivalences and tensions within 'humanism' in terms of a) the agency and primacy of 'the human' who is shown here as not making, but accepting, an history outside of 'the human', and b) divisions within the same 'mankind'.

14. The 'invisible empire' refers to discriminatory amnesia about Empire and is a core constituent of the dominant white discourse about Britishness. It constructs histories of the British Empire in ways that obscure its coercion and exploitation (Wemyss, 2008). Also see Wemyss (2009), which shows how East London has been constituted as a place independent of, and outside, the violence of the British Empire.

15. Gilroy (2004) rightly sees this as relevant to other European nations too.

16. This is not to say that there is any dearth of opinions which deny a lasting impact of colonialism (see for example Runciman 1997).

17. Discussing the British obsession with Hitler and 'the great anti-Nazi war', Gilroy argues that it is symptomatic of the nation's 'inability even to face, never mind actually mourn, the profound change in circumstances and moods that followed the end of the Empire and consequent loss of imperial prestige' (2004: 96, 98).

18. For example, an article by Sarah Cassidy in the *Independent*, 17 February 2003 noted: 'A report by Ofsted, the school inspection body, warned that the "Hitlerisation" of courses threatened to damage understanding of history, and could result in pupils leaving school ignorant of key events'. Tony Halpin's article in *The Times*, 22 December 2005 noted that 'Pupils learnt about little else in GCSE courses except the fate of Nazi Germany and of Henry VIII and his wives, according to the annual report of the Qualifications and Curriculum Authority (QCA)'. Ofsted has recently reiterated that primary school history 'lacks narrative' (BBC news, 13 March 2011). However, under the current government's initiative, the proposed 'narrative' is likely to simply eulogise British 'achievements' and further invisibilise the long and exploitative history of slavery and colonialism.

19. Debate on this issue was held, for example, in a series of lectures and discussions on 'Teaching history' by the Royal Society of Arts (RSA), London during 2007.
20. A study on coverage of Africa by US television networks, similarly, shows a relatively low coverage of issues relating to Africa with the focus primarily on conflicts and disasters (Golan, 2008).
21. This was observed throughout the interviews. Asking respondents to read something carefully invariably led them to ask more. This throws light on a plausible factor that influences INGOs' decisions on messages. If the purpose of a message is narrow, i.e. just fundraising, the easy option is to keep the message 'simple' by way of less information, emotional content or tautological/circulatory information which merely describes the symptoms or details while giving the impression of providing more information. This avoids the risk of further questions or doubts.

8 Towards Reflexive Understandings

1. The phrase first appeared in 2008. See, for instance, Oxfam: 'Be Humankind' in *Metro*, 9 June 2008, page 32 and recently in 'Epic. Oxfam Trailtrekker 2011', *Metro*, 3 February 2011.
2. *Metro*, 7 February 2011, page 34.
3. The expression has been modified and appropriated from the title 'Distant voices, still lives', a movie directed by Terence Davies (1988).
4. I draw here on Boaventure de Sousa Santos's book title: *Another knowledge is possible* (2007).

BIBLIOGRAPHY

ActionAid (2006). *Focus on Images* (ActionAid communications toolkit). London, ActionAid UK.

Alam, S. and Matin, N. (1984). 'Limiting the women's issue in Bangladesh: the Western and Bangladesh legacy', *South Asia Bulletin*, 4(2): 1–10.

Alcock, P. (2006). *Understanding Poverty*. Basingstoke, Palgrave Macmillan.

Althusser, L. (1984). *Essays on Ideology*. London, Verso.

Anheier, H.K. (2005). *Nonprofit Organizations: Theory, Management, Policy.* London, Routledge.

Anthias, F. and Yuval-Davis, N. (1989). *Woman-Nation-State*. London, Macmillan.

Appadurai, A. (1990). 'Disjuncture and Difference in the Global Cultural Economy', in Mike Featherstone (ed.) *Global culture: Nationalism, Globalization and Modernity.* London, Sage.

Apter, A. (2002). 'On Imperial Spectacle: The Dialectics of Seeing in Colonial Nigeria', *Comparative Studies in Society and History*, 44(3): 564–596.

Arnold, D. (1988). *Famine: Social Crisis and Historical Change.* Oxford, Basil Blackwell.

Ashcroft, B., Griffiths, G. and Tiffin, H. (1989) *The Empire Writes Back: Theory and Practice in Post-Colonial Literatures.* London, Routledge.

Ashcroft, B., Griffiths, G. and Tiffin, H. (1998) *Key Concepts in Post-Colonial Studies.* London, Routledge.

Ashcroft, B. and Ahluwalia, P. (2001). *Edward Said.* London, Routledge.

Bagchi, A. (2002) 'The other side of foreign investment by imperial powers: transfer of surplus from colonies', *Economic and Political Weekly*, 8 June 2002.

Baggini, J. (2008). 'Spongers', *New Humanist*, 123(2), March/April 2008. http://newhumanist.org.uk/1738.

Barnes, C. (1992). *Disabling Imagery and the Media: An Exploration of the Principles for Media Representations of Disabled People.* Halifax, The British Council of Organisations of Disabled People with Ryburn Publishing Limited.

Barthes, R. (1977). *Image, Music, Text.* Essays Selected and Translated by Stephen Heath. London, Fontana.

— (1993). *Mythologies.* Translated by Annette Lavers. London, Vintage.

— (2000). *Camera Lucida: Reflections on Photography.* Translated by Richard Howard. London, Vintage.

Batliwala, S. and Dhanraj, D. (2007). 'Gender myths that instrumentalise women: a view from the Indian front line', in Andrea Cornwall, Elizabeth Harrison and Ann Whitehead (eds) *Feminisms in Development: Contradictions, Contestations and Challenges.* London, Zed Books.

BBC News (2011). 'Ofsted: Primary school history "lacks narrative"', 13 March 2011. http://www.bbc.co.uk/news/education-12711145

Beitz, C.R. (1999). *Political Theory and International Relations.* Princeton, Princeton University Press.

Beneria, L. (2003) *Gender, Development, and Globalization: Economics as if All People Mattered.* London, Routledge.

Benthall, J. (1993). *Disasters, Relief and the Media.* London, I.B.Tauris.

Berger, J. (1972). *Ways of Seeing: Based on the BBC television series with John S. Berger.* London, British Broadcasting Corporation and Penguin Books.

Bhabha, H.K. (1994). *The Location of Culture.* London, Routledge.

Bhambra, G.K. (2007). *Rethinking Modernity: Postcolonialism and the Sociological Imagination.* Basingstoke, Palgrave Macmillan.

Black, M. (1992). *A Cause for our Times: Oxfam the first 50 years.* Oxford, Oxford University Press.

Blaut, J.M. (2000). *Eight Eurocentric Historians.* New York, The Guilford Press.

Boltanski, L. (1999). *Distant Suffering: Morality, Media and Politics.* Cambridge, Cambridge University Press.

Breckenridge, C.A. (1989). 'The Aesthetics and Politics of Colonial Collecting: India at World Fairs', *Comparative Studies in Society and History*, 31(2): 195–216.

Breckenridge, C.A. and Van der Veer, P. (1993). 'Orientalism and the Postcolonial Predicament', in Carol A. Breckenridge and Peter van der Veer (eds) *Orientalism and the Postcolonial Predicament.* Philadelphia, University of Pennsylvania Press.

Brigg, M. (2002). 'Post-development, Foucault and the colonisation metaphor', *Third World Quarterly*, 23(3): 421–436.

Burke, P. (1990). 'The Spread of Italian Humanism', in Anthony Goodman and Angus MacKay (eds) *The impact of Humanism on Western Europe.* London, Longman.

Burnell, P. (1992/1993). 'Debate: NGOs and Poverty – Third World Charities in a Changing World/ Third World Charities in Britain towards 2000', *Community Development Journal*, 27/28(3): 290–302 / 66–81.

CAF (2004). *Charting the Charity Universe.* Charities Aid Foundation (CAF) (read with UK International Development NGOs: A Profile of the Sector, Liz Goodey, CAF, August 2004), UK.

CAF and BOND (2004). *UK International Development NGOs – A profile of the sector.* Researchers: Liz Goodey and Cathy Pharoah. Charities Aid Foundation (CAF) and British Overseas NGOs for Development (BOND).

CAF and NCVO (2005). *UK Giving 2004/05: Results of the 2004/05 survey of individual charitable giving in the UK.* Charities Aid Foundation (CAF) and National Council for Voluntary Organisations (NCVO), UK. http://www.cafonline.org/pdf/UKGiving200405.pdf

CAF and NCVO (2010). *UK Giving 2010: An overview of charitable giving in the UK, 2009/10.* Charities Aid Foundation (CAF) and National Council for Voluntary Organisations (NCVO), UK. http://www.cafonline.org/pdf/UK%20Giving%202010_101210.pdf

Calhoun, C. (2003) 'The Class Consciousness of Frequent Travellers: Towards a Critique of Actually Existing Cosmopolitanism', in Daniele Archibugi (ed.) *Debating Cosmopolitics.* London, Verso.

Campbell, D. (2007). 'Geopolitics and Visuality: Sighting the Darfur conflict', *Political Geography*, 26(4): 357–382.

Campbell, T. (2007). 'Poverty as a Violation of Human Rights: Inhumanity or Injustice?', in Thomas Pogge (ed.) *Freedom from Poverty as a Human Right.* Oxford, Oxford University Press.

Cassidy, S. (2003). ' "Hitlerisation" is damaging pupil's historical knowledge' (Report on the findings of a study by the Office for Standards in Education, Children's Services and Skills [Ofsted]). The *Independent*, 17 February 2003. http://findarticles.com/p/articles/mi_qn4158/is_20030217/ai_n12678532/pg_1?tag=artBody;col1

Chambers, R. (1983). *Rural Development: Putting the Last First.* Harlow, Longman.

Chandra, R. (1992). *Industrialization and Development in the Third World.* London, Routledge.

Charity Commission (2002–2008). *Register of Charities.* http://www.charity-commission.gov.uk/

Chatterjee, P. (2007). 'Interview with Partha Chatterjee', in Nermeen Shaikh (interviewer) *The Present as History: Critical Perspectives on Contemporary Global Power.* New York, Columbia University Press.

Chouliaraki, L. (2006). *The Spectatorship of Suffering.* London, Sage Publications.

Clark, D.J. (1993). *New Openings Survey I.* http://www.djclark.com/change/newopen.html

— (2003). *New Openings Survey II.* http://www.djclark.com/change/newopen.html

Clark, T. (1997). *Art and Propaganda in the Twentieth Century: The Political Image in the Age of Mass Culture.* London, Weidenfeld.

Coetzee, J.M. (2007). *Diary of a Bad Year.* London, Vintage Books.

Cohen, S. (2001). *States of Denial: Knowing about Atrocities and Suffering.* Cambridge, Polity.

Cohen, S. and Seu, B. (2002). 'Knowing Enough Not to Feel Too Much: Emotional Thinking about Human Rights Appeals', in Mark Philip Bradley and

Patrice Petro (eds) *Truth Claims: Representation and Human Rights.* London, Rutgers University Press.

Cohn, B.S. (1996). *Colonialism and its Forms of Knowledge: The British in India.* Princeton, NJ, Princeton University Press.

Comaroff, J.L. and Comaroff, J. (2007). 'Introduction: The Portraits of an Ethnographer as a Young Man', in John L. Comaroff, Jean Comaroff and Deborah James (eds) *Picturing a Colonial Past: The African Photographs of Isaac Schapera.* Chicago, University of Chicago Press.

Conrad, P. (1992). 'Medicalisation and social control', *Annual Review of Sociology*, 18: 209–232.

Corbridge, S. (1998). '"Beneath the Pavement Only Soil": The Poverty of Post-Development', *Journal of Development Studies*, 34(6): 138–148.

Cornwall, A. (2005). 'Love of the heart: Tales from Raizes Vivas Brazil', ActionAid International Report in the Series *Critical Stories of Change.* December 2005. www.actionaid.org/503/further_resources.html

Cornwall, A. and Molyneux, M. (2006). 'The Politics of Rights – Dilemmas for Feminist Praxis: an introduction', *Third World Quarterly*, 27(7): 1175–1191.

Davies, N. (1999). *The Isles: A History.* London, Macmillan.

Davis, M. (2001). *Late Victorian Holocausts: El Nino Famines and the Making of the Third World.* London, Verso.

De Graaf, M. (1987). 'Context, constraint or control? Zimbabwean NGOs and their environment', *Development Policy Review*, 5: 277–301.

De Sousa Santos, B., Nunes, A.J. and Menenzes, M.P. (2007). 'Introduction: Opening Up the Canon of Knowledge and Recognition of Difference', in Beauventura de Sousa Santos (ed.) *Another Knowledge is Possible: Beyond Northern Epistemologies.* London, Verso.

De Waal, A. (1989). *Famine That Kills: Darfur, Sudan, 1984–1985.* Oxford, Clarendon.

— (1997). *Famine Crimes: Politics and the Disaster Relief Industry in Africa.* London, African Rights.

Deacon, D., Pickering, M., Golding, P. and Murdock G. (1999). *Researching Communications: A Practical Guide to Methods in Media and Cultural Analysis.* London, Arnold.

Dean, H. and Taylor-Gooby, P. (1992). *Dependency Culture: The Explosion of a Myth.* Hemel Hempstead, Harvester.

Dean, H. and Melrose, M. (1999). *Poverty, Riches and Social Citizenship.* Basingstoke, Macmillan Press.

Debord, G. (1994). *The Society of the Spectacle.* Translated by Donald Nicholson-Smith. New York, Zone Books.

Devereux, S. (2007). 'Introduction: From "old famines" to "new famines"', in Stephen Devereux (ed.) *The New Famines: Why Famines Persist in an Era of Globalisation.* London, Routledge.

DFID (2000). *Viewing the World: A Study of British television coverage of developing countries.* Department for International Development, UK.

DFID (2007). *Public Attitudes towards Development: Knowledge and attitudes concerning poverty in developing countries, 2006.* ONS Omnibus Survey produced by the Office for National Statistics on behalf of Department for International Development, UK.

DiMaggio, P.J. and Powell, W.W. (1991). 'The Iron Cage Revisited: Institutional Isomorphism and Collective Rationality in Organizational Fields', in Walter W. Powell and Paul J. DiMaggio (eds) *The Institutionalism in Organizational Analysis.* Chicago, University of Chicago Press.

Dirks, N.B. (1996). 'Foreword' to Bernard S. Cohn's *Colonialism and its Forms of Knowledge: The British in India.* New Jersey, Princeton University Press.

Dogra, N. (2007a). '"Reading NGOs visually" – Implications of visual images for NGO management', *Journal of International Development,* 19(2): 161–171.

— (2007b). 'Cross-connections or crossed-connections? Representations of global poverty and international development by British development NGOs'. Unpublished paper presented at the Conference on Non-Governmental Organisations and Politics in Contemporary Britain organised by Database of Archives of Non-governmental Organisations (DANGO), Birmingham, UK, 4–5 July 2007.

Douzinas, C. (2007). *Human Rights and Empire: The Political Philosophy of Cosmopolitanism.* Abingdon, Routledge-Cavendish.

Dyer, R. (1993). *The Matter of Images: Essays on Representations.* London, Routledge.

Eade, D. and Williams, S. (1995). *The Oxfam Handbook of Development and Relief.* Oxford, Oxfam Publications.

Easterly, W. (2006). *The White Man's Burden: Why the west's efforts to aid the rest have done so much ill and so little good.* Oxford, Oxford University Press.

Edkins, J. (2000). *Whose Hunger? Concepts of Famine, Practices of Aid.* Minneapolis, University of Minnesota Press.

Edwards, M. (2002). '"Does the Doormat Influence the Boot?" Critical Thoughts on UK NGOs and International Advocacy', in Michael Edwards and Alan Fowler (eds) *The Earthscan Reader on NGO Management.* London, Earthscan.

Edwards, M., Hulme, D. and Wallace, T. (2000). 'Increasing Leverage for Development: Challenges for NGOs in a Global Future', in Tina Wallace and David Lewis (eds) *New Roles and Relevance: Development NGOs and the Challenge of Change.* West Hartford, CT, Kumarian Press.

Edwards, M. and Hulme, D. (2002). 'NGO Performance and Accountability: Introduction and Overview', in Michael Edwards and Alan Fowler (eds) *The Earthscan Reader on NGO Management.* London, Earthscan.

Eriksen, T.H. (2001). *Small Places, Large Issues: An introduction to social and cultural anthropology.* London, Pluto.

Escobar, A. (1995). *Encountering Development: The Making and Unmaking of the Third World.* Princeton, NJ, Princeton University Press.

Fairclough, N. (1995). *Media Discourse.* London, E. Arnold.

Fanon, F. (1990). *The Wretched of the Earth.* London, Penguin.

Fenton, N., Golding, P. and Radley, A. (1993). *Charities, Media and Public Opinion: A research report.* Loughborough, Communication Research Centre, Department of Social Sciences.

Ferguson, J. (1994). *The Anti-Politics Machine: 'Development', Depoliticisation and Bureaucratic Power in Lesotho.* Minneapolis, University of Minnesota Press.

Ferguson, N. (2004). *Empire: How Britain Made the Modern World.* London, Penguin.

Fowle, F. (2002) 'Cecile Walton's "Romance"', *Woman's Art Journal,* 23(2) [Autumn, 2002–Winter, 2003]: 10–15.

Fox, D.J. (1998) *An Ethnography of Four Non-governmental Development Organisations: Oxfam America, Grassroots International, ACCION International, and Cultural Survival Inc.* Lewiston New York, The Edwin Mellen Press.

Fox, K. (2004). *Watching the English: The Hidden Rules of English Behaviour.* London, Hodder and Stoughton.

Frank, A.G. (1998). *ReOrient: Global Economy in the Asian Age.* Berkeley, University of California Press.

Gilman, S. (1985). *Difference and pathology: stereotypes of sexuality, race and madness.* Ithaca NY, Cornell University Press.

Gilroy, P. (1995). *There ain't no Black in the Union Jack: The Cultural Politics of Race and Nation.* London, Routledge.

— (2004). *After Empire: Melancholia or Convivial Culture?* London, Routledge.

Goffman, E. (1979). *Gender Advertisements.* London, Macmillan.

Golan, J.G. (2008). 'Where in the World is Africa? Predicting Coverage of Africa by US Television Networks', *The International Communication Gazette,* 70(1): 41–57.

Golding, P. and Middleton, S. (1982). *Images of Welfare: Press and Public Attitudes to Poverty.* Oxford, Robertson.

Gopal, P. (2006). 'The story peddled by imperial apologists is a poisonous fairy-tale', *Guardian,* Wednesday 28 June 2006. http://www.guardian.co.uk/commentisfree/story/0,,1807649,00.html

Gowan, P. (2003). 'The New Liberal Cosmopolitanism', in Daniele Archibugi (ed.) *Debating Cosmopolitics.* London, Verso.

Grillo, R.D. (1997). 'Discourses of Development: The View from Anthropology', in Ralph D. Grillo and Roderick L. Stirrat (eds) *Discourses of Development: Anthropological Perspectives.* Oxford; New York, Berg.

Guijt, I. and Shah, M.K. (1998). 'Waking Up to Power, Conflict and Process', in Irene Guijt and Meera Kaul Shah (eds) *The Myth of Community: Gender Issues in Participatory Development.* London, Intermediate Technology Publications Ltd.

Hall, C. (2002) *Civilising Subjects: Metropole and Colony in the English Imagination 1830–1867.* Cambridge, Polity.

Hall, S. (1992a) 'Introduction' and 'The West and the Rest: Discourse and Power', in Stuart Hall and Bram Gieben (eds) *Formations of Modernity.* Cambridge, Polity Press.

— (1992b) 'Race, culture, and communications: Looking backward and forward at Cultural Studies', *Rethinking Marxism – a journal of economics, culture and society*, Spring, 5(1): 10–18.

— (1993) 'Encoding, Decoding', in Simon During (ed.) *The Cultural Studies Reader*. London, Routledge.

— (1997) *Representation: Cultural Representations and Signifying Practices*. London, Sage.

— (2007) 'Preface' to Paul Gilroy's *Black Britain: A Photographic History*. London, Saqi in association with gettyimages.

Halpin, T. (2005). 'Hitler is "dominating teaching of history"' (The annual report of the Qualifications and Curriculum Authority (QCA).) *The Times*, 22 December 2005 http://www.timesonline.co.uk/tol/news/uk/article778700. ece)

Hancock, G. (1991). *Lords of Poverty: The free-wheeling lifestyles, power, prestige and corruption of the multi-billion dollar aid business*. London, Mandarin.

Harcourt, B.E. (2001). *Illusion of Order: The False Promise of Broken Windows Policing*. Cambridge, MA, Harvard University Press.

Heuman, G. and Walvin, J. (2003). 'Introduction to Part One: The Atlantic Slave Trade', in Gad Heuman and James Walvin (eds) *The Slavery Reader*. London, Routledge.

Hobart, M. (1993). 'Introduction: the growth of ignorance?', in Mark Hobart (ed.) *An Anthropological Critique of Development: The Growth of Ignorance*. London, Routledge.

Hobson, J.M. (2004). *The Eastern Origins of Western Civilization*. Cambridge, Cambridge University Press.

Hudson, A. (2002). 'Advocacy by UK-Based Development NGOs', *Nonprofit and Voluntary Sector Quarterly*, 31(3): 402–418.

Hutnyk, J. (2004). 'Photogenic Poverty: Souvenirs and Infantilism', *Journal of Visual Culture*, 3(1): 77–94.

Inikori, J.E. and Engerman, S.L. (1992). 'Introduction: Gainers and Losers in the Atlantic Slave Trade', in Joseph E. Inikori and Stanley L. Engerman (eds) *The Atlantic Slave Trade: Effects on Economies, Societies, and Peoples in Africa, the Americas, and Europe*. Durham, Duke University Press.

Intangible Business (2006). *The UK's Most Valuable Charity Brands*. http://www.charitytimes.com/pages/ct_news/news%20archive/December_05_news/141205%20table.htm; http://www.guardian.co.uk/society/2007/jan/10/charities.voluntarysector1; http://www.intangiblebusiness.com/Reports/The-UKs-Most-Valuable-Charity-Brands-2006~379.html

Jaffe, H. (1985). *The History of Africa*. London, Zed Books.

Jhally, S. (1987). *The Codes of Advertising: Fetishism and the Political Economy of Meaning in the Consumer Society*. London, Frances Pinter.

John, M. (2004) 'Gender and Development in India, 1970s–1990s', in M. Chaudhuri (ed.) *Feminism in India*. New Delhi, Kali for Women and Women Unlimited.

Jones, J.P. (2007). *When Ads Work: New Proof that Advertising Triggers Sales.* Armonk NY, M.E. Sharpe.

Kabeer, N. (1994). *Reversed Realities: Gender Hierarchies in Development Thought.* London, Verso.

— (2000). The *Power to Choose: Bangladeshi Women and Labour Market Decisions in London and Dhaka.* London, Verso.

Kelleher, M. (1997). *The Feminization of Famine: Expressions of the Inexpressible?* Cork, Cork University Press.

Korten, D.C. (1990). *Getting to the 21st Century: Voluntary Action and the Global Agenda.* West Hartford, Kumarian Press.

Kothari, U. (2002) 'Feminist and Postcolonial Challenges to Development', in Uma Kothari and Martin Minogue (eds) *Development Theory and Practice: Critical Perspectives.* Hampshire, Palgrave.

Kothari, U. and Minogue, M. (2002) 'Critical Perspectives on Development: An Introduction', in Uma Kothari and Martin Minogue (eds) *Development Theory and Practice: Critical Perspectives.* Hampshire, Palgrave.

Kraidy, M.M. (2003). 'Transnational advertising and international relations: US press discourses on the Benetton "We on Death Row" campaign', *Media, Culture & Society,* 25(2): 147–165.

Kress, G. and van Leeuwen, T. (1996). *Reading Images: The Grammar of Visual Design.* London, Routledge.

Kumar, S. (1996). 'Accountability: what is it and do we need it?', in Stephen P. Osborne (ed.) *Managing in the Voluntary Sector: A handbook for managers in charitable and non-profit organizations.* London, International Thomson Business Press.

Leclau, E. (1989). 'Preface' to Slovaj Zizek's *The Sublime Subject of Ideology.* London, Verso.

Lever, J. (1997). 'Charity Law', in Paul Palmer and Elizabeth Hoe (eds) *Voluntary Matters: Management and Good Practice in the Voluntary Sector.* London, The Directory of Social Change.

Lewis, D. (2007). *The Management of Non-Governmental Development Organizations: An Introduction.* London, Routledge.

Lewis, R. (1996). *Gendering Orientalism: Race, Femininity, and Representation.* London, Routledge.

Lidchi, H.J. (1994). 'All in the Choosing Eye: charity, representation and developing world'. Unpublished PhD Thesis. London, The Open University.

Lidchi, H. (1999). 'Finding the right image: British Development NGOs and the regulation of imagery', in Tracey Skelton and Tim Allen (eds) *Culture and Global Change.* London, Routledge.

Lissner, J. (1977). *The Politics of Altruism.* Geneva, Lutheran World Foundation.

— (1981). 'Merchants of misery', *New Internationalist,* 100: 23–25.

Lister, R. (2004). *Poverty.* Cambridge, Polity.

Lloyd, T. (2001) *Empire: The History of the British Empire.* London, Hambledon and London.

Lutz, C.A. and Collins, J.L. (1993) *Reading National Geographic*. London, University of Chicago Press.

Luxemburg, R. (2004). 'The historical conditions of accumulation', in Peter Hudis and Kevin Anderson (eds) *The Rosa Luxemburg Reader*. New York, Monthly Review Press.

Lyon, A. (2005). 'Misrepresentations of Missing Women in the U.S. Press: The Rhetorical Uses of Disgust, Pity, and Compassion', in Wendy S. Hesford and Wendy Kozol (eds) *Just Advocacy? Women's Human Rights, Transnational Feminisms, and the Politics of Representation*. New Jersey: Rutgers University Press.

MacKeith, J. (1992). 'Raising Money or Raising Awareness? Issues and tensions in the relationship between fund-raisers and service-providers.' Unpublished paper. London, London School of Economics.

MacKenzie, J.M. (1984). *Propaganda and Empire: the Manipulation of British Public Opinion, 1880–1960*. Manchester, Manchester University Press.

Mamdani, M. (2004). *Good Muslim, Bad Muslim: America, the Cold War, and the Roots of Terror*. New York, Pantheon Books.

Marx, K. (1981). *Capital: Volume III*. Translated by David Fernbach. London, Penguin Books in association with *New Left Review*.

Mayer, R. (2002). *Artificial Africas: Colonial Images in the Times of Globalisation*. Hanover and London, University Press of New England.

McCarthy, F.E., Abdullah, T. and Zeidenstein, S (1979). 'Program assessment and the development of women's programs: the views of action workers', in Hanna Papanek and Rounaq Jahan (eds) *Women and Development: Perspectives from South and South East Asia*. Dhaka, Bangladesh Institute of Law and International Affairs.

McClintock, A. (1995). *Imperial Leather: Race, Gender, and Sexuality in the Colonial Contest*. New York, Routledge.

McIntyre, K. (2002) 'Geography as Destiny: Cities, Villages, and Khmer Rouge Orientalism', in Jane Haggis and Susanne Schech (eds) *Development: A Cultural Studies Reader*. Oxford, Blackwell Publishers.

Melhuus, M. and Stolen, K.A. (1996) 'Introduction', in Marit Melhuus and Kristi A. Stolen (eds) *Machos, Mistresses, Madonnas: Contesting the Power of Latin American Gender Imagery*, London, Verso.

Messaris, P. (1997). *Visual Persuasion: The Role of Images in Advertising*. Thousand Oaks, CA, Sage Publications.

Meyer, J.W. and Rowan, B. (1991). 'Institutionalized Organizations: Formal Structure as Myth and Ceremony', in Walter W. Powell and Paul J. DiMaggio (eds) *The Institutionalism in Organizational Analysis*. Chicago, University of Chicago Press.

Minear, L. (1987). 'The other mission of NGOs: education and advocacy', *World Development*, 15(Supplement): 189–200.

Minogue, M. (1997). 'Theory and Practice in Public Policy and Administration', in Michael J. Hill (ed.) *The Policy Process: A Reader*. New York, Prentice Hall/Harvester Wheatsheaf.

Mitchell, T. (1989) 'The World as Exhibition', *Comparative Studies in Society and History*, 31(2): 217–236.

— (1991) 'America's Egypt: Discourse of the Development Industry', *Middle East Report*, 169: 18–34.

— (2002) *Rule of Experts: Egypt, Techno-politics, Modernity*. Berkeley, University of California Press.

Molyneux, M. (1985) 'Mobilization without Emancipation? Women's Interests, the State, and Revolution in Nicaragua', *Feminist Studies*, 11(2): 227–254.

Moeller, S.D. (1999). *Compassion Fatigue: How the Media Sell Misery, War, and Death*. New York, Routledge.

Mohanty, C. (1991). 'Cartographies of Struggle: Third World Women and the Politics of Feminism', in Chandra Talpade Mohanty, Ann Russo and Lourdes Torres (eds) *Third World Women and the Politics of Feminism*. Bloomington, Indiana University Press.

— (1995). 'Under Western Eyes: Feminist Scholarship and Colonial Discourses', in Bill Ashcroft, Gareth Griffiths and Helen Tiffin (eds) *The Post-colonial Studies Reader*. London, Routledge.

Moser, C. (1993). *Gender Planning and Development: Theory, Practice & Training*. London, Routledge.

Mudimbe, V.Y. (1988) *The Invention of Africa: Gnosis, Philosophy and the Order of Knowledge*. Bloomington, Indiana University Press.

— (1994) *The Idea of Africa*. Bloomington, Indiana University Press.

Nandy, A. (1983). *The Intimate Enemy: Loss and Recovery of Self under Colonialism*. Oxford, Oxford University Press.

Nederveen Pieterse, J. (1992). *White on Black: Images of Africa and Blacks in Western Popular Culture*. New Haven, Yale University Press.

— (1998). 'My Paradigm or Yours? Alternative Development, Post-Development, Reflexive Development', *Development and Change*, 29: 343–373.

Newsinger, J. (2006). *The Blood Never Dried: A People's History of the British Empire*. London, Bookmarks.

Oguibe, O. (1998). 'Photography and the Substance of the Image', in Nicholas Mirzoeff (ed.) *The Visual Culture Reader*. London, Routledge.

Oxfam (2006a). *The art of self defence for Oxfam supporters: How to rid the world of those annoying myths about Oxfam*. Oxford, Oxfam.

Oxfam (2006b). *The little book of communication*. Oxford, Oxfam.

Oxfam (2006c). *Be that change (brand booklet)*. Oxford, Oxfam.

Parmar, P. (2003) 'Hateful Contraries: Media Images of Asian Women', in Amelia Jones (ed.) *The Feminism and Visual Culture Reader*. London, Routledge.

Pilger, J. (2003). 'Foreword' to Mike Curtis' *Web of Deceit: Britain's Real Role in the World*. London, Vintage.

Plantenga, D. (2004) 'Gender, identity and diversity: learning from insights gained in transformative gender training', in Caroline Sweetman (ed.) *Gender, Development and Diversity*. Oxford, Oxfam GB.

Pogge, T. (2002). *World Poverty and Human Rights – Cosmopolitan Responsibilities and Reforms.* Cambridge, Polity.

— (2004). '"Assisting" the global poor', in Deen K. Chatterjee (ed.) *The Ethics of Assistance: Morality and the Distant Needy.* Cambridge, Cambridge University Press.

Preiswerk, R. and Perrot, D. (1978). *Ethnocentrism and History: African, Asia and Indian America in Western Textbooks.* New York, NOK Publishers International.

Radley, A. and Kennedy, M. (1997). 'Picturing Need: Images of Overseas Aid and Interpretations of Cultural Difference', *Culture & Psychology*, 3(4): 435–460.

Ramamurthy, A. (2003) *Imperial Persuaders: Images of Africa and Asia in British Advertising.* Manchester, Manchester University Press.

Rathgeber, E.M. (1990) 'WID, WAD, and GAD: Trends in Research and Practice', *Journal of Developing Areas*, XX1V, July.

Rawls, J. (1999). *The Laws of Peoples.* Cambridge, MA, Harvard University Press.

Rigby, P. (1996). *African Images: Racism and the End of Anthropology.* Oxford, Berg.

Ritchin, F. (1990). 'The Lyric Documentarian', in *An Uncertain Grace: Photographs by Sebastião Salgado.* Essays by Eduardo Galeano and Fred Ritchin. London, Thames & Hudson.

Robinson, M.A. (1994). 'International Aid Charities in Britain', in Susan K.E. Saxon-Harrold and Jeremy Kendall (eds) *Researching the Voluntary Sector.* London, Charities Aid Foundation.

Rosen, S.L. (2000). 'Japan as Other: Orientalism and Cultural Conflict', *Intercultural Communication*, 4.

Runciman, G.W. (1997). *A Treatise on Social Theory, Volume 3: Applied Social Theory.* Cambridge: Cambridge University Press.

Sachs, W. (1997). 'Introduction', in Wolfgang Sachs (ed.) *The Development Dictionary: A Guide to Knowledge as Power.* London, Zed Books.

Said, E.W. (1994). *Culture and Imperialism.* London, Vintage.

— (1995). *Orientalism.* Harmondsworth, Penguin.

— (1997). *Covering Islam: How the media and the experts determine how we see the rest of the world.* London, Vintage.

Schech, S. and Haggis, J. (2000). *Culture and Development: A Critical Introduction.* Oxford, Blackwell Publishers.

Schech, S. and Haggis, J. (2002). 'Introduction: Pathways to Culture and Development', in Jane Haggis and Susanne Schech (eds) *Development: A Cultural Studies Reader.* Oxford, Blackwell Publishers.

Schwandt, T.A. (1994). 'Constructivist, Interpretivist Approaches to Human Inquiry', in Norman K. Denzin and Yvonna S. Lincoln (eds) *Handbook of Qualitative Research.* London: Sage.

Scott, C.V. (1995). *Gender and Development: Rethinking Modernization and Dependency Theory.* Boulder, CO, Lynne Rienner Publishers.

Seaton, J. (2005). *Carnage and the Media: The Making and Breaking of News about Violence*. London, Allen Lane.

Sen, A. (1981). *Poverty and Famines: An Essay on Entitlement and Deprivation*. Oxford, Oxford University Press.

— (1995). *Inequality Reexamined*. Oxford, Oxford University Press.

— (1999). *Commodities and Capabilities*. Oxford, Oxford University Press.

— (2001). *Development as Freedom*. Oxford, Oxford University Press.

— (2006). *The Argumentative Indian: Writings on Culture, History and Identity*. London, Penguin Books.

Senillosa, I. (1998). 'A new age of social movements: a fifth generation of non-governmental organization in the making?', *Development in Practice*, 8(1): 40–53.

Shaw, Martin. (1996). *Civil Society and Media in Global Crises: Representing Distant Violence*. London, Pinter.

Shohat, E. and Stam, R. (1994). *Unthinking Eurocentrism: Multiculturalism and the Media*. London, Routledge.

Shohat, E. and Stam, R. (1998). 'Narrativizing Visual Culture: Towards a polycentric aesthetics', in Nicholas Mirzoeff (ed.) *The Visual Culture Reader*. London, Routledge.

Silverstone, R. (1999). *Why Study the Media?* London, Sage.

— (2005). 'The Sociology of Mediation and Communication', in Craig Calhoun, Chris Rojek and Bryan Turner (eds) *The SAGE Handbook of Sociology*. London, Sage.

— (2007). *Media and Morality: On the rise of the Mediapolis*. Cambridge, Polity Press.

Smillie, I. (1995). *The Alms Bazaar: Altruism under fire – non profit organizations and international development*. London, Intermediate Technology Publications Ltd.

Smith, M. (2004). 'Contradiction and change? NGOs, schools and the public faces of development', *Journal of International Development*, 16(5): 741–749.

Smith, M. and Yanacopulos, H. (2004). 'The Public Faces of Development: An Introduction', *Journal of International Development*, 16(5): 657–664.

Sogge, D. (1996). 'Settings and Choices' and 'Northern Lights', in David Sogge (ed.) with Kees Biekart and John Saxby, *Compassion and Calculation: The Business of Private Foreign Aid*. London, Pluto Press with Transnational Institute (TNI).

Sontag, S. (1979). *On Photography*. London, Penguin Books.

Soper, K. (1986). *Humanism and Anti-Humanism*. London, Hutchinson.

Spivak, G.C. (1988). 'Can the subaltern speak?', in Cary Nelson and Lawrence Grossberg (eds) *Marxism and the Interpretation of Culture*. Basingstoke, Macmillan Education.

— (2007). 'Interview with Gayatri Chakravorty Spivak', in Nermeen Shaikh (interviewer) *The Present as History: Critical perspectives on contemporary global power*. New York, Columbia University Press.

Stubbs, P. (2003). 'International Non-State Actors and Social Development Policy', *Global Social Policy*, 3(3): 319–348.

Trinh, T. Minh-ha (2003). 'DIFFERENCE: "A special third world women issue"', in Amelia Jones (ed.) *The Feminism and Visual Culture Reader*. London, Routledge.

Tvedt, T. (1998). *Angels of mercy or development diplomats?: NGOs and foreign aid*. Oxford, James Curry.

Visvanathan, N. (1997). 'Introduction to Part 1', in Nalini Visvanathan, Lynn Duggan, Laurie Nisonoff & Nan Wiegersma (eds) *The Women, Gender and Development Reader*. London, Zed Books.

VSO (2002). *The Live Aid Legacy: The developing world through British eyes – A research report*. London, Voluntary Services Overseas (VSO).

Wemyss, G. (2008) 'White memories, white belonging: competing colonial anniversaries in postcolonial east London', *Sociological Research Online*. September 2008.

— (2009) *The Invisible Empire: White Discourse, Tolerance and Belonging*. Farnham, Ashgate.

Wetherell, M. and Potter, J. (1992). *Mapping the Language of Racism: Discourse and the legitimation of exploitation*. Hertfordshire: Harvester Wheatsheaf.

White, S. (2002). 'Thinking race, thinking development', *Third World Quarterly*, 23(3): 407–419.

Wieringa, S. (1995). *Subversive Women*. London, Zed Books.

Williams, R. (1976). *Keywords: A Vocabulary of Culture and Society*. London, Fontana Press.

Wilson, J.Q. and Kelling, G.L. (1982). 'Fixing Broken Windows', *The Atlantic Monthly*, March 1982.

Wolff, L. (1994). *Inventing Eastern Europe: The Map of Civilization on the Mind of Enlightenment*. Stanford, Stanford University Press.

Wood, G. (1985). 'The Politics of Development Policy Labelling', *Development and Change*, 16(3): 347–373.

Woods, A. (2000). *Facts about European NGOs Active in International Development*. Paris, Organisation for Economic Cooperation and Development (OECD).

Wrangham, R.P. (2005). 'Negotiating meaning and practice in the Zambézia agricultural development project, Mozambique', Ph.D. Thesis. London, London School of Economics.

Young, K. (1992). *Gender and Development Readings*. Ottawa, Canadian Council for International Cooperation.

Young, R. (1990). *White Mythologies: Writing History and the West*. London, Routledge.

— (2001). *Postcolonialism: An Historical Introduction*. Oxford, Blackwell.

Ziai, A. (2004). 'The ambivalence of post-development: between reactionary populism and radical democracy', *Third World Quarterly*, 25(6): 1045–1060.

INDEX

Images and figures are highlighted in italics after the page number, e.g. sponsorship 37*i2.2*